This collection of illuminating and provocative essays explicitly engages with the ways notions about gender and responsibility are deeply implicated in understandings of myriad forms of lethal violence, from the violence of individual actors to the violence of the state. Implicitly, these analyses also reveal how our understandings of lethal violence shape constructions of gender and criminal responsibility; and they require us to consider the violence of legal interpretation in both its productive and destructive forms. The international and interdisciplinary scope is impressive, informative, and imperative.

—**Rosemary Gartner**, *Centre for Criminology and Sociolegal Studies, University of Toronto, Canada*

Homicide, Gender and Responsibility

The crime of homicide has long animated academic debate, community concern and political attention. The discussion has often centered on the perceived (in)adequacy of legal responses to homicide, questions of culpability, and divergent representations of victims and offenders. Within this, notions of gender, responsibility and justice are pivotal. This edited collection builds on existing scholarship by examining these concerns not only in the context of the 'private' world of domestic murder but also in the more 'public' world of the state, the corporation, war, and genocide. In so doing this book draws from key frameworks of criminological thought, legal analysis and empirical evidence to critically examine the relationship between homicide, gender and responsibility.

Bringing together leading international criminology and legal scholars, this collection provides a unique contribution to the academic and policy engagement with what is, more often than not, an ordinary and mundane crime. Analysing the crime in a variety of different social contexts alongside an in-depth and critical analysis of the interconnections between the ordinary act of lethal violence, gender and notions of responsibility, this book will be of interest to students, scholars and policymakers working in criminology and socio-legal studies.

Kate Fitz-Gibbon is a senior lecturer in criminology in the School of Social Sciences at Monash University, Victoria, Australia.

Sandra Walklate is Eleanor Rathbone Chair of Sociology at the University of Liverpool, UK.

Routledge Studies in Crime and Society

Homicide, Gender and Responsibility

An international perspective

Edited by Kate Fitz-Gibbon and Sandra Walklate

Routledge
Taylor & Francis Group

LONDON AND NEW YORK

First published 2016
by Routledge
2 Park Square, Milton Park, Abingdon, Oxon OX14 4RN

and by Routledge
711 Third Avenue, New York, NY 10017

Routledge is an imprint of the Taylor & Francis Group, an informa business

British Library Cataloguing in Publication Data
A catalogue record for this book is available from the British Library

Library of Congress Cataloging-in-Publication Data
Names: Fitz-Gibbon, Kate (Lecturer in criminology) editor. | Walklate,
    Sandra, editor.
Title: Homicide, gender and responsibility : an international perspective /
    edited by Kate Fitz-Gibbon and Sandra Walklate.
Description: New York : Routledge, 2016. | Series: Routledge studies in
    crime and society
Identifiers: LCCN 2015042636 | ISBN 9781138843479 (hardback) |
    ISBN 9781315730981 (e-book)
Subjects: LCSH: Homicide—Great Britain. | Sex role—Great Britain. |
    Criminal justice, Administration of—Great Britain. | Responsibility—
    Great Britain.
Classification: LCC HV6535.G7 H66 2016 | DDC 364.152—dc23
LC record available at http://lccn.loc.gov/2015042636

ISBN: 978-1-138-84347-9 (hbk)
ISBN: 978-1-315-73098-1 (ebk)

Typeset in Times New Roman
by Apex CoVantage, LLC

Printed and bound in Great Britain by
TJ International Ltd, Padstow, Cornwall

Contents

**Blurring the boundaries between homicide, gender and
responsibility**   95

5   **Murderousness in war: from My Lai to Marine A**   97
    SANDRA WALKLATE AND ROSS MCGARRY

6   **'He seems to come out as a personally cruel person':**
    perpetrator re-presentations in direct murder cases at the ICTY   113
    ANETTE BRINGEDAL HOUGE

7   **Lethal violence and legal ambiguities: deaths in custody in**
    Australia's offshore detention centres   130
    ALISON GERARD AND TRACEY A. KERR

8   **Attributing criminal responsibility for workplace fatalities**
    and deaths in custody: corporate manslaughter in Britain
    and Ireland   148
    DAVID M. DOYLE AND JOE MCGRATH

    Concluding thoughts on homicide, gender and responsibility   171
    SANDRA WALKLATE AND KATE FITZ-GIBBON

    Index   181

Illustrations

About the editors

Kate Fitz-Gibbon is a senior lecturer in criminology in the School of Social Sciences at Monash University (Victoria, Australia). Her research examines legal responses to lethal violence, the law of homicide and the impact of criminal law reform across Australian and international jurisdictions. This research has been undertaken with a focus on gender, responsibility and justice. Dr Fitz-Gibbon has advised on homicide law reform reviews in several Australian jurisdictions. Recent publications include: *Homicide Law Reform, Gender and the Provocation Defence* (2014, Palgrave Macmillan) and *Homicide Law Reform in Victoria: Retrospect and Prospects* (edited with Arie Freiberg, 2015, The Federation Press).

Sandra Walklate is Eleanor Rathbone Chair of Sociology at the University of Liverpool (United Kingdom) and adjunct professor at QUT in Brisbane. Internationally recognised for her work in victimology and research on criminal victimisation, her recent publications include: *Victims: Trauma, Testimony, Justice* (2015, Routledge with Ross McGarry), *The Contradictions of Terrorism* (2014, Routledge with Gabe Mythen) and *Criminology and War: Transgressing the Borders* (edited collection, Routledge, 2015, with Ross McGarry). She is currently Editor in Chief of the *British Journal of Criminology*.

Contributors

Anette Ballinger is a lecturer in the School of Social Science and Public Policy at Keele University. She is the author of the award-winning book *Dead Woman Walking: Executed Women in England & Wales, 1900–1955* (Ashgate: 2000) (Hart Socio-Legal Prize 2001). She has written numerous book chapters and journal articles on the subject of gender and punishment in modern history, and her new book, entitled *Capitalising on Punishment: Gender, Truth and State Power*, will be published by Ashgate later this year.

Myrna Dawson, Professor, Department of Sociology & Anthropology, University of Guelph, is also Director of the Centre for the Study of Social and Legal Responses to Violence (www.violenceresearch.ca) and Co-Director of the Canadian Domestic Homicide Prevention Initiative (www.cdhpi.ca). Her recent projects examine intimacy, violence and the law as well as the rise and impact of domestic violence death review committees. Her recent articles appear in *Trauma Violence & Abuse*, *Child Abuse & Neglect* and the *Journal of Research in Crime & Delinquency*.

David M. Doyle is a lecturer at the Department of Law, Maynooth University. David read History and Politics at University College Dublin (UCD), where he graduated with BA and MA degrees, before completing a Bachelor of Laws degree (with first class honours) and his doctorate at the National University of Ireland, Galway. A previous recipient of an Irish Research Council (IRC) doctoral scholarship, David was also an IRC Marie Skłodowska-Curie Elevate Fellow at the University of Oxford and an IRC Postdoctoral Fellow at the UCD Sutherland School of Law. His most recent article was published in the *Journal of British Studies* (July 2015).

Alison Gerard is Associate Professor in Law and Director of the Centre for Law at Charles Sturt University. She completed her masters in International Humanitarian Action with the Institute for International Law of Peace and Armed Conflict at Bochum University, Germany. Her research focuses on social justice issues including the securitisation of migration and deaths in custody. Alison's latest book, *The Securitisation of Migration and Refugee Women* published by Routledge in 2014, examines the experiences of women who have travelled from Somalia to the EU to seek refugee protection. Gerard is a lawyer and contributor to the Border Crossing Observatory, hosted by Monash University.

Anette Bringedal Houge is a PhD research fellow at the Department of Criminology and Sociology of Law, Faculty of Law, University of Oslo. Her main research interests are mass violence and war crimes in general and sexual violence in particular. Her PhD research project on conflict-related sexual violence addresses what re-presentation work feminist legal strategies are based upon, and the imageries of perpetrators and victims that the ensuing court processes produce.

Tracey A. Kerr is a PhD candidate at the School of Humanities and Social Sciences, Charles Sturt University. Her thesis is focusing on human rights and state crime implications of Australia's offshore immigration detention regime. Tracey holds a BA from Boston University, a JD from Northeastern University, an LLM (Human Rights and Social Justice) from the University of New South Wales and an MPH from the University of Sydney.

Ross McGarry is Lecturer in Criminology within the Department of Sociology, Social Policy and Criminology at the University of Liverpool. He has written widely on criminology, victimology and critical military studies in international journals, including the *British Journal of Criminology* and *Armed Forces and Society*. He is the co-editor (with Sandra Walklate) of *Criminology and War: Transgressing the Borders* from Routledge and the forthcoming *Palgrave Handbook on Criminology and War* and is the co-author of *Victims: Trauma, Testimony and Justice*. He is currently writing a monograph for the New Directions in Critical Criminology series from Routledge entitled *Criminology and the Military*.

Joe McGrath is a lecturer at the Sutherland School of Law, University College Dublin. A recipient of the Irish Research Council doctoral scholarship, he completed his PhD on corporate and financial regulation at University College Cork in 2011. He also graduated with a first class honours Bachelor of Civil Law (BCL) from University College Cork in 2007. His first monograph, *Corporate and White Collar Crime in Ireland: A New Architecture of Regulatory Enforcement*, was published by Manchester University Press in 2015.

Julie Stubbs is a criminologist and Professor in the Faculty of Law at the University of New South Wales. Her research focuses mostly on women's involvement in criminal justice, as victims and offenders. Her publications include research on domestic violence, sexual assault, homicide and defences to homicide, restorative justice and incarceration. Her forthcoming books include: *Justice Reinvestment: Winding Back Imprisonment* (Palgrave Macmillan; co-authored with Brown, Cunneen, Schwartz and Young) and *Australian Violence* (Federation Press, co-edited with Tomsen).

Acknowledgements

This edited collection brings to life an idea first conceptualised over warm cups of coffee and collaborative discussions between the editors in Liverpool in February 2014. Inspired by the notion of the continuum of violence developed by Liz Kelly, we sought to bring together scholars working to understand responses to lethal violence committed across a range of contexts and jurisdictions.

We would like to thank all of the contributors to this collection. We are absolutely delighted to bring together a truly international group of scholars across a number of interdisciplinary borders. The breadth and quality of the research contributed, we believe, will provide a valuable resource for those interested in the study of homicide, gender and responsibility. In particular, we would like to thank Anette Bringedal Houge, who joined the project at the last minute and whose excellent individual contribution provides an invaluable perspective to the collection.

Thank you to our colleagues for their ongoing support and for providing the research space for us to bring this collection together. We also wish to thank Emily Briggs for her interest in this project from the outset and for assisting to bring it to fruition with Routledge.

Finally, we would like to take this opportunity to thank our families, in particular Mick and Ron, whose support and encouragement is always appreciated.

Kate Fitz-Gibbon and Sandra Walklate
October 2015

Abbreviations

ABS	Australian Bureau of Statistics
ACCT	Assessment, Care in Custody and Teamwork
ACT	Australian Capital Territory
AustLII	Australian Legal Information Institute
BLS	Bureau of Labor Statistics
BWS	Battered women's syndrome
CPS	Crown Prosecution Service
DIBP	Department of Immigration and Border Protection
DPP	Director of Public Prosecutions
DVDRT	Domestic Violence Death Review Team
ECHR	European Convention of Human Rights
ESAW	European Statistics on Accidents at Work
HAS	Health and Safety Authority
HMCIP	Her Majesty's Chief Inspector of Prisons for England and Wales
HMPS	Her Majesty's Prison Service
HREOC	Human Rights and Equal Opportunity Commission
HRW	Human Rights Watch
HSE	Health and Safety Executive
ICTY	International Criminal Tribunal for the former Yugoslavia
IP	Intimate partner
IPH	Intimate partner homicide
IPH DV	Intimate partner homicide in which there was a history of domestic violence
IPV	Intimate partner violence
LRC	Law Reform Commission
NOMS	National Offender Management Service
NSW	New South Wales
PNG	Papua New Guinea
PPO	Prison and Probation Ombudsman for England and Wales
PTSD	Posttraumatic stress disorder
RRA	Regional Resettlement Agreement

SMT   Senior Management Team
UNDP   United Nations Development Programme
UNHCR   United Nations High Commissioner for Refugees
VLRC   Victorian Law Reform Commission
VSC   Victorian Supreme Court
YOI   Young Offender Institution

Introduction

Homicide, gender and responsibility

Kate Fitz-Gibbon and Sandra Walklate

Debate surrounding legal responses to the crime of homicide has often centred on the perceived (in)adequacy of the law's response to murder (particularly in high-profile cases), questions of culpability and divergent representations of victims and offenders. Within this debate, notions of gender, responsibility and justice have been focal. As important as these issues are, they have often been of immediate concern only when considering fairly circumscribed understandings of murder: those considered to be 'domestic'. This book expands on this debate by examining these concerns not only in the context of the 'private' world of familial homicide but also in the more 'public' world of the state, the corporation, war and genocide. In so doing this book draws from key frameworks of criminological thought, legal analysis, empirical evidence and rigorous research to critically examine the relationships among and responses to homicide, gender and responsibility.

Through this collection, we seek to expand on the work of Kelly (1988) to argue that the myriad contexts within which homicide is committed can be envisaged as occurring along a continuum. Kelly conceptualised the 'continuum of violence' in her feminist analysis of women's experiences of sexual violence victimisation. Through this notion, Kelly explored shared commonalities across different forms of sexual violence, in particular the presence of gender inequality, men's power and women's resistance. Kelly's work has since given rise to a body of work that has further explored this continuum, particularly in relation to sexual violence (e.g. Cockburn, 2009; Cowburn, 2011). The importance of gender in exploring violence along a continuum is aptly captured by Cockburn (2009: 158), who argues:

> Since gender relations shape the dynamics of every site of human interactions, from the household to the international arena, a gender lens tends to reveal a connectedness between the many kinds and occasions of violence. One seems to flow into the next, as if they were a continuum.

Building on this idea of different contexts of violence existing along a continuum and similarly recognising the importance of a gendered analysis, we posit that to date lethal violence, and the many different contexts in which it can occur, has been largely examined in silos – public and private homicide, local and global homicide, intimate and stranger homicide. Offering a break from this traditional approach, this book considers constructions of responsibility and gendered dimensions in response to the perpetration of lethal violence across a range of contexts: between intimate partners, by children, by soldiers in war, by corporations, within official institutions such as detention centres and as part of genocide. In putting the concepts of gender and responsibility in the same critical frame, the purpose of this book is to add some conceptual nuances to understanding how the everydayness of such violence and responses to it are stitched into the fabric of ordinary life, thus adding to Kelly's (2011) call for better conceptual maps of gender and (sexual) violence.

In examining representations of responsibility along a continuum, this book is not strictly concerned with the legal categorisation of homicides according to offence category (murder, capital murder, manslaughter) or the term of punishment imposed. Nor does it advocate that official allocations of responsibility denote an accurate reflection of individual culpability. Rather it focuses on providing a critical analysis of how constructions of gender and responsibility frame our understandings of the event of lethal violence and allocations of individualised and collective culpability for such actions. In this respect, the collection invites you to think beyond the law's response and to consider how the representation of responsibility for homicide and the actions of those involved may be influenced by gendered (mis)understandings.

Why gender?

The past three decades have seen increasing recognition of violence as a gendered phenomenon. This recognition is evident at several levels – in respect of documenting differences in how the sexes perpetrate and experience violence, identifying variances apparent in how the legal system responds to male and female violent offenders and victims and in terms of the presence and influence of gender inequality at sites of violence. In relation to the first of these focuses that men both perpetrate homicide and are victimised at far greater rates than their female counterparts is a well-documented trend internationally that has remained relatively stable in recent times. Where differences arise, however, is in how the sexes experience and perpetrate lethal violence as well as variances in perpetrator motivations. In exploring structures of violence, Cockburn (2009: 162) succinctly argues the reasons underpinning male violence:

> Men take part in violence for many reasons – for money, for honor, patriotism, or brotherhood, in self-defense, for liberation, to liberate others. But male positioning in patriarchal gender systems and the masculine identities they generate underwrite all these reasons. Indeed, many versions of masculinity in the world's varied cultures are constituted in the practice of fighting: to be a "real" man is to be ready to fight and ultimately to kill and to die.

This view is supported by broader, empirical research, which has observed that men are likely to kill in response to a threat to their masculine honour, as a performance of power or in response to a loss of control (Morgan, 2002; Polk, 1994). Women, on the other hand, are more likely to perpetrate homicide following victimisation and in the context of vulnerability. As Daly and Chesney-Lind (1988: 520) identified nearly three decades ago, it is often difficult 'to separate victimisation from offending', which denotes a very different relationship to power and to gendered scripts.

Recognising the differences in the social contexts which lead to the perpetration of lethal violence by men and women inevitably leads to questions concerning how such differences should be, and indeed are, reflected in allocations of responsibility. Is the woman who kills her domestic abuser less responsible for the same act committed by a man upon an unfaithful spouse? Should children who have been raised in domestically abusive households be considered less responsible for their own perpetration of homicide? Or the solider, trained to kill in the masculinised context of war but who uses those skills in a non-combative scenario? In navigating our way through these questions, this book seeks to cast light on how gendered understandings and experiences of violence permeate representations of responsibility.

Adding a further layer to this focus on gender requires recognition of research that has examined the connection between gender inequality and violence against women (see, e.g. Carrington, 2015; Cockburn, 2009; Connell, 2005; Strauss, 1994; Whaley and Messner, 2002; Whaley et al., 2013). Feminist theorists have argued that patriarchal belief systems which present women as inferior simultaneously condone the perpetration of male violence where the performance of violence serves to demonstrate power and elevate status (Whaley and Messner, 2002: 190; see also Carpenter and Ball, 2012: 74–76). This link between gender and violence has been explored with specific reference to sexual violence, as described by Cockburn (2009: 170) in her exploration of a continuum of violence in pre-conflict, conflict and postwar sites:

> [G]ender links violence at different points on a scale reaching from the person to the international, from the home to the back street to the maneuvers of the tank column and the sortie of the stealth bomber: battering and marital rape, confinement, "dowry" burnings, honor killings, and genital mutilation in peacetime; military rape, sequestration, prostitution, and sexualized torture in war.

Following Cockburn's (2009) blurring of the conventional boundaries between public violence and private violence, here we explore this further by documenting how gendered assumptions and stereotypes can be influential in framing constructions of responsibility for homicide. Drawing out themes of power and masculinity, this book examines where gendered narratives of violence remain visible in responses to homicide. So, moving beyond the traditionally private world of domestic murder, the second half of the book examines where gendered assumptions are also present in official accounts of and responses to homicide committed in public spaces at a local and global level. In exploring this, and in moving beyond the questions of gender inequality and rates of violence, we are concerned with documenting how stereotypes that promote and reinforce gender inequality are influential in allocations, constructions and interpretations of responsibility.

This focus on gender, however, should not be interpreted as limiting the scope of this book. While several chapters do examine more *traditional* sites of gendered violence, such as the male use of violence against an intimate partner, this is not the exclusive focus of this collection. Chapters included within offer an analysis of the construction of responsibility in the less explored gendered domains of lethal violence, such as homicides that implicate the state and corporations and in the context of war. The resulting analyses reveal nuances in gendered responses to and constructions of homicide across time, place and context.

Why responsibility?

Contestations surrounding the responsibility of homicide offenders are particularly evident in the contemporary era of the twenty-four-hour news cycle, where responsibility for a high-profile incident of lethal violence can be debated and allocated prior to the formal arrest, charge or trial of the person(s) involved. The disjunct that can emerge among official, legal and community allocations of responsibility was clearly borne out in the period immediately following the jury's acquittal of George Zimmerman for the shooting death of Trayvon Martin in Florida (United States). The February 2012 shooting of the unarmed seventeen-year-old student by Zimmerman, a neighbourhood watch coordinator, attracted media attention worldwide (Barry et al., 2012; Lee, 2013; Wiggins, 2012). In June 2013 a jury acquitted Zimmerman of all charges, supporting his case that he had acted in self-defence (State of Florida v George Zimmerman [2013] case 592012CF001083A). Despite the jury's acquittal, significant debate surrounding Zimmerman's responsibility persisted (James and Smyth, 2014), alongside calls for a conviction to be sought in federal court, implicates the failure of the court to secure justice. Ongoing debate surrounding Zimmerman's degree of responsibility in the killing of Martin despite the finalisation of the case in the legal realm is not unique. Criminal justice acquittals, or indeed convictions, do not always transfer to mirrored allocations of responsibility in public debates about high-profile homicide incidents. This is evident from the continued debate in the United States surrounding the lethal actions of OJ Simpson and Casey Anthony, in Australia following the Gordon Wood case, and in Italy following the convictions and recent acquittal of Amanda Knox. Community responses in each of these cases demonstrate that official accounts of responsibility are not always easily digestible and that while guilt or innocence may be dichotomised in law, in community perceptions a person deemed not responsible for an act by law may still be perceived morally responsible outside the realm of law.

While the media undoubtedly play a key role in communicating perceptions of responsibility in individual cases of this kind to the wider community, it is also recognised that the operation of the law, and the ongoing maintenance of gendered discourses in our criminal courts, reinforces perceptions of an offender's – and in some cases a victim's – perceived level of responsibility for the homicide perpe-trated. This is particularly controversial when considered in the context of lethal violence that to date has been the subject of less consideration in legal inquiry – for example, lethal violence perpetrated 'illegally' by a soldier during war, by a state and/or others in cases of genocide and the role of business corporations in perpetrating acts of such violence. While these contexts of homicide have been the subject of recent debates in several international jurisdictions (see e.g., Cor-lett, 2013; Field and Jones, 2014; Price, 2014; van der Wilt, 2015), sparked largely by media attention surrounding key cases, those debates have yet to examine the ways in which gender and responsibility are represented and the consequential adequacy of the law's response. By bringing together an exploration of homicide in the private and public spheres, this book directly addresses this gap.

In adopting a focus on responsibility, this collection contributes to over two decades of feminist advocacy that has sought to bring to light gendered influ-ences in the operation of the law and the introduction of law reform that seeks to bring the experiences of traditionally silenced populations within the bounds of the criminal law. For this purpose, we explore responsibility as synonymous with accountability – this may involve being held to account by a legal standard (*criminal responsibility*) or being held to be in breach of a moral standard (*moral responsibility*) (Lacey, 2001). While the former has attracted most attention in the context of homicide research and legal scholarship, both are important in terms of understanding how responsibility for homicide is constructed along a continuum of lethal violence. Moreover, we take each of these understandings of responsibil-ity to be constituted one within the other.

Holding offenders of domestic and sexual violence against women to account has been a focus of significant debate, and in the realm of homicide law such con-cerns have sparked a plethora of law reform activity over the last twenty years, particularly in relation to the complete and partial defences to murder (Carline and Easteal, 2014; Fitz-Gibbon and Stubbs, 2012; Graycar and Morgan, 2005; Horder, 1992; Ramsey, 2010; Sheehy et al., 2012). One of the key goals of such reform has been to ensure that responsibility as apportioned by law reflects the gendered nature of lethal violence between intimate partners. This goal has animated law reform efforts in the United Kingdom, Australia, Canada and New Zealand, which have on the one hand sought to restrict the partial defence of provocation to prevent jealous and controlling men who killed their female intimate partners from evading a conviction for murder, while on the other hand expanding the complete defence of self-defence to ensure that it is able to better accommodate the experiences of women who kill an abusive partner to provide a more just avenue to acquittal (see, e.g. Law Commission, 2005, 2007; Morgan, 2002; Victorian Law Reform Commission, 2004). Despite this level of reform, overcoming the law's inability to adequately reflect on and respond to the gendered nature of homicide has proven a difficult task. Doctrinal reform, such as that mentioned here, has often failed to distance the law of homicide from concerns that the gendered narratives employed within the criminal courts reinforce stereotypical assumptions about masculinity, femininity, victim blaming and men's power over women (for research examining the impact of this in the Australian context, see *inter alia* Fitz-Gibbon, 2014; Tyson, 2013). Frustration at the law's inability to accurately reflect women's experiences of violence is well captured by Stubbs and Wangmann (2015), who, in her analysis of victims of domestic violence within legal processes, argues that 'legal narratives are constructions which cannot ever hope to capture the complexities, the nuances and the ambiguities of women's lives'.

While not focused on the operation of legal categories per se, this book demonstrates how in official allocations of responsibility, the actions of those involved can be privileged or, conversely, silenced. Examining official responses to violence and suffering, Aradau (2004) refers to the 'politics of pity' to explain how through the policy intervention process governments can legitimise or de-legitimise the suffering of others. It is through the latter that the suffering and pain of victims is rendered invisible by the official response. Aradau's work is salient here in our examination of responsibility for homicide on the less explored end of the continuum. In questioning the extent to which states, corporations and institutions are held responsible in official responses to a homicide, this book considers the extent that the state and/or law is able to provide an effective mechanism through which responsibility for homicide can be held to account.

Set against the backcloth of what is already known about the nature and extent of sexual violence (Kelly, 1988) and the nature of violence more generally (the continuum of violence; Cockburn, 2009), this book explores the extent to which the domains of private homicide and public homicide become blurred when set against attributions of responsibility. We argue that this is particularly the case when such attributions are understood as both gendered and a product of the state's legally informed responses to such violence. These concepts – private homicide, public homicide, gender and responsibility – provide the key framework for the chapters that follow. To explore those constructions of responsibility and gender across contexts of homicide, this book falls into two parts. Reflecting the subtitle of this book, the contributions contained across the two parts adopt a truly international approach which balances focused case studies from Australia, Canada, Ireland, England and Wales, Vietnam and Afghanistan with a consideration of the broader international persepctive.

About this book

Part I, 'Making Sense of the Boundaries between Homicide, Gender and Responsibility', examines the gendered operation of homicide law and the changing nature of the law's response to 'domestic' murder. This is undertaken across four chapters with a focus on examining gendered understandings and representations of domestic homicide victims and offenders. These chapters illustrate why, despite over two decades of scholarship and legislative reform that has had gender in mind, it remains debatable to what extent a gendered analysis of murder has offered a more accurate representation of this offence and a more just response to its occurrence. This reform has largely taken the 'private' realm as the focus of its concern, and the four chapters in Part I reflect those preoccupations.

In Chapter 1, Anette Ballinger uses the homicide case of Ruth Ellis and David Blakely as a lens through which to unwrap the gendered nature of responsibility and its ongoing relationship with the law of provocation. Ellis was the last woman to be executed in England and Wales, and the law's response to her use of lethal violence against her lover, David Blakely, has continued to animate scholarly debate despite its having occurred over half a century ago. Ballinger reconsiders the issue of (ir)responsibility and the impact of discourses of masculinity and femininity on legal proceedings and the categorisation of a homicide offence as murder or manslaughter. The resulting feminist analysis invites the reader to challenge the inherently masculine nature of law and, in particular, the problematic construction of the 'reasonable man' within criminal law.

In Chapter 2, Julie Stubbs examines the three key themes of murder, gender and responsibility to provide a detailed discussion of the perpetration of lethal violence by men and women in the domestic context alongside the limits of criminal law in adequately responding to acts of domestic homicide and understanding divergences in how men and women perpetrate and experience violence. Highlighting the importance of recognising differences in how we conceptualise domestic homicide and intimate partner homicide, Stubbs traces the extent to which law reform introduced in Australia, the United States and elsewhere has been able to improve the ability of the courts to adopt a gendered lens in understanding and responding to domestic homicide. In the second half of the chapter, Stubbs adopts an intersectional framework, which draws on recent homicide statistics to cast light on the overrepresentation of indigenous persons as both victims and offenders. A factor that Stubbs argues highlights the pressing need for responses that recognise violence as racialised and promote prevention policies away from the realm of criminal law.

Continuing this analysis of domestic homicides, in Chapter 3, Myrna Dawson provides an intricate analysis of forty Canadian sentencing judgments for persons convicted of the murder of a spouse. Her analysis examines the proliferation and impact of stereotypes about intimacy and violence in the law's response to intimate partner homicides, with a particular focus on how such stereotypes influence sentencing decisions surrounding a defendant's culpability, the need for public protection and evaluations of practical constraints of the system. Dawson's analysis points to a positive trend of judicial emphasis on the seriousness of intimate partner violence as a social issue; however, the analysis also reveals the continued proliferation of stereotypes about violence and intimacy in legal portrayals of intimate homicide.

In Chapter 4, Kate Fitz-Gibbon extends the analysis of private homicides to critically examine allocations of responsibility and discourses of hegemonic masculinity in the narratives employed during the sentencing of children convicted of homicide offences. Locating her analysis in the international context, Fitz-Gibbon argues that Australia – like England and Wales – has adopted an inherently punitive approach to understanding and responding to lethal violence committed by children. Drawing on an analysis of a decade of sentencing judgments from Victoria (Australia), she argues that the actions of children who kill are judicially framed at sentencing in line with stereotypical notions of dangerous and irresponsible masculinity and collective violence. In the second half of her analysis, however, Fitz-Gibbon argues that a judicial discourse of understanding offers a more effective lens through which childhood experiences of vulnerability, fear and social isolation can be illuminated and a more nuanced allocation of individual responsibility can ensue.

In Part II, 'Blurring the Boundaries between Homicide, Gender and Responsibility', the contributors consider less explored contexts of lethal violence and explore the extent to which varied contexts of lethal violence offer different insights into the role of gender and the allocation of responsibility for such acts. The first of these explorations, by Sandra Walklate and Ross McGarry in Chapter 5, examines the perpetration of murder in war. Using two case studies – the My Lai massacre during the Vietnam War and the conviction of 'Marine A' for the murder of a Taliban member in September 2011 – Walklate and McGarry provide a nuanced analysis of what is (and importantly, what is not) made visible in official allocations of responsibility for lethal violence in armed combat. Tracing the role of the law in war, the authors draw on the work of Sarat, Hobbes and Walklate to demonstrate why allocations of responsibility for lethal violence committed between soldiers is no longer 'simple or straightforward' and indeed why domestic armed conflict and international laws fail to offer an effective lens through which responsibility for such violence can be constructed. Weaving a detailed analysis of their two chosen case studies, Walklate and McGarry's chapter reveals the gendered role of the state in responding to murder in war alongside the complexities inherent in determining state responsibility versus that of the individual soldier for murder committed in armed combat.

Continuing the examination of lethal violence perpetrated in conflict settings, in Chapter 6 Anette Bringedal Houge provides a detailed reading of homicide case law from the ICTY. This case law is used as a means to explore constructions of individual responsibility and the influence of gender and militarism in murder cases dealt with under international law. Opening with a quote from Jonathan Littell's novel, *The Kindly Ones*, Houge's analysis examines how defendant perpetrators are represented and their actions explained by legal practitioners, including judges, prosecutors and defence counsel. This case analysis is compared with her earlier research examining the production of legal narratives in cases of sexual war violence (Houge, 2015). The resulting comparative discussion explores whether narratives of justification and neutralisation are more likely to emerge in cases of illegitimate killing while also considering the ways in which vulnerability is constructed along gendered lines throughout this legal setting.

In Chapter 7, Alison Gerard and Tracey Kerr provide a detailed examination of intersections of gender, race and sovereignty in official responses to the death of an Iranian asylum seeker at an Australian-funded, offshore detention centre on Manus Island (Papua New Guinea). The chapter traces the securitisation of migration internationally and the unique dangers that resulting policies pose to the welfare of asylum seekers. This backdrop is then used to frame their intricate analysis of official responses to the February 2014 death in custody of Reza Barati. Examining three sources of official Australian government representations of Barati's death, Gerard and Kerr argue that the spread of legal ambiguities in offshore detention settings has impacted on official accountability and constructions of responsibility. Their conclusion that such policies have the practical impact of dispersing and outsourcing responsibility for lethal violence resonates beyond the Australian context to deaths that occur in detention and correctional settings globally.

In the final chapter, David Doyle and Joe McGrath provide a comparative analysis of divergent means of imposing criminal responsibility for corporate manslaughter in Ireland and England and Wales and, in doing so, point to the obstacles encountered in challenging individualised notions of responsibility in the law. Beginning with a background examination of the recent legislative reform that has impacted on how responsibility is allocated for work-related fatalities in Britain and Ireland, the chapter then extends the work of Horder (2012) to examine the extent to which prison services can be held responsible for deaths in custody. While Doyle and McGrath point to the difficulties that may be experienced in attempts to extend criminal liability to prison services, their argument illuminates the inability of such legislation to offer a deterrent for such deaths and the need to reconstruct deaths in custody as a public health issue if effective prevention strategies are to emerge.

The conclusion builds on the work of Kelly (1988) and Cockburn (2009) by considering how the varied contexts of lethal violence examined throughout this book can be understood along a continuum of lethal violence. Drawing out the common themes of gender and responsibility explored throughout, the conclusion also considers how individualised versus collective responsibility is constructed along this continuum as well as the influence of power and structural gender inequality and the role of official institutions in denying responsibility.

References

Barry, D., Kovaleski, S. F., Robertson, C. and Alvarez, L. (2012) Race, tragedy and outrage collide after a shot in Florida. *New York Times*, 1 April.

Carline, A. and Easteal, P. (2014) *Shades of Grey – Domestic and Sexual Violence Against Women: Law Reform and Society*. London: Routledge.

Carpenter, B. and Ball, M. (2012) *Justice in Society*. Sydney: The Federation Press.

Carrington, K. (2015) *Feminism and Global Justice*. London: Routledge.

Cockburn, C. (2009) The continuum of violence. In Linke, U. and Smith, D. T. (eds.) *Cultures of Fear: A Critical Reader*. London: Pluto Press, pp. 158–173.

Connell, R. W. (2005) Change among the gatekeepers: Men, masculinities, and gender equality in the global arena. *Signs*, 30(3): 1801–1825.

Corlett, J. A. (2013) U.S. responsibility for war crimes in Iraq. *Responsibility and Punishment*, 34: 225–246.

Cowburn, M. (2011) Perceiving the continuum of sexual harm and the need for varied responses to sexual violence. *International Journal of Offender Therapy and Comparative Criminology*, 55(2): 179–181.

Daly, K. and Chesney-Lind, M. (1988) Feminism and criminology. *Justice Quarterly,* 5(4): 497–538.

Field, S. and Jones, L. (2014) Are directors getting away with manslaughter? Emerging trends in prosecutions for corporate manslaughter. *Business Law Review,* 35(4): 158–163.

Fitz-Gibbon, K. (2014) *Homicide Law Reform, Gender and the Provocation Defence: A Comparative Perspective.* Hampshire, UK: Palgrave Macmillan.

Fitz-Gibbon, K. and Stubbs, J. (2012) Divergent directions in reforming legal responses to lethal violence. *Australian and New Zealand Journal of Criminology,* 45(3): 318–336.

Graycar, R. and Morgan, J. (2005) Law reform: What's in it for women? *Windsor Yearbook of Access to Justice,* 23(2): 393–419.

Horder, J. (1992) *Provocation and Responsibility.* Oxford: Clarendon Press.

Horder, J. (2012) *Homicide and the Politics of Law Reform.* Oxford: Oxford University Press.

James, J. and Smyth, K. (2014) If George Zimmerman were found guilty, would the criminal justice system be considered just? In Fasching-Varner, K. J., Reynolds, R. E., Albert, K. A. and Martin, L. L. (eds.) *Trayvon Martin, Race and American Justice: Writing Wrong.* Rotterdam: Sense Publishers, pp. 107–112.

Kelly, L. (1988) *Surviving Sexual Violence.* Oxford: Polity Press.

Kelly, L. (2011) Preface: Standing the test of time? Reflections on the concept of sexual continuum. In Brown, J. and Walklate, S. (eds.) *Handbook of Sexual Violence.* London: Routledge, pp. xvii–xxvi.

Lacey, N. (2001) Responsibility and modernity in criminal law. *Journal of Political Philosophy,* 9: 249–276.

Law Commission (2005) *A New Homicide Act for England and Wales?* Consultation Paper No. 177. London.

Law Commission (2007) *The Partial Defence of Provocation.* Report 98. Wellington, New Zealand.

Lee, C. (2013) Making race salient: Trayvon Martin and implicit bias in a not yet post-racial society. *North Carolina Law Review,* 91: 101–157.

Morgan, J. (2002) *Who Kills Whom and Why: Looking beyond Legal Categories.* Occasional Paper. Melbourne: Victorian Law Reform Commission.

Polk, K. (1994) *When Men Kill: Scenarios of Masculine Violence.* Melbourne: Cambridge University Press.

Price, L. (2014) Finding fault in organisations – reconsidering the role of senior managers in corporate manslaughter. *Legal Studies,* 35(3): 385–407.

Ramsey, C. B. (2010) Criminal law: Provoking change – comparative insights on feminist homicide law reform. *Journal of Criminal Law and Criminology,* 100(1): 33–109.

Sheehy, E., Stubbs, J. and Tolmie, J. (2012) Defences to homicide for battered women: A comparative analysis of laws in Australia, Canada and New Zealand. *Sydney Law Review,* 34: 467–492.

Strauss, M. A. (1994) State-to-state differences in social inequality and social bonds in relation to assaults on wives in the United States. *Journal of Comparative Family Studies,* 25: 7–24.

Stubbs, J. and Wangmann, J. (2015) Competing conceptions of victims of domestic violence within legal processes. In Wilson, D. and Ross, S. (eds.) *Crime, Victims and Policy.* Hampshire: Palgrave Macmillan, pp. 107–132.

Tyson, D. (2013) *Sex, Culpability and the Defence of Provocation.* Abingdon, UK: Routledge.

van der Wilt, H. (2015) Srebrenica: On joint criminal enterprise, aiding and abetting and command responsibility. *Netherlands International Law Review*. doi: 10.1007/ s40802–015–0036–8

Victorian Law Reform Commission (2004) *Defences to Homicide: Final Report*. Melbourne.

Whaley, R. B. and Messner, S. F. (2002) Gender equality and gendered homicides. *Homicide Studies*, 6(3): 188–210.

Whaley, R. B., Messner, S. F. and Veysey, B. M. (2013) The relationship between gender equality and rates of inter- and intra-sexual lethal violence: An exploration of functional form. *Justice Quarterly*, 30(4): 732–754.

Wiggins, O. (2012) A rallying cry for justice in teen's death. *Washington Post*, 25 March.

1 A question of provocation or responsibility?

Revisiting the case of Ruth Ellis and David Blakely

Anette Ballinger

Despite having taken place in 1955, the execution of Ruth Ellis continues to occupy academic scholarship, true crime publications and other aspects of popular media (Ballinger, 1996, 2000, 2012; BBC1, 1999; Goodman and Pringle, 1974; Hancock, 1989; Rose, 1993). More specifically, it has remained a reference point for criminological and legal debates concerning murder and manslaughter both in England and Wales and elsewhere in the world operating within a similar criminal justice system. Not only was Ellis the last woman to be executed in England and Wales, but her case had a direct impact on the law in that it was central to the introduction of the defence of diminished responsibility as part of the reforms within the 1957 Homicide Act and has since acted as a benchmark against which understandings of provocation and responsibility have evolved.

However, there is another aspect of this case which has been less explored – the issue of responsibility and *ir*responsibility as opposed to diminished responsibility. This change of focus widens the scope for a more critical analysis to include not only Ruth Ellis, but also the man she killed, her lover, David Blakely. In this chapter I argue that this alternative focus allows the operation of legal and popular discourses in relation to gender to become visible, particularly through the defence of provocation. Ultimately, this reveals the taken-for-granted and hidden assumptions in respect of the gendered nature of irresponsibility and its relationship to what counts as provocation.

In order to facilitate this analysis, the chapter will explore how responsibility and irresponsibility were deeply implicated in this case through discourses and constructions of masculinity and femininity which gave meaning to – and underpinned – the legal proceedings that ensued. In so doing, this chapter offers a feminist analysis of responsibility/irresponsibility and their impact on courtroom proceedings. This will illustrate how, in the very act of *under-emphasising* irresponsibility in Blakely's behaviour and *over-emphasising* the responsible behaviour of Ruth Ellis, the court played its part in marginalising social issues of power, reducing them to legal understandings of individual responsibility, ultimately leaving the wider questions of gender divisions and patriarchal control untouched and ignored. Despite an increased and renewed interest in the Ellis case forty-eight years after her execution in 2003, when her appeal was heard and dismissed, there has been little or no attempt to explore such questions.

Since the question of how the 'reasonable man' would act, and indeed re-act, both to and in certain circumstances was and remains a key concept within English law, descriptive details about Ruth and David's relationship are necessary in order to document the exact circumstances that culminated in David's death.

The case

After being involved in a volatile, violent and exploitative relationship with David Blakely for nineteen months, Ruth finally shot him outside a pub in Hampstead on Easter Sunday, 1955. Towards the end of their relationship, David's erratic behaviour towards Ruth had intensified, increasingly relying on both psychological cruelty and physical violence (Ballinger, 1996, 2000; Goodman and Pringle, 1974). This culminated in Ruth suffering a miscarriage after what was to become her last beating, ten days prior to the shooting (Medical Report, 13 June 1955, DPP2/2430). As a direct consequence of their relationship, he had also left her homeless and penniless. To elaborate, at twenty-five years of age, David was three years younger than Ruth, and unlike her, came from a privileged, upper-middle-class background, evidenced, for example, by his public school education and private income. This ensured that he did not need to seek regular employment but instead was able to live a 'playboy' lifestyle, focusing his attention on motor racing, alcohol and women (see e.g. Ballinger, 2012: 447; Ellis with Taylor, 1995: 69; Hancock, 1989: 57). According to virtually all published accounts, David was regarded as a shallow, immature character (see e.g. Goodman and Pringle, 1974; Healey, 1985; Jakubait with Weller, 2005). Unwilling to hold down a permanent job, and permanently short of money as a result of having invested his personal allowance in building a racing car, David moved in with Ruth after only two weeks, letting her support him. This did not curtail his interest in other women. Apart from being officially engaged to Mary Dawson, a woman from his own social class, he was also involved in various affairs while sharing Ruth's flat (Ballinger, 1996: 13, 2000). The last few weeks of their complex relationship were taken up by, on the one hand, David promising Ruth marriage in the light of Ruth's pregnancy, and, on the other, his disappearance for days during which he would be involved in another sexual relationship (DPP2/2430).

Despite having promised to return to Ruth for the Easter holidays, he finally disappeared altogether – moving in with friends and refusing all contact with her. 'In a state of nervous exhaustion and mentally drained for these uncertainties' following this final 'protracted period of contradictory and provocative behaviour' which had left her 'seething, furious and powerless for three days', and having 'suffered the additional humiliation of being removed' by police officers outside the house of the friends where David was staying, Ruth shot him after eventually managing to locate him outside the Magdala pub in Hampstead (Ballinger, 2000: 298).

Coming from a lower social class than David, and described variously as 'a model', 'a club-hostess' and a 'typical West End tart' (Marks and Van den Bergh, 1990: 148), the implication was clear – Ruth was a particular 'type' of woman – 'young, blonde, attractive and immoral' (Farran, as cited in Ballinger, 1996: 13). Nonetheless, she was well paid as manager of the Little Club, which provided her with accommodation. Both were lost as a result of her relationship with David, who would visit the club during her working hours and frequently became inebriated and violent towards her, either in the bar or within earshot in the flat above. As their relationship deteriorated, so the extent of David's financial exploitation increased, to the point where he let Ruth settle his bills (DPP2/2430: 46). Thus, upon her arrest, 'the woman who once had pounds to waste had six-pence in copper in her bag . . . and nothing in the bank' (Hancock, 1989: 185). She also had to rely on the charity of her friend, Desmond Cussen, to pay the rent for her flat.

On taking responsibility

To reiterate a point made above, the descriptive details regarding Ruth and David's relationship presented here should not be interpreted as a moral judgement upon either of their characters – instead, it is intended to provide necessary context to the analysis that follows.

When analysing Ruth's conduct following the shooting, it is scarcely possible to point to another case in which the perpetrator of a crime took more responsibility for her actions. Thus, immediately after the shooting, Ruth handed the gun over to Alan Thompson, an off-duty police officer, with the words: 'Please take this gun and arrest me' (Morton, 2015: 402). When, during her trial, she was asked by the prosecutor, Mr Humphreys: 'Mrs Ellis, when you fired that revolver at close range into the body of David Blakely, what did you intend to do?' she replied: 'It is obvious that when I shot him I intended to kill him' (DPP2/2430). As noted by one jury member: 'Mrs Ellis herself . . . admitted she meant to kill him' (cited in Marks and Van den Bergh, 1990: 162).

She not only took full responsibility for her crime, she fully accepted her punishment to the point where she refused to plead for mercy or allow the instigation of an appeal on her behalf. Instead she wrote from her prison cell: 'I say a Life for a Life'. . . . 'I am quite happy with the verdict' (letters reproduced in Goodman and Pringle, 1974: 74 and *Daily Express*, 14 July 1955). In short, while she had pleaded 'not guilty' due to provocation, she undoubtedly took full responsibility for her action. However, as the law stood in 1955, the provocation defence was ruled out due to the 'trigger event' having taken place several days earlier, hence, the presiding judge, Mr Justice Havers, ruled that 'the whole doctrine relating to provocation depends on the fact that it causes . . . sudden and temporary loss of self-control (DPP2/2430: 68). In other words, no allowance could be made for a 'cooling off' period between the time of the provocation and the act carried out in response to it (Carline, 2005a: 16). With the benefit of hindsight, it is clear that this ruling is a reflection of how the subject of the 'reasonable man' was constructed, requiring that retaliation must be immediate and in proportion to the level of provocation endured (Carline, 2005b: 217).

The question, however, remains why the appeal was dismissed forty-eight years later, during an era when the diminished responsibility defence is taken for granted and legal changes have become established, in an attempt to take account of women's 'slow burn' experience of provocation (Munro, 2007: 134). In 2003 the appeal judges answered this question when they ruled that the appeal should be dismissed on the grounds that 'we must apply the substantive law of murder as *applicable at the time*, disregarding the changes brought about by the Homicide Act 1957' (*Ellis v R*, 2003: 9, emphasis added). The judges fully accepted there was 'unchallenged evidence that over a significant period of time the deceased had subjected Mrs Ellis to violent conduct', including the beating that preceded the miscarriage, and had she retaliated *immediately*, the judge would have been obliged to leave the issue of provocation to the jury (*Ellis v R*, 2003: 10–11).

Within a liberal system of law, where 'facts speak for themselves' (Inglis, 2003: 172), the judges' reasoning that 'it is not possible to take the purely statutory defence of diminished responsibility created [in] 1957 and apply it as if it had been enacted at the date of the killing or the date of the trial' (*Ellis v R*, 2003: 9) appears self-explanatory and beyond common sense. To have ruled otherwise would have left the door open to innumerable future appeals of other cases tried prior to 1957. This point was further reinforced when the appellant's barrister also argued that Ruth was suffering from BWS, a factor that would now be taken into consideration. Unsurprisingly, this argument was rejected, for it seems entirely unrealistic – inconceivable even – to expect a court to accept an appeal based on terms and concepts such as 'domestic violence' or BWS, neither of which had entered popular or legal discourse at the time of the trial. In short, the rationale behind rejecting the appeal appears entirely justifiable and correct – both legally and ethically.

Yet, the case continues to capture the popular imagination and to trouble commonsense notions of justice, mercy and fair play. How, therefore, can we explain the chasm between this logical and reasonable legal resolution of the case and the persistent, deeply felt notion that Ruth Ellis suffered an injustice at the hands of the criminal justice system, and thus ultimately at the hands of the state? It is to this question that the chapter now turns.

Neutral yet gendered – the legal versus the social: theoretical implications

The Ellis case remains troubling because it appears to provide firm evidence of the 'mismatch between the normative expectations of state law and the endless plurality of social life' (Davies, 2007: 152). Such a 'mismatch' forces us to consider, even conclude, that law is unable to fulfil its promise to deliver justice for all, which raises the question:

> Are we to accept a position of compromise, which states . . . that law necessarily does violence to people's lives by forcing complex narratives into simplified normative frames? (Davies, 2007: 156)

To elaborate, Weait (2007: 29) explains that the principles of neutrality and equality are inherent to, and form the basis of, formal law because the very foundation of liberal legal thought rests on the assumption that in matters concerned with establishing responsibility, 'one's sex, gender, race, ethnicity, sexuality, relationships with others – in short one's lived identity – are irrelevant, and must be so'. Thus, by definition, the law cannot be 'concerned with what it is to be a human being . . . nor can it be concerned with what a human-being-responsible actually means' since, ultimately, to do so would undermine the very foundations on which it is built and which are 'necessary for its continued functioning' (ibid.: 30). In other words, 'to seek substantive justice by particularising the legal subject [is] doomed to failure' (ibid.: 44), since, to expect individual experiences and their social reality to be reflected through the adjudicative process would undermine the very rule of law. Thus, 'the construction of subjectivity and responsibility through law can only provide an account of subjectivity and responsibility *for* law, and this account is one that will inevitably occlude the reality, and deny the relevance, of inequality, specificity and partiality' (ibid.: 23, added emphasis). This must be so, since 'factors by which "difference" is constructed are social in character, rather than legally recognised' (Davies, 2007: 161).

Weait's (2007) explanation of the inherent logic of liberal law, and how the legal subject and responsibility are constructed within it, makes perfect sense, even common sense, thereby eloquently demonstrating how our understanding of the criminal law is taken as a given – within post-Enlightenment culture it is difficult to conceive of how it could be otherwise. As noted by Davies (2007: 156), 'the liberal positivist approach to law and its subjects is incredibly resilient', not least due to 'its rhetorical attractiveness [and] its adaptability in the face of changing socio-political contexts'. Thus, 'the moral and political traditions within which it is embedded' is precisely what 'precludes us from thinking differently, laterally and imaginatively about the very conduct, consequences and people that are the object of its repression, censure and condemnation' (Weait, 2007: 21). Yet, despite the law's ability to repress contradictions (Davies, 2007: 163), alternative discourses can, and do, challenge and resist official state-defined 'truths' (Inglis, 2003), and I shall argue that the Ellis case represents a moment when people *did* and *do* think differently and that this can, to a considerable extent, account for the continued preoccupation with the case in both public consciousness and academic analysis.

The gendered nature of provocation:
when 'being responsible' doesn't pay

> Once masculinity appears as a specific position, not just the way things are, its judgements will be revealed in process and procedure, as well as adjudication and legislation (Mackinnon, as cited in Collier, 2010: 15 f/n).

So far it has been established that formal law is based on the discourses of neutrality and equality and thus refuses to take inequality, specificity, partiality and wider social divisions into account. As noted above, for defenders of the dominant social order, this must be so to avoid undermining the very foundations on which law is built. Yet, it is also this very feature that presents a problem for women, because by definition, this involves ignoring the 'pre-existing gender-power imbalance' inherent within a heteropatriarchal society (Atwell, 2007: 5).

The law – via legal reasoning – arguably reinforces this imbalance through the 'channelling' of social power – 'law genders us, classes us' – for example, by excluding its own 'inbuilt corruptions of neutrality such as its hetero-normative symbolism' (Davies, 2007: 161, 156, 163). As Mackinnon notes, 'law's purported neutrality is simply a mask for the "masculinity" of its judgements' (as cited in Collier, 2010: 15). Within this context, 'the reasons for according some interactions epistemic privilege while others are sidelined are ideological, discursive, and aesthetic, not rational' or neutral (Davies, 2007: 163).

Additionally, the gendered nature of the provocation defence has been a concern for feminist scholars for several decades. Radford, for example, has observed that '[j]udicial sympathy for the human fallibility of provoked men is not afforded so generously to battered women' (as cited in Morrissey, 2003: 98). Morrissey (ibid.: 93) adds that the defence of provocation contains an 'explicit masculinist bias'. This is unsurprising, since the origins of the entire legal system date back to an era when women formally belonged to men and thus had no legal status of their own (Ballinger, 2005: 78). Historically, therefore, law was 'constructed around a masculine subject and an associated set of masculine characteristics' that reflected male norms and values (Davies, 1997: 28). Indeed it is still the case that 'Western legal systems are constructed around the advancement of male pursuits and the resolution of male disputes' (Morrissey, 2003: 70). Within this context the provocation defence can be traced back to the seventeenth century, when the ultimate form of provocation was for a husband to find himself cuckolded. In such circumstances, 'delivering a fatal blow was regarded as fully morally justified, such was the affront to a man's honour' (Burton, 2001: 254). The subjectivity of men who react immediately and violently to what they perceive as provocation, as in this example, has thus 'been legally valued over that of their male and female victims and arguably over the subjectivity of women who have been assaulted for years' and eventually kill their partners (Davies, 2007: 161). Indeed, only six years prior to the Ellis case did the judiciary accept that the provocation defence could also be applied to women who had killed their partners (Taylor, as cited in O'Donovan, 1991: 226). This defence therefore provides a clear illustration of 'the manner in which law has been constructed from a male perspective, according to male standards, so that it either excludes, devalues or distorts women's experiences and motivations' (Fox, 1995: 171). Thus, while a 'reasonable' man can be provoked into murder by suspected or actual infidelity through the subject position 'If I can't have her, no one else can' (Campbell, 1992: 99), a woman claiming provocation after finding herself in identical or similar circumstances, even if combined with being a victim of battery, is likely to have such a claim dismissed on the grounds that to do otherwise would provide 'a licence to kill' (Lees, 1992: 272).

In short, while it was accepted that a 'reasonable man' may be unable to control his emotions in such circumstances, a woman who claims provocation in similar situations was, and arguably still is, constructed as out for revenge, since unlike dominant constructions of masculinity, anger and rage are not part of the construction of acceptable femininity (Morrissey, 2003: 98; Lees, 1992: 268). The construction of masculinity, however, allows a man to 'remain reasonable, whilst losing mastery of his mind under provocation. . . . He feels powerful enough to defend himself or to lose his temper. This construct is built into the law as a definition of the defence to homicide' (O'Donovan, 1993: 428). Implicit to this construction is the notion that a man can remain 'reasonable' yet irresponsible, unlike the 'vengeful' woman who remains in control, plotting premeditated revenge – she is entirely *responsible*. The only way to escape such responsibility is through relying on another stereotypical subject position – the hysterical, helpless, pathological woman whose behaviour is driven by her overwrought, irrational emotions. Thus, despite battered women having a long history of offering rational and 'reasonable' explanations for retaliating against violent partners (Ballinger, 2005), the judiciary has an equally long history of dismissing, invalidating or re-interpreting such explanations in order to 'render them harmless' (Allen, 1987). This process of replacing agentic explanations with pathological excuses not only distracts attention away from the responsible reasoning behind the retaliation and instead emphasises 'a diseased mind' – it also neutralises the threat that retaliating women pose to the dominant discourses of heteropatriarchy (Ballinger, 2005: 67). Within legal discourse, there is thus an absence of subject positions for retaliating women outside the two gender stereotypes of – on the one hand – the passive, helpless victim to be pitied rather than punished, who cannot be regarded as a responsible agent for pathological reasons (Allen, 1987: 93), and – on the other – the cold-blooded femme fatale out to seek revenge at any cost (Ballinger, 1996).

This lack of available subject positions for responsible, yet less blameworthy, retaliating women impacted on the Ellis trial and ultimately resulted in consequences which continue to haunt contemporary criminal justice systems. Furthermore, despite the law's extraordinary ability to preclude 'us from thinking differently' as noted above, then, as now, the majority of the public *did* think differently – if the evidence available in the National Archives is accepted as an accurate measure of public opinion at the time about this case – and this difference arguably plays a key role in explaining why the case continues to be publicly debated 60 years after the execution of Ruth Ellis.

Responsible agent or forced to kill?[1]

Providing numerous case-study examples of the gendered nature of the provocation defence, Lees (1992) argued that when men rely on this defence, it is the character of their female victim that comes under scrutiny and that when infidelity is alleged, independent corroboration is frequently not considered necessary – the word of the man is simply accepted. As Burton (2001: 254) observes: 'There are plenty of examples in the late twentieth century of men successfully pleading provocation relying on what their partners allegedly said to them.'

Having studied a number of cases in which a plea of provocation was accepted when utilised by men, Lees (1992: 277) concluded that decisions are made in court based on the assumptions that there are limits to the amount of nagging, insubordination, withdrawal of sexual services or suspected/actual infidelity that 'the ordinary man can be expected to put up with . . . and that murder is a reasonable response to' such behaviour – imagined or otherwise. Thus, the fact that 'men are far more likely to kill because of jealousy and possessiveness, and are more likely to premeditate and carefully plan the homicides than are women' (Morrissey, 2003: 69) has not prevented the provocation defence from being accepted:

> In some of the case-studies provocation was accepted despite evidence of premeditation as in the case of Leslie Taylor who phoned his wife to tell her he was coming before proceeding to stab her.
>
> (Lees, 1992: 278)

The gender-specific acceptance of what counts as provocation identified here can be linked to Smart's concept of the phallocentric nature of the law – that is, regardless of which side of the law the men in the courtroom stand on, they all share the site of hegemonic masculinity (Connell, 1987), and from this site 'women's bodies are sexualised terrain' (Smart, 1989: 38). This 'fratriarchy' among men (Remy, 1990), regardless of whether they are members of the judiciary, victims or defendants, helps to explain why the presence of all the key 'triggers' in the Ellis case – infidelity, jealous possessiveness, attempts to end a relationship – that justify the provocation defence when men kill their partners were not accepted as evidence of provocation where she was concerned, for as Walker has observed:

> The idea that a woman could kill her partner and still meet the legal standard of reasonableness . . . is a reality few people want to acknowledge, let alone accept.
>
> (as cited in Morrissey, 2003: 98)

To elaborate, three separate yet interrelated aspects of Ruth Ellis' conduct and behaviour can be understood to have interacted with, and reinforced each other, and combined with a phallocentric judiciary, they played a key part in sealing her fate. They are the highly gendered aspects of her physical appearance, personal demeanour and sexual reputation. Their interrelation was so intense that at times it was difficult to separate them out, as exemplified in the *News of the World*:

> Ruth Ellis was an attractive young woman. Of her kind. But what was her kind? Experienced. Worldly. Sexually provocative. The kind of woman you would expect to find in places like The Little Club.
>
> (8 October 1972: 10)

When she appeared in the courtroom, it soon became clear that this was not a woman prepared to play the traditional role of the pathologically damaged helpless victim, lacking responsibility for her actions:

> Instead of a dejected young woman, tired-looking, sombre and about to stand trial for her life, she looked like she was attending the premiere of a West End show.
>
> (Marks and Van Den Bergh, 1990: 134)

Ruth's demeanour matched her appearance, for, as had been the case upon her arrest, in the courtroom she once again took full responsibility for the killing of David:

> I was feeling just a little – in a peculiar mood then: rather nasty mood. . . . I had an idea I wanted to kill him. . . . When I put the gun in my bag I intended to find David and shoot him. I thought I had missed him, so I fired again. He was still running, and I fired a third shot.
>
> (Trial transcript reproduced in Goodman and Pringle, 1974)

As noted above, she had also stated that her intentions were 'obvious' when she placed the gun in her bag – 'to shoot David'. Such declarations led *The Sunday People* to observe:

> Her crime was not that of a sexual innocent suddenly discovering man's inhumanity to woman. It seemed like the vengeance of a cool sophisticate, proud of her lone act of savagery.
>
> (2 December 1973)

Similarly, Hancock (1989: 14) observed that she described 'the shooting of the man with whom she had been living, like a male motorist reporting the running down of a stray dog'. Thus, her demeanour, her apparent lack of remorse and failure to seek redemption ensured that she would become embedded in the 'femme fatale' subject position – a cold-blooded killer ruled by rationality rather than emotions. This was further reinforced by her repeated attempts to take full responsibility for her act. For example, when her mother attempted to persuade her to plead insanity, she responded: 'It's no use Mother. I was sane when I did it. And I meant to do it' (Mrs Nielson interviewed in the *Sunday Dispatch*, 26 June 1955). She not only took full responsibility for her crime – making no attempt to excuse it – she attempted 'to prove that she had been morally justified in killing David' because of his treatment of her (Goodman and Pringle, 1974: 42):

> He was at Tanza Road with Anthony and Carole Findlater without me. He had promised never to go there without me. . . . It never occurred to David to come back and face me. The hero of the race track was terrified of an angry woman.
>
> (Ellis, as cited in *Daily Mirror*, 16 July 1955: 9)

While this may have sounded like a rather feeble excuse for committing murder from the viewpoint of those working inside a heteropatriarchal judicial system, it is nonetheless the case that much of the time her explanations were virtually indistinguishable from the justifications provided by male killers, whose defence of provocation, as outlined above, was and is frequently accepted in court:

> I no longer thought of David as the man I loved, but as someone who was trying to make a fool of me. I felt humiliated and frustrated.
>
> (*Daily Mirror*, 16 July 1955: 9)

Words, phrases and explanations such as feeling 'humiliated', 'frustrated' and 'made a fool of' echo what was considered acceptable excuses in Lee's (1992: 278) research when men kill their partners:

> He had felt 'totally humiliated at what she had done in front of my family' and received a six-year sentence for manslaughter.

In another case, 'a non-stop form of humiliation and degradation . . . drained every bit of self respect from a grown man' (Lees, 1992: 277). Having had his defence of provocation accepted, Nicholas Boyce received a sentence of six years for manslaughter after having dismembered his wife's body, cooked parts of it 'and dumped them in plastic bags in several parts of London' (Lees, 1992: 275). In Ruth's case, however, feeling humiliated and 'made a fool of' could not be made to match the defence of provocation. On the contrary, the more she attempted to explain herself, the more she appeared to comply with the definition on which criminal responsibility depends: the capacities of understanding, reason and control (Lacey, 1998: 111) – as when, for example, she emphasised her achievements and independence prior to meeting David, and the loss of both as a consequence of allowing him into her life:

> When I first fell in love with David, I was the successful manageress of a prosperous club. I had admirers, money in the bank, and a lovely flat. Now all I had was a bed-sitting room, no money, no job, and a man who swore he loved me one day and couldn't be bothered to collect me on time the next week.
>
> (*Daily Mirror,* 16 July 1955)

Rather than generating respect, this level of independence, when found in women, can itself be interpreted as 'provocation', even in contemporary culture:

> The women who pose the greatest threat to masculinity are those who assert or appear to assert independence. Any assertions of independence from or resistance to male control may incite or "provoke" male violence. . . . This is not to assume a biological explanation of male supremacy but to assert that violence is central to the construction of masculinity under patriarchy.
>
> (Radford, 1992: 265)

Within the context of the socio-political climate of the 1950s – a period of intense snobbery and concern about 'the apparent breakdown of family values and moral decay' (Ballinger, 2000: 311) – the impact of female assertions of independence and resistance to male control was intensified, and did nothing to reduce the impact of Ruth's apparent unconventional attitude and lifestyle: a single mother at seventeen who had lacked respectability since then as a result of her career as a nightclub hostess, and who had furthermore taken a lover younger than herself from a higher social class, yet failed to defer to him, but on the contrary, considered herself his equal (ibid.).

In sum, apart from having failed to adhere to the dominant discourses of appropriate femininity in terms of respectability, sexuality and domesticity, Ruth had also failed to demonstrate any of the 'appropriate' feminine emotions such as tearfulness, nervousness or hysteria which could have 'rendered her harmless' (Allen, 1987) by reducing her responsibility. On the contrary, her sanity, and thus her responsibility, indeed her very rationality, were formally confirmed by various medical experts whose repeated searches for signs of hysteria failed. Even the psychiatrist employed on behalf of the defence found that 'she had not a *sufficiently* hysterical personality to solve her problem by a complete loss of memory' (Medical Report, 3 May 1955, emphasis added). One month later the medical officer at Holloway Prison examined her and confirmed that 'her behaviour has been rational' and 'she thought she was being unfairly treated by the deceased to whom she had shown much kindness in the past' (Medical Report, 3 June 1955). A third medical expert reported that 'her mood was not disturbed, she showed no depression . . . had no history of violent behaviour, uncontrolled outbursts of temper, or undue aggression (Medical Report, 13 June 1955). In short, her demeanour simply did not match her defence of provocation but was instead interpreted as confirmation that she was a calculating, rational and ruthless killer (Ballinger, 2000: 299).

Reinforcing patriarchy through the (non)defence of Ruth Ellis

Despite his violent and faithless conduct, David Blakely remained an almost invisible presence in the courtroom. Thus, despite regularly beating Ruth and being responsible for her miscarriage, getting involved with her while still engaged to another woman and, in turn, having various other affairs while living with her, his victim status remained intact. From the very beginning of Mr Stevenson's opening speech for the defence, he told the jury that 'it is always an unpleasant thing to say anything disagreeable about someone who is dead' (DPP2/2430). This comment would seem entirely incompatible with proving that Ruth had endured provocation, nonetheless the trial transcript provides many examples of Mr Stevenson's determination to undermine his own client's defence. For example, when he cross-examined Desmond Cussen about the violence Ruth had suffered, he neither referred to David's faithless and violent behaviour nor asked who had been responsible for her injuries. Instead, he specifically stated that he did not want to hear the 'details' of the very behaviour that is crucial in establishing provocation:

Have you ever seen any marks or bruises on her?
Yes.
How often?
On several occasions.
Have you sometimes helped her to disguise them with make-up and that sort of thing?
Yes . . .

Did you help to disguise bruises on her shoulders?
Yes.
I do not want to press you for *details*, but how often have you seen that sort of mark on her? (Emphasis added)
It must be on half a dozen occasions.
Did you on one occasion take her to Middlesex Hospital?
Yes, I did.
Why was that?
She came back when she was staying in my flat, and when I arrived back I found her in a very bad condition.
In what respect?
She had definitely been very badly bruised all over the body.
And did she receive treatment for that condition at Middlesex Hospital?
Yes.

(DPP2/2430)

As to who might have inflicted such injuries, the jury learned nothing. Nor did they hear the evidence of Dr Hill, who had noted 'multiple bruises on both arms and legs, the left hip and around the eyes . . . [and] a more severe bruise over her left ankle', to whom Ruth explained 'that she had been beaten up by a friend who was a racing driver' (Goodman and Pringle, 1974: 24–25). In fact, none of the hospital staff were called upon to give evidence, as were none of the women with whom Ruth suspected David was having an affair. On the contrary, Mr Stevenson specifically stated that no names were to be mentioned in court:

> . . . did you have occasion to complain to Blakely about his conduct with any other women? I do not want you to mention any names, but did you?
>
> (DPP2/2430)

This reluctance to establish concrete evidence of the two most common causes of provocation, violence and unfaithfulness, was repeated when Mr Stevenson examined Ruth:

> Again I do not want to mention any names, but . . . was some [*sic*] some trouble about a young woman?
> *Yes.*
> And again without mentioning names was that a woman down at Penn or Beaconsfield?
> *Yes*
>
> (DDP2/2430)

Thus, as a result of Mr Stevenson's abject failure to establish the very evidence that would have helped to prove provocation, David's promiscuous and faithless conduct remained almost entirely invisible to the jury. This observation is not intended to support victim blaming. Instead it is intended to support the arguments above, concerning the level of 'irresponsibility' afforded to men which was rein-forced by the double standards of morality where men and women are concerned, for when Ruth was engaged in flirtatious behaviour in the course of her work as a club hostess, she was called a prostitute. David's behaviour, however, was con-sidered that of a 'playboy' (see e.g. Hancock, 1989: 80). Indeed, his violence was explained, if not justified, by her conduct, for the beatings were – in his words – caused by Ruth 'tarting around the bar' where she worked, which made him 'very jealous' (DPP2/2430). A shift in focus from David's violence to Ruth's 'provoca-tive' behaviour which 'explained' his jealousy can therefore be observed in court proceedings. This in itself is largely a gender-specific phenomenon, for if the roles had been reversed and a man had killed his female partner, the victim's behaviour was likely to be a focus of the trial in order to legitimise the perpetrator's violence and diminish his guilt (Lees, 1992: 272; Ballinger, 2000: 310; Coates and Wade, 2004: 3). Furthermore, this shift in focus reiterates the gender-specific acceptance of provocation based on 'faithless conduct or disenchantment' (Burton, 2003: 280), and thus confirms Lees's (1992: 282) observation that:

> [w]hen the victim is a man, allegations about his sexual infidelity would just not be taken seriously, and it is doubtful whether they would even be raised.

In fact the legal process in this case not only operated to reinforce the gendered nature of the provocation defence, it actively engaged in the *rewriting* of the spe-cific behaviour that was presented as evidence of provocation, a process which served to render any responsibility or irresponsibility on David's part even more invisible. Thus, dismissing the defence of provocation Mr Justice Havers ended his summing up with these words:

> According to our law . . . it is no defence for a woman who is charged with [the] murder of her lover to prove that she was a jealous woman and had been badly treated by her lover and was in ill-health, and, after her lover promised to spend the Easter holidays with her, he left her without any warning and refused to communicate with her, or that he spent holidays with his friend or in the company of another woman, or if he was committing misconduct with another woman, or that as a result of that she became furious with him and emotionally upset and formed an intention to kill him which she could not control. None of these facts individually afford any defence, nor do they all collectively afford any defence.
>
> (DPP2/2430)

In this rewriting of the evidence by the presiding judge, financial exploitation and ruin, mental cruelty and regular physical violence were translated into being 'badly treated'; suffering a miscarriage after a beating by the baby's father was translated into 'ill-health'; and repeated unfaithfulness with a number of other women was rewritten as 'committing misconduct with another woman'. As noted above, the mere suspicion or unsubstantiated accusations of 'faithless conduct and disenchantment' have afforded a defence of provocation in numerous cases where male perpetrators are concerned. However, the social construction of gender, the gendered nature of both law and responsibility/irresponsibility and the 'trivalisation of domestic violence performed by men' (Morrissey, 2003: 69) ensured that there was no subject position available for Ruth Ellis in which she could be 'at once responsible and agentic, yet vindicated and absolved' (Morrissey, 2003: 68). Meanwhile, David himself, as well as his conduct and behaviour, remained largely invisible in the courtroom, to the point where it was considered inappropriate, even by Ruth's defence counsel, to say anything 'unpleasant' about him.

In short, there was an utter downplaying of David's irresponsible behaviour, a feature that plays directly into the social construction of masculinity, as can be seen for example in the number of good-natured, non-condemning words and phrases that describe male irresponsibility – horseplay, laddish behaviour, 'being a bit of a cad', 'boys will be boys'. Behaviour and actions, or indeed non-actions such as failing to return to Ruth as promised, and more generally, failing to take responsibility for ending the relationship (if indeed that was his wish), his erratic and deceptive two-timing behaviour, his financial exploitation of Ruth, his failure to take forthcoming fatherhood seriously, were either ignored during the trial, or when discussed, were presented as entirely unremarkable throughout the trial transcript (DPP2/2430). Thus, in every respect, the very behaviour and actions that could have provided substance to the provocation defence were ignored. As Ruth's daughter, Georgie, wrote forty years after the trial:

> The harm that David Blakely inflicted upon my mother had been but peripherally touched upon and thinly portrayed. Thereafter, it had been glossed over by a parade of almost irrelevant trivia that had nothing to do with Ruth's state of mind, nor with that which had driven her to exterminate her perfidious lover.
>
> (Ellis with Taylor, 1995: 189)

Ultimately, according to the prosecution *and* the defence, Ruth had all three of the ingredients required to demonstrate criminal responsibility noted above – understanding, reason and control – in abundance, while David apparently had none. Once again, the intention here is not to argue this case on the territory of victim blaming. Rather, the intention is to provide a wider, critical context for the crime, and to challenge the unproblematic manner in which the legal system separates victim and offender categories, and instead to argue that 'victimisation and criminality form a continuum of experience' (Atwell, 2007: 5). There is a strong body of evidence to suggest that a large section of the public did exactly that and, in contrast to the legal system, refused to see the case as one of 'stark simplicity' as claimed by the prosecution (DPP2/2430). This challenge to the guilty verdict helps to explain the continuing academic and popular interest in the case and Ruth's execution.

Thinking differently: resistance and opposition to an 'open and shut' case

While legal personnel had displayed a deep unwillingness to challenge the 'stark simplicity' of this case, it provoked resistance, hostility and outrage within the public, nationally and internationally. Spontaneous petitions for a reprieve appeared throughout the country. In one case, more than 100,000 Britons signed a petition 'to reduce the charge against her from murder to manslaughter' (*Police Review,* 22 August 1986). More generally, her execution was met with resistance from publications as diverse as the *Daily Mirror* (30 June 1955) and the *Lancet* (23 July 1955). A large crowd protested outside Holloway Prison the night before Ruth's execution, chanting 'Evans – Bentley – Ellis' – thus situating her case amongst what was eventually to be officially recognised as two miscarriages of justice – the executions of Timothy Evans and Derek Bentley (*The Times,* 13 July 1955).

More specifically, the National Archives holds two folders which contain the letters written by individuals, or in some cases co-authors, about the case and sent to the Home Office prior to Ruth's execution. According to Lizzie Seal (2011: 494), of the 610 letters received, 552 (90%) are in favour of reprieve and 58 (10%) are against it. There is therefore concrete evidence to suggest that far from being accepted by the public as an 'open and shut' case, a substantial number of individuals found what they perceived to be a lack of justice deeply offensive. One letter writer noted that rather than having carried out the crime 'with cool deliberation and determination, she was, I believe, under the stress of an overpowering emotion which swept her completely off balance and deprived her temporarily of normal reasoning'. Given the level of betrayal she had experienced, it was no surprise to find that there was 'an overwhelming strong sense of monstrous outrage and injury' (letter, 4 July 1955, HO291/235). Another author wrote that 'even if she fired to kill, it was a crime of hot, not cold, blood' (letter, 23 June 1955, HO291/236). Yet another writer argued that 'a cold blooded killer would try hard to escape the consequences of the crime', unlike Ruth, who made no attempt to defend herself (letter, undated, HO291/235).

At a different level, a letter cited by Seal (2011: 498) revealed its author to be critical of Lord Havers' decision to disallow the provocation defence:

> . . . a pregnant woman may be punched into a miscarriage and dangerous haemorrhage, swindled and all this counts for nothing and contributes nothing to a womans [*sic*] mind.

Many others emphasised David's violence – 'the woman has been brutally used by the male' (letter, 1 July 1955, HO291/235) – thus 'this poor girl has been tortured enough even before the crime' by a man 'unworthy' of her passion (letter, 5 July 1955, HO291/235). 'She has at least been as much sinned against, as sinning', observed another author (letter, 6 July 1955, HO291/235).

During an era when the discourse of domestic violence barely existed, Seal (2011: 498) observes that there were in fact many battered women who identified with Ruth:

> I understand her desperation to do this act because only a woman understands that has been in the same position like myself and millions of others beaten by our husbands.

Conversely, a number of letter writers compared and contrasted Ruth's punishment with that of other murderers whose crime they perceived to be worse, such as the case of 'a brutal murderer . . . who in the words of Sir Winston Churchill, "pushed the body of a young girl ignominiously through a porthole", after he had raped and murdered her', yet had escaped the death penalty (letter, 28 June 1955, HO291/236).

These letters, taken together with the various protests and petitions prior to the execution, provide substantial evidence of a strong opposition to Ruth's punishment and thus suggest that the legitimacy of the legal system was under threat by those who considered her punishment unfair – particularly within the context of David's mistreatment of her (Seal, 2011: 501). Thus, to return to the initial argument made above, the Ellis case can be understood as a powerful representation of the mismatch between normative expectations of law and the plurality of social life. The very principles of neutrality and equality on which law is based, and which do not permit it to be 'concerned with what it is to be a human being' (Weait, 2007: 29), were also the very reasons for placing legitimacy of the justice system in danger while simultaneously confirming the futility of seeking 'substantive justice by particularising the legal subject' (Weait, 2007: 44). In a sense the refusal to pathologise Ruth's crime carried its own danger, because by disallowing concern with what it is to be human, and instead imposing an apparent technical neutrality onto the case, the underlying patriarchal rationale, deeply embedded within law, was momentarily made visible to the public. Connell (1994) has explained that the law does not work in the interests of men in a simplistic manner. Rather it is the functioning of state procedure that is patriarchal. Thus, the more objective state procedures appear to be, 'the more effectively patriarchal they are' (Connell, 1994: 145). While these processes usually remain hidden, the blatant disregard for the wider context within which this killing took place momentarily threatened to expose the problematic aspect of legal 'objectivity' and 'neutrality'. Indeed, Atwell (2007: 5) observes:

> The problem is a system that treats a crime as a "snapshot", a separate event in which one must be either victim or offender but cannot be both. Such a perspective . . . neglects to address the reality where women have experienced victimisation . . . by individuals.

The victimisation experienced by Ruth Ellis, however, was all too apparent to the public who refused to accept that David carried no responsibility whatsoever, as exemplified by Marks and Van den Bergh's (1990: 188) observation that:

> David was a conceited braggart, living off women and afraid of facing up to the scenes his behaviour inevitably provoked.

The chasm between the legal resolution of the case and the deeply felt notion within the public conscience that the law was presiding over an injustice of the highest order was thus wider than ever and has remained a persistent feature of the case ever since, serving as a constant reminder that there are limits to legal legitimacy.

Conclusion

> Male dominance 'is perhaps the most pervasive and tenacious system of power in history. . . . [I]t is metaphysically nearly perfect. Its point of view is the standard for point-of-viewlessness, its particularity the means of universality' (Mackinnon, as cited in Collier, 2010: 15 f/n).

The Ruth Ellis/David Blakely case has demonstrated the difficulties retaliating women face in presenting themselves as responsible agents. There simply was, and arguably still is, no subject position available where a retaliating woman can be at once responsible and culpable, yet less blameworthy without losing sight of agency (Hudson, 2002: 22).

As a result of their status as both victims and perpetrators – both guilty and blameless – women like Ruth Ellis force us to confront this absence of subject positions within a phallocentric legal system. In her case the failure to 'render her harmless' or at least less blameworthy, was greatly exacerbated by her social class and deviant femininity. Eaton has observed that 'the defence of provocation reflects the defendant's relationship to the social world. . . . "[S]hould this relationship follow an acceptable pattern it will be used to show that the defendant is not really a criminal since the social identity in question is basically conformist"' (Eaton, as cited in Lees, 1992: 283). However, if this pattern is considered unconventional, that in itself may be presented as grounds for provocation, and the batterer's violence may be excused on the grounds that he was subject to intolerable pressure:

> Sexist concepts about the nature of men and women's roles in the family, and about the acceptability of male violence, as a reaction to any behaviour deemed to be insubordinate to male authority, legitimise the violence they purport to protect women from.
>
> (Lees, 1992: 283)

Moreover, the outcome of the appeal demonstrated that nearly half a century after her execution took place, these arguments remain relevant. Thus, despite formal equality in law, substantial equality remains in short supply for women, and becomes particularly visible through the crime of spouse killing. The long history of condoning female-spouse killings through the provocation defence demonstrates that 'patriarchal narratives of provocation have been incorporated into law and recognised by its hierarchy' (Davies, 2007: 161). Thus, within the wider context of the heteropatriarchal social order, men killing female partners are perceived as *defenders* of the nuclear family through their attempts to prevent their spouses from leaving. In sharp contrast, women like Ruth Ellis who engage in identical behaviour stand as a direct challenge and threat to the heteropatriarchal social order:

> A woman who kills her male partner threatens the social fabric of her culture, such an act disturbs, challenges and questions the modern western incarnations of the ideologies of family, marriage and heterosexuality.
>
> (Morrissey, 2003: 97)

Indeed, such a women can be understood as a threat to the legal foundations itself on which the assumption of the universal subject of reason rests, for as Downing (2013: 102) notes:

> [T]he very assumption of the existence of a universal subject of reason reveals a masculinist bias in law, given that women have historically been excluded from male philosophy's definition of perfect rationality.

Little wonder, then, that Ruth's particular crime was threatening in the extreme, for to those who followed the case, it appeared that she had acted according to a reasoning usually reserved for men, as discussed above – rage, faithless conduct and disenchantment, jealousy and possessiveness (Atwell, 2007: 6). While this was, and remains, perfectly intelligible to the public in general and feminist theorists in particular, it has proved impossible so far to build a legal argument of the case that is compatible with popular and academic understanding. This is because the legal construction of responsibility, with its focus on understanding, reason and control, 'while important in enabling us better to understand the logic and the principles, which inform criminal law – is necessarily constrained in its understanding of what "being responsible" means' (Weait, 2007: 21). From this point of view, advances made to feminise understandings of provocation in many adversarial jurisdictions still fall short in terms of appreciating that which underpins provocation itself: responsibility. Coates and Wade (2004: 3) have observed:

> The tenets of the interactional and discursive view of violence and resistance encompass both the actions of the offender and the victim. . . . The 'degree of responsibility' apportioned to any offender depends only in part upon his or her actions. It hinges also on how both the offender's and the victim's actions are represented linguistically in police reports, legal arguments, testimony, related judgements, and more broadly in professional and public discourse.

Thus, 'the legal subject of adjudication' can be framed only according to the 'law's own institutionalised logic and the moral and political traditions within which it is embedded' (Weait, 2007: 29, 21). These traditions are patriarchal in nature, hence it is unsurprising that 'the law sees and treats women the way men see and treat women' (Mackinnon, as cited in Collier, 2010: 15). As such, these traditions do not include subject positions for a responsible, rational, non-hysterical, yet abused and victimised female pleading provocation, who refuses to rely on stereotypical feminine theatrics in an attempt to avoid punishment. Nor is this likely to change in the near future, for as noted above 'the criminal law is itself a conservative institution the function of which is not to liberate but to repress, censure and condemn' (Weait, 2007: 21). Thus, demands for legal changes which address gender inequality cannot create new subject positions for retaliating women such as Ruth Ellis, because such a strategy merely increases the power of law (Ballinger, 2012: 464). Fitz-Gibbon and Pickering (2012: 166), for example, found that legal changes introduced in Australia in 2005 to take account of 'loss of control' were overwhelmingly taken up by men. Similarly, following the replacement of the provocation defence with 'loss of control' in England and Wales in 2010, Edwards (2010: 224) commented:

> Given that there is no change in the nomenclature, we can expect a mirror image of the behaviour and legal descriptors that passed for loss of self-control under the old law of provocation to be replicated.

Thus, to avoid, deny and transcend the law's ability to 're-gender' legal reforms, it is crucial that the 'law's power to define and disqualify' and 'its ability to redefine the truth' are challenged (Smart, 1989: 164). This will involve a challenge to the deeply embedded concepts of rationality and responsibility, since they themselves are inherently masculine. As Smart (ibid.: 87) observed:

> Law is not rational because men *are* rational, but law is constituted as rational as are men, and men as the subjects of the discourse of masculinity come to experience themselves as rational [emphasis in original].

Only after such fundamental challenges to the very foundations on which a heteropatriarchal legal system is built can new legal subject positions for women like Ruth Ellis be imagined and realised which bear a closer resemblance to public perception than is currently the case. Only then will the Ruth Ellis case be 'open and shut' and justice finally delivered to her memory.

Acknowledgement

Many thanks to Kate Fitz-Gibbon and Sandra Walklate for their helpful comments, and to Joe Sim for his encouragement and support throughout the preparation of this chapter.

Note

1 This sentence is borrowed from Morrissey (2003: 92).

References

Allen, H. (1987) Rendering them harmless: The professional portrayal of women charged with serious violent crimes. In Carlen, P. and Worrall, A. (eds.) *Gender, Crime and Justice.* Milton Keynes: Open University Press, pp. 81–94.

Atwell, M. W. (2007) *Wretched Sisters: Examining Gender and Capital Punishment.* New York: Peter Lang.

Ballinger, A. (1996) The guilt of the innocent and the innocence of the guilty: The cases of Marie Fahmy and Ruth Ellis. In Myers, A. and Wight, S. (eds.) *No Angels.* London: Pandora, pp. 1–28.

Ballinger, A. (2000) *Dead Woman Walking.* Aldershot: Ashgate.

Ballinger, A. (2005) Reasonable women who kill: Re-interpreting and re-defining women's response to domestic violence in England and Wales, 1900–1965. *Outlines: Critical Social Studies*, 7(2): 65–82.

Ballinger, A. (2007) Masculinity in the dock: Legal responses to male violence and female retaliation in England and Wales, 1900–1965. *Social & Legal Studies*, 16(4): 459–481.

Ballinger, A. (2012) A muted voice from the past: The "Silent Silencing" of Ruth Ellis. *Social & Legal Studies,* 21(4): 445–467.

BBC1. (1999) *Ruth Ellis: A Life for a Life.* Broadcast, 28 November.

Burton, M. (2001) Intimate homicide and the provocation defence – endangering women? R. v. Smith. *Feminist Legal Studies*, 9: 247–258.

Burton, M. (2003) 'Sentencing Domestic Homicide upon Provocation: Still "Getting Away with Murder"' *Feminist Legal Studies* 11, 279–89.

Campbell, J. (1992) 'If I can't have you, no one can': Power and control in homicide of female partners. In Radford, J. and Russell, D. E. H. (eds.) *Femicide: The Politics of Woman Killing.* Buckingham: Open University Press, pp. 99–113.

Carline, A. (2005a) Women who kill their abusive partners: From sameness to gender construction. *Liverpool Law Review,* 26: 13–44.

Carline, A. (2005b) Zoora Shah: An 'unusual woman'. *Social & Legal Studies,* 14(2): 215–238.

Coates, L. and Wade, A. (2004) Telling it like it isn't: Obscuring perpetrator responsibility for violent crime. *Discourse & Society,* 15(5): 499–526.

Collier, R. (1995) *Masculinity, Law and the Family.* London: Routledge.

Collier, R. (2010) *Men, Law and Gender: Rethinking the 'Man of Law'.* London: Routledge.

Connell, R. W. (1987) *Gender & Power.* Cambridge: Polity Press.

Connell, R. W. (1994) The state, gender and sexual politics: Theory and appraisal. In Radke, H. L. and Stam, H. J. (eds.) *Power/Gender.* London: Sage, pp. 136–173.

Davies, M. (2007) Beyond unity. In Munro, V. and Stychin, C. F. (eds.) *Sexuality and the Law: Feminist Engagements.* London: Glasshouse, pp. 151–170.

Downing, L. (2013) *The Subject of Murder: Gender, Exceptionality and the Modern Killer.* Chicago: University of Chicago Press.

Edwards, S. (2010)'Anger and Fear as Justifiable Preludes for Loss of Self-Control *Journal of Criminal Law* 74(3) 223–241.

Ellis, G. with Taylor, R. (1995) *Ruth Ellis, My Mother.* London: Smith Gryphon Publishers.

Fitz-Gibbon, K. and Pickering, S. (2012) Homicide law reform in Victoria, Australia: From provocation to defensive homicide and beyond. *British Journal of Criminology,* 52(1): 159–180.

Fox, M. (1995) Legal responses to battered women who kill. In Bridgeman, J. and Millns, S. (eds.) *Law and Body Politics.* Aldershot: Dartmouth, pp. 171–200.

Goodman, J. and Pringle, P. (1974) *The Trial of Ruth Ellis.* London: David & Charles.

Hancock, R. (1989) *Ruth Ellis: The Last Woman to be Hanged.* London: Weidenfeld and Nicolson.

Healey, T. (1985) *Crimes of Passion.* London: Hamlyn.

Hudson, B. (2002) Gender issues in penal policy and penal theory. In Carlen, P. (ed.) *Women and Punishment.* Cullompton: Willan Publishing, pp. 21–46.

Inglis, T. (2003) *Truth, Power and Lies.* Dublin: University College Dublin Press.

Jakubait, M. with Weller, M. (2005) *Ruth Ellis: My Sister's Secret Life.* London: Robinson.

Lacey, N. (1998) *Unspeakable Subjects: Feminist Essays in Legal and Social Theory.* Oxford: Hart Publishing.

Lees, S. (1992) Naggers, whores and libbers: Provoking men to kill. In Radford, J. and Russell, D.E.H. (eds.) *Femicide: The Politics of Woman Killing.* Buckingham: Open University Press, pp. 267–288.

Marks, L. and Van Den Bergh, T. (1990) *Ruth Ellis: A Case of Diminished Responsibility?* Harmondsworth: Penguin.

Messing, J. T. and Heeren, J. W. (2009) Gendered justice: Domestic homicide and the death penalty. *Feminist Criminology,* 4(2): 170–188.

Morrissey, B. (2003) *When Women Kill: Questions of Agency and Subjectivity.* London: Routledge.

Morton, J. (2015) *Justice Denied.* London: Robinson.

Munro, V. (2007) *Law and Politics at the Perimeter* Oxford: Hart Publishing.

O'Donovan, K. (1991) Defences for battered women who kill. *Journal of Law and Society,* 18(2): 219–239.

O'Donovan, K. (1993) Law's knowledge: The judge, the expert, the battered woman, and her syndrome. *Journal of Law and Society,* 20(4): 427–437.

Radford, J. (1992) 'Womanslaughter: A licence to kill? The Killing of Jane Asher' In Radford, J. and Russell, D.E.H. (eds.) *Femicide: The Politics of Woman Killing.* Buckingham: Open University Press, pp. 253–266.

Remy, J. (1990) Patriarchy and fratriarchy as forms of androcracy. In Hearn, J. and Morgan, D. (eds.) *Men, Masculinities & Social Theory.* London: Unwin Hyman, pp. 43–54.

Rose, J. (1993) *Why War?* Oxford: Basil Blackwell.

Seal, L. (2011) Ruth Ellis and public contestation of the death penalty. *Howard Journal of Criminal Justice,* 50(5): 492–504.

Smart, C. (1989) *Feminism and the Power of Law.* London: Routledge.

Weait, M. (2007) On being responsible. In Munro, V. and Stychin, C. F. (eds.) *Sexuality and the Law: Feminist Engagements.* London: Glasshouse, pp. 19–50.

National archive documents, newspapers and other periodicals

DDP2/2430

HO291/235

HO291/236

Ellis v R (2003) EWCA Crim 3556

Daily Express, 14 July 1955

Daily Mirror, 30 June 1955; 16 July 1955

Lancet, 23 July 1955

News of the World, 8 October 1972

Police Review, 22 August 1986

Sunday Dispatch, 26 June 1955

Sunday People, 2 December 1973

Times, 13 July 1955

2   Murder, manslaughter and domestic violence

Julie Stubbs

Taking a cue from the title of this book, this chapter is organised around the three themes of murder, gender and responsibility. It begins by considering the shifting boundary between murder and manslaughter and, contrary to common wisdom, the lack of consensus around these terms. The focus then shifts to gender and a consideration of gendered patterns in homicide and femicide using the overlapping categories of domestic homicide and intimate partner homicides. It also demonstrates the value of more complex conceptions of gender to understanding patterns in homicide using an intersectional framework to explore the differential vulnerability of women to homicide. The third theme, responsibility, is examined by reference to legal responses to domestic homicide and intimate partner homicides for battered women. While some women have benefited from law reforms and shifts in legal practices, women who do not conform to idealised notions of what it means to be a battered woman or other 'benchmarks' continue to be disadvantaged.

Murder and manslaughter: the shifting boundary

As Ngaire Naffine (2009) has noted, criminal law theorists commonly approach murder and rape from the presumption that they are 'core crimes' for which there is agreement about the behaviour and its moral culpability. Within this body of work, murder is taken to be 'self evidently blameworthy'. However, Naffine (2009: 229) argues that 'actual legal norms and practices' and 'what happens to real people' demonstrate that there is 'less clarity and certainty' about these core wrongs than criminal law theorists typically assert. Empirical research demonstrates that 'persons accused of homicide exhibit a wide range of moral culpability' which demonstrates the need 'to re-examine stereotyped views of "murderers" in which variations in culpability pass unexamined' (Wallace, 1986: 180).

What constitutes murder is not settled but has varied over time and currently differs across jurisdictions in important respects. What comes to be legally designated as murder is substantially determined by the availability and operation of defences and partial defences. These vary markedly within Australia and across similar nations. A flurry of reform over recent decades has added to this diversity as jurisdictions have adopted different responses (Fitz-Gibbon and Stubbs, 2012).

Even within a given jurisdiction the direction of reforms has been inconsistent over this period. For instance, reforms adopted in NSW over the past three decades have shifted the boundary between murder and manslaughter, at times contracting the category of murder by expanding manslaughter and at other times reducing the basis for manslaughter and thus shifting cases into the category of murder (Brown et al., 2015: 50–51). The following examples are illustrative.

In 1982, statutory reforms made the partial defence of provocation more widely available to some defendants, such as women who had been abused, by removing the requirement of 'immediacy', thus allowing a course of conduct over time and not just the final act to be recognised as provocation. At the same time, judges were given some discretion to depart from the mandatory life sentence for murder where there were mitigating circumstances that diminished the offender's culpability.[1] These changes were in line with recommendations made by the NSW Taskforce on Domestic Violence (1981). In 1987 the High Court decision in *Zecevic v DPP (Vic)*, (1987) 162 CLR 645, simplified the rules for self-defence which opened up the prospect of an acquittal for some battered women, but it also narrowed the category of manslaughter by abolishing the partial defence of excessive self-defence. However, in 2002 excessive self-defence was reintroduced in NSW, thus widening the category of manslaughter, although this shift was made with no reference to domestic homicide. In 2014, reforms to provocation were introduced with the intention of restricting the availability of that partial defence by preventing its use in some circumstances, such as 'infidelity, leaving a relationship or a non-violent sexual advance' and imposing a new threshold of extreme provocation that requires, *inter alia*, that the provocative conduct amount to a serious indictable offence (Hazzard, 2014). This new threshold, together with other aspects of the reform package,[2] imposes additional hurdles for battered women and all others who are not excluded from relying on the partial defence to reduce murder to manslaughter.

Australian debates around defences to homicide have been driven largely by concerns about domestic violence, intimate partner homicide and so-called homosexual advance killings. Social movement activism has been significant in highlighting some defences and some forms of homicide, often in reaction to high-profile cases that have generated unease about how the law has been applied (Fitz-Gibbon and Stubbs, 2012). There has been substantial criticism of provocation being available too readily in undeserving cases such as abusive men who have killed an intimate partner and men who appear to kill other men out of homophobia (Coss, 2006; Howe, 1997). There also has been criticism that self-defence and provocation have not been interpreted and applied in an expansive enough way to recognise the desperate circumstances faced by some battered women who kill their abusers (Douglas, 2012; Sheehy et al., 2012). However, while there may be a strong sense that there is a need to differentiate among killings that are not morally equivalent, there is less clarity around what principles should be applied and what this means for the law and legal practice. Debates about whether the partial defence of provocation should be abolished, retained or modified and the way in which the debate has been resolved differently in different jurisdictions

(Fitz-Gibbon, 2014; Select Committee on the Partial Defence of Provocation, 2013; Victorian Law Reform Commission, 2004) provide prominent examples of the lack of consensus on this issue. As Alan Norrie (2005: 59) has argued, there 'is an important gap between legal concepts used to judge deaths, and the moral quality of the killings. . . . Legal categories have to be teased and twisted to reflect the moral quality of killings in particular cases.'

For some scholars the answer to differentiating among killings that are not moral equivalents lies not in different categories of homicide but in sentencing. Others oppose this approach, raising concerns about 'fair labelling' (Leader-Elliott, 2015). They argue that the distinction between murder (and in some jurisdictions between gradations of murder) and manslaughter is meaningful and should be retained to reflect different levels of moral blame (Crofts, 2007). Consistent with the appeal to fair labelling, feminist legal scholars have long sought to have legal categories more adequately reflect women's lives (Graycar and Morgan, 2002). Leaving the task to sentencing is also controversial on the basis that it detracts from the role of juries (Crofts and Loughnan, 2013). In addition, the shift is predicated on the assumption that judicial officers have sufficient discretion to reflect such distinctions in sentencing, and yet there are few jurisdictions in which judicial discretion to sentence in murder cases is unfettered. Murder continues to carry a mandatory life sentence in some jurisdictions – e.g. section 305 of the Criminal Code 1899 of Queensland, presumptive life in others, e.g. section 279(4) of the Criminal Code of Western Australia; section 102 of the Sentencing Act 2002 of New Zealand – or is constrained by minimum terms, baselines – e.g. section 5A of the Sentencing Act 1991 of Victoria – or precedent in other jurisdictions, while there is typically wide discretion in sentencing manslaughter. There has been a lack of political will to review constraints on judicial discretion in sentencing for murder in many jurisdictions (Fitz-Gibbon and Stubbs, 2012: 323; Quick and Wells, 2012: 338) and indeed the state of Victoria has recently introduced new restrictions in the form of baseline sentences.

Gender, homicide and femicide

Most homicides involve men killing other men, and relatively few women resort to homicide. However, men and women kill and are killed in circumstances that are typically very different. Australian homicide researchers made early and significant contributions to recognising '[q]ualitatively distinct homicides' associated with relationships between the victim and offender and situational contexts and gendered patterns in homicide (Wallace, 1986: 177–80; see also Polk, 1994). For instance, Wallace's study based on homicides in NSW from 1968 to 1981 found that the largest category of homicides were domestic, that is, committed by family members, but female victims were almost two and half times more likely than male victims to be killed in a domestic homicide. Women almost exclusively killed family members. Men were also more likely to kill a family member, but domestic homicides made up just one-third of cases in which men killed, since men killed in a wider range of circumstances (Wallace, 1986: 72–74).

The term 'femicide' has been important in bringing to the fore the gendered dimensions often obscured by the gender-neutral term 'homicide'. Feminist activists introduced the term 'femicide' to name the 'misogynist killing of women by men' (Radford, 1992: 3) and to draw connections with other forms of sexual violence as identified by Liz Kelly's (1988) continuum of violence. However, in this chapter as elsewhere in my work, I also want to keep in sight matters in which women kill in response to domestic violence. Violence against women and girls occurs in the context of structural inequalities, but violence also reinforces gendered inequality (Kelly, 2005). Just as femicides cannot be adequately understood as isolated individual events, battered women's resort to lethal violence also needs to be contextualised with reference to gendered inequality. Thus this chapter deals with both femicides and those homicides by women that arise in the context of domestic violence, with attention especially to intimate partner homicides.

Domestic homicide and intimate partner homicide as distinctive

Domestic homicide, intimate partner homicide and domestic violence–related homicides are often conflated in media and public discourse. These are distinguishable but overlapping categories, although the definitions are not fixed and are often determined by laws which differ by jurisdiction. For instance, Websdale (1999: 3) notes that in the US, definitions of domestic homicide commonly include family members but exclude boyfriends/girlfriends who do not live together. By contrast, in some Australian states and territories the legal definition of domestic relationship for the purpose of domestic violence laws is very broad. In NSW, it includes current and former partners, including same-sex partners, current or past intimate (not necessarily sexual) relationships, other family members, residents in the same household or residential care facility and carers, according to the NSW Crimes (Domestic and Personal Violence) Act 2007, section 5. All of those relationships are included in the category of domestic homicide. Domestic homicides occur across a range of relationships and in various circumstances. While homicides of children, siblings or parents are instances of domestic homicide, they are not the focus of this chapter.

Within some studies, intimate partner homicides are defined as a subcategory of domestic homicide and typically include current or former intimate partners of the offender. Studies vary as to whether they include boyfriends/girlfriends, extramarital lovers or new partners, and thus the category of intimate partner violence might not be totally subsumed within domestic homicide. Common conceptions of domestic homicide and intimate partner homicide risk providing an incomplete account that excludes other parties killed in the context of violence within the primary relationship – for instance, friends sheltering a victim of domestic violence or new partners of estranged spouses.

Commonly, public concern and policy have focused on domestic violence–related homicides, especially those that occur in intimate partner relationships. One reflection of heightened concern about domestic violence–related homicides has been the adoption of domestic violence death review mechanisms in several nations; through the identification of patterns in homicides, these mechanisms are intended to prevent deaths and improve systems and services (Bugeja et al., 2013). The DVDRT in NSW examined all homicide incidents for the period 2000–2010 (*n* = 833) and found an identifiable history of domestic violence in the cases of 48 percent of female victims and 17 percent of male homicide victims. Almost 80 percent of females as compared with 35 percent of males who were killed in a domestic violence homicide were killed by an intimate partner. Males were also commonly killed by their new partner's former partner, by a son or stepson or, in the case of children, by a parent (DVDRT, 2015: vii).

Intimate partner homicide

While the common term 'intimate partner homicide' is gender neutral, these homicides are anything but gender neutral. A recent systematic review of intimate partner violence in sixty-six countries found that the number of female victims of IPH exceeded the number of male victims in all but two countries, and in all countries 'women's main risk of homicide is from an intimate partner' (Stöckl et al., 2013: 862, 863). However, consistent with evidence that homicide is shaped by social, historical and cultural norms and practices (Wallace, 1986: 177), the gender ratio between male and female victims differs among countries and over time.

The US is exceptional in that the number of men and women killed in intimate partner homicides is much closer than in other countries. One leading US study reported that the sex ratio of killing, as measured by the number of women who killed husbands per 100 men who killed their wives, was 75, whereas this ratio was typically between 30 and 40 in comparable countries (Websdale, 1999: 9 citing Wilson and Daly, 1992). Stöckl et al. (2013: 864) noted that the gender ratio in the US had changed since 1975 due to the substantial reduction in the number of male victims of intimate partner homicide, but a more modest decrease for women victims. They attributed this trend to improvements in services and support to women victims of domestic violence, providing more options to escape a violent relationship, which has reduced the number of male victims.

Gender patterns in intimate partner violence also differ according to other social categories. Rates are commonly higher among racialised groups, although not uniformly so. For instance, in the US, African Americans are overrepresented as victims and offenders in intimate partner homicides, with a disproportionate involvement by African American women as offenders, while Latinos have low rates. Researchers differ as to how they interpret these findings, pointing to different cultural values and levels of socioeconomic disadvantage in different communities and to the differential oppression experienced by African American women (Websdale, 1999: 6–7, 10).

Within Australia, homicide rates also differ markedly by race. While Indigenous homicide rates have declined, as have homicide rates generally, Indigenous people remain substantially overrepresented as victims and offenders (Bryant and Cussen, 2015: 24). The proportion of IPH is greater where both parties are Indigenous (38 percent) than non-Indigenous (20 percent), and Indigenous victims (78 percent female, 44 percent male) are much more likely than non-Indigenous victims (64 percent female, 22 percent male) to be killed in a domestic or family violence incident (Cussen and Bryant, 2015: 5). While offence rates have fallen for Indigenous women too, the proportion of women offenders is higher for Indigenous homicides (20 percent) than non-Indigenous homicides (12 percent, Cussen and Bryant, 2015: 7). It is especially notable that the Indigenous female rate exceeds the rate for non-Indigenous men, demonstrating that the commonplace assumption that male rates necessarily exceed female rates is simplistic. Research findings that Filipino women in Australia are disproportionately victims of IPH, with rates almost six times those of other women (Cunneen and Stubbs, 2004), also indicate complexity in the way in which gender relations may be associated with homicide and the value of an intersectional framework (see further below).

Researchers have identified common features of intimate partner homicides. Allison Wallace's NSW study (1986) demonstrated that most intimate partner homicides are committed by men; a history of prior domestic violence by the male offender is common, and many of the homicides occur at around the time of separation. An 'overwhelming' feature of these cases was 'the widespread use of violence by men to control their wives' activities' (Wallace, 1986: 179). Subsequent Victorian research confirmed these findings and drew on developing theories of masculinity (Polk, 1994). Polk and Ranson (1991: 21) also found that men who killed an intimate partner often did so out of jealousy and sexual possession in what was often 'the ultimate attempt to exert power and control' over their partner. There were no women in their study who killed out of jealousy or possessiveness; most did so out of self-protection (Polk and Ranson, 1991: 23); they argue that 'the role of gender is powerful, and must play a central role in any theoretical explanation' (24).

The more recent study of domestic violence homicides in NSW noted above found that among intimate partner homicides in which there was evidence of IPH DV, all female victims were killed by men. Two-thirds of female victims were killed by a current intimate partner, but in almost half of those cases there was evidence that separation was being considered. In the other one-third of cases, women were killed by a former partner, mostly within three months of the end of the relationship. Indigenous women constituted 12 percent of IPH DV cases and thus were considerably overrepresented, as they make up less than 3 percent of the NSW population. Among male victims, 17 percent were killed by a male intimate partner and the remainder by a female intimate partner; 91 percent were killed by a current partner. In all but one of the cases in which a woman killed a male partner, there had been previous domestic violence by the deceased man, and in seven cases the female had also 'occasionally' used domestic violence (data supplied to the author by DVDRT). 'There were no cases where a woman was a domestic violence abuser who killed a male domestic violence victim' (DVDRT, 2015: 4). All same-sex IPH DV cases involved men. Indigenous men were substantially overrepresented (34 percent).

The largest number of domestic violence homicides that were not IPH included other family members, most commonly children, but a substantial number included new intimate partners of the perpetrator's former partner. Dobash and Dobash (2015: 254) also noted the number of 'collateral murders' that occurred in the context of intimate partner conflict and the need for greater recognition of these cases in studies of IPH.

The findings of these Australian studies are consistent with the international literature. Websdale (1999: 26) provides a summary of common precursors to intimate partner homicide. These include:

> a history of domestic violence, which often results in the increasing entrapment of women; the separation, estrangement or divorce of the parties; obsessive possessiveness and morbid jealousy by the abusive partner; threats to commit intimate partner homicide; prior agency involvement, including police and courts; depression, the criminal history of perpetrators; and the use of alcohol or drugs or both.

Women who commit intimate partner violence commonly do so out of self-preservation; unlike men, women rarely kill following separation or on discovery (or suspicion) of infidelity (Websdale, 1999: 19). A recent US study of women who killed an intimate partner confirmed that most did so in self-defence and that women rarely killed out of sexual proprietariness (Belknap et al., 2012).

Researchers have consistently found that women are more vulnerable to IPH at the time of separation (Mahoney, 1991; Stark, 2007; Wallace, 1986). Johnston and Hotton (2003: 61) reported, based on Canadian data, that women accounted for 75 percent of victims of homicides between intact spouses but 91 percent where spouses were estranged. While women were at heightened risk of IPH following separation, that was not the case for men (Johnston and Hotton, 2003: 70). Women who were estranged were mostly killed in their own homes; men were more likely than women to track down and kill their former partner, consistent with themes of proprietariness and jealousy (Johnston and Hotton, 2003: 80). Similarly in their study of British murder cases, Dobash and Dobash (2015: 63) found that '[m]any of the women saw separation as the ending of an intimate relationship while the men did not. Instead, these men viewed separation as inappropriate and unacceptable and as a challenge to their ongoing possession of, and authority over, their woman partner.'

Dobash and Dobash's study (2015) is notable for several reasons: the authors examined differences among men who committed intimate partner murders and between these offenders and those convicted of other types of murder, and considered differences between lethal and nonlethal intimate partner violence.

Men who killed intimate female partners commonly had a history of previous violence against the women, but some did not and their killing appeared to 'come out of the blue' (Dobash and Dobash, 2015: 64). Men with no prior convictions (approximately 25 percent) differed from those who had prior convictions in numerous ways. They appeared 'more conventional' – they were less likely to have had problems across the life course and were more likely to be educated and employed – but they shared other characteristics, including their orientation to women. In almost half of cases there was evidence of previous violence which had gone undetected or had not been acted on (Dobash and Dobash, 2015: 81). In all, 70 percent of men who murdered an intimate partner had been violent in a previous relationship (ibid.: 82). For IP murderers as compared with other murderers, 'issues of gender and gender relations stand out. . . . Male authority and control over women, and particularly women partners, provides a foundation for extreme forms of possessiveness that are related to a variety of behaviors from extreme forms of control to physical and sometimes sexual violence used against women partners' (Dobash and Dobash, 2015: 99). They found that 'men who murder women tend to "specialize" in perpetrating violence against women' (Dobash and Dobash, 2015: 249). They also found that contrary to common belief, these were not necessarily cases of 'an incremental shift or slip from a nonlethal to a lethal outcome'. Instead men who killed intimate partners often had a 'fixed firm intention to kill' which involved a shift from the intent 'to keep or reclaim their partner to one fixed on her death' (Dobash and Dobash, 2015: 254). And 'these men often saw themselves as victims who had been wronged and, as such, were embittered and indignant. They viewed themselves as acting in a moral universe wherein their anger and violence was appropriate and justified' (Dobash and Dobash, 2015: 254).

Explaining gendered patterns of domestic homicide and intimate partner homicide

While gendered patterns in domestic homicide and intimate partner homicide are well established, there is little consensus about theoretical frameworks that might explain the patterns. Theorists commonly point to the role of gendered inequality but differ in their approach. Websdale (1999: 208) emphasises patriarchal relations but also recognises that marginalised men may resort to violence to assert masculine status and control. Some theorists hypothesise that greater gender equality is likely to be associated with reduced rates of IPH of females, while others propose that at least in the short term, backlash against shifts to greater gender equality may increase the number of women killed in IPH (Eriksson and Mazerolle (2013). One commonly advanced theory draws on evolutionary biology to explain factors such as higher rates of the killing of female intimate partners after estrangement, where wives are younger, in common law unions rather than marriages and where there are children from a woman's previous relationship. Wilson and Daly (1998) contend that the patterns in IPH arise from sexual proprietariness related to men's concerns to ensure their paternity and guard against women's infidelity or desertion; cross-cultural differences in rates are attributed to variations in social circumstances. Eriksson and Mazerolle (2013) have proposed a version of general strain theory which they argue accounts for gender patterns in IPH through examining differences in strains, emotions and coping strategies of men and women.

As noted above, gendered relations are associated with intimate partner homicide in complex ways, and thus an intersectional framework offers tools for analysis. Intersectionality has become shorthand for the interplay of gender and other social categories such as race, class, sexuality and disability and is said to address 'the most central theoretical and normative concern within feminist scholarship: namely, the acknowledgement of differences among women' (Davis, 2008: 70). The framework arose from challenges by African American scholars (Collins, 2000; Crenshaw, 1991) to the failure of mainstream feminism to reflect women's diversity and of antiracism to engage adequately with gender. While it is subject to debate and has been interpreted in different ways (Cho et al., 2013), it has significantly influenced criminological research on violence (Sokoloff and Dupont, 2005; Stubbs and Tolmie, 1995).

My colleague Chris Cunneen and I used an intersectional framework to research the heightened vulnerability of Filipino women to intimate partner homicide in Australia, a vulnerability that was not shared by Filipino men or by other immigrant women (Cunneen and Stubbs, 2004). Most of the women had migrated to Australia as sponsored partners of Australian men who were not from the Philippines, and their deaths commonly occurred in the context of domestic violence. We examined the way in which the intersection of race, gender and the international political economy that underpins migration situates the immigrant Filipino woman so that she has limited prospects for resistance or opposition to a violent partner. This framework helped us to identify that culturally defined conceptions of male desire and racialised constructions of femininity, together with relative economic power, were at play in Australian men's pursuit of a Filipino partner, often using Internet marriage marketing sites, and in their attempts to exercise control of their partners through violence. The vulnerability of these women had transnational, local, symbolic and material dimensions. Redressing that vulnerability would require not just holding men accountable for their violence within the criminal justice system, but also rethinking aspects of immigration policy, commercial marriage brokerage, improving services and supports for immigrant women and significant cultural change.

Law, responsibility and intimate partner homicide

Empirical evidence indicates a wide range of moral culpability among those who kill and complex patterns in homicides related to gender and other social relations, but also some common themes. How well does law respond to these factors in cases of intimate partner homicide? Three decades of research, activism and law reform intended to offer a fairer and more just response to cases of intimate partner homicide appear to have had some limited effects.

Activism and law reform efforts concerning intimate partner femicide have largely focused on closing down opportunities for undeserving men to access defence strategies and thus achieve reductions in sentences for their acts. These strategies have not always been successful, as recent Victorian experience with respect to a new, and now abolished, offence of 'defensive homicide' suggests

(Department of Justice, 2013). However, perhaps it is not surprising that what was intended as a safety net for battered women who killed an abuser but who could not meet the threshold for self-defence was used mainly by men who killed other men, often while intoxicated, as these are common cases (Leader-Elliott, 2015). Experience in Western Australia also depicts a disturbing development. In that state, 'one-punch laws' were introduced to fill a perceived gap in manslaughter, resulting from the defence of accident which exists in that state and directed towards the typical case of a young intoxicated man killing another man – the maximum penalty is ten years. However, an unintended consequence has been the diversity of circumstances in which cases have arisen under this provision and that 40 percent of cases have been against men who killed their partners or ex-partners – and in circumstances where they had a history of prior violence and abuse. The highest sentence recorded was five years. These were not the types of matters contemplated when the one-punch laws were drafted. That most of these matters involved a guilty plea (Quilter, 2014: 25) highlights ongoing concerns about prosecutorial discretion, a process that is largely opaque.

In contrast to efforts to restrict defences in cases of femicide, advocacy and law reform undertaken on behalf of battered women who kill has proposed various strategies to open up the law to women, reshape legal categories such as self-defence to more accurately reflect women's lives, situate women's offending in its social context and reshape what counts as evidence in legal decision making. Some reforms have been limited and risk falling short because they fail to acknowledge the complex ways in which substantive homicide law, defences, evidentiary rules and sentencing interact, while others have been more comprehensive. Leader-Elliott (2015: 166) has described the package of family violence reforms developed by the Victorian Law Reform Commission (2004) as 'among the most significant achievements in Australian criminal law reform over recent decades'. The reforms included, *inter alia*, 'a conceptual structure for the admission of evidence of violence' and a clear statement that in family violence cases the threat need not be 'imminent'. In Queensland, wide-ranging evidence of the effects of domestic violence has been ruled admissible, and while this lacks a statutory basis, this development has been a significant advance (Douglas, 2012).

Some jurisdictions have adopted a more expansive version of self-defence that may better accommodate the circumstances faced by some battered women (Sheehy et al., 2012) although in reformulating the law on self-defence Victoria has a more restrictive definition than in NSW (Leader-Elliott, 2015). In Victoria the defence is not available unless the defendant feared death or really serious injury (section 332M of the Crimes Act of 1958 (Vic)). Queensland took the distinctive approach of introducing a new defence, 'Killing for preservation in an abusive relationship' (section 304B, Criminal Code Act of 1899 [Qld]), which reduces murder to manslaughter and may be available for non-confrontational killings where self-defence does not apply in that state. However, it has attracted controversy on several grounds, including because in other states in Australia these elements would be the basis for an acquittal, and it may undermine the prospect of an acquittal based on self-defence, but in practice it seems to have limited application (Douglas, 2012; Easteal and Hopkins, 2010; Edgely and Marchetti, 2011).

A common feminist strategy has been to introduce evidence of the social context of the accused person's actions, commonly through the use of expert evidence, in order to allow a fair assessment of those actions. Domestic violence is typically long-term and cumulative and operates within and reinforces wider circumstances of inequality and social entrapment. The coercion that battered women experience cannot be realistically understood in terms of the immediate circumstances surrounding the homicide event (Stark, 2007). Battered woman syndrome was introduced for this purpose. The Canada Supreme Court decision in *R v Lavallee* (1990), which was particularly influential in Australia, endorsed such an approach. Justice Ratushny, who subsequently conducted a review of self-defence cases in Canada, wrote that the significance of *Lavallee* was not in the recognition of expert evidence concerning battered woman syndrome: 'Rather, its real significance for the law of self-defence lies in the fact that the Court took a broad view of the evidence that is relevant to the legal elements of that defence (1997: 26, per Ratushny J).

Battered woman syndrome has been used successfully in some cases, especially using experts fully conversant in domestic violence and its effects, but is often narrowly construed as evidence of psychological impairment with less attention to social context. In the latter case it can work against the requirements of specific defences, for instance to demonstrate that the accused person's behaviour was reasonable. A major US review was critical of battered woman syndrome but affirmed the value of social context evidence in assisting the courts to assess battered women's self-defence claims fairly (US Department of Justice and US Department of Health and Human Services, 1996). However, Schneider (2000: 147) has identified profound resistance from some criminal law scholars to the 'affirmative recognition of the significance of social context, and the necessary interrelationship between individual action, social context and social responsibility', since such recognition 'challenges fundamental assumptions about "free will" in the criminal law'.

Social context evidence that situates an accused woman's actions may be especially important for those women who don't meet idealised constructions of what it means to be 'a battered woman' and to challenge stereotypes. Naffine's (2009: 222) criticisms of the approach to homicide taken by some criminal law theorists also take up concerns about idealised constructions at odds with the complexities and messiness of the lives of real people, including women facing desperate circumstances arising from domestic violence.

Feminist scholarship and victimology has long recognised that idealised conceptions of the victim have worked to the disadvantage of those who fall short of the ideal. For instance, Merry (2003: 353) noted that domestic violence victims need to 'conform to the law's definitions of rational and autonomous reactions to violence'. The ideal battered woman 'follows through, leaves the batterer, cooperates with prosecuting the case, and does not provoke violence, take drugs or drink, or abuse children' (Merry, 2003: 353). A battered woman who kills an abuser may well fall short on some of these measures. However, the battered woman who kills faces other hurdles; she is both victim and offender and must meet the specific legal tests related to the defence she is mounting. For instance, a plea of self-defence commonly requires that her actions were necessary and reasonable. However, evidence of the extent of the threat that she faced and the impact of the abuse upon her may well undermine her claim to self-defence; where such evidence is taken to indicate trauma and impaired psychological functioning arising from abuse, her action may be seen to be unreasonable and due to impairment. This dilemma has been at the heart of debates about BWS and its limitations (Sheehy et al., 1992). That BWS reflects white, middle-class standards to the disadvantage of other women and especially racialised women has begun to be recognised (Allard, 1991; Douglas, 2012; Stubbs and Tolmie, 1995, 2005).

The very substantial overrepresentation of some racialised women among battered women charged with homicide is a significant concern. Australian research has found marked differences in how Indigenous women's cases proceed – for instance, they rarely go to trial and most of the women charged plead to manslaughter (Stubbs and Tolmie, 2005). While it cannot be inferred from this that they are subject to unwarranted differential treatment, some of these women appeared to have a possible case for self-defence. Indigenous women are said to be 'the most legally disadvantaged group in Australia' (ATSIC 2003 cited by Human Rights and Equal Opportunity Commission, Aboriginal & Torres Strait Islander Social Justice Commissioner, 2005: 14) and may face additional pressures to plea bargain. While some of these women might have the prospect of going to trial on self-defence, their capacity to plea bargain is likely to be affected substantially by the range of partial defences available. In the absence of partial defences, they may face substantially longer sentences if convicted of murder.

Some proponents of the abolition of provocation have argued that battered women's interests can best be met by extending self-defence; however, not all battered women's cases will meet the criteria for self-defence, even on an expanded definition. Where partial defences don't exist, such as in New Zealand, women have little or no basis for entering a guilty plea to manslaughter. New Zealand has a much higher proportion of battered women convicted of murder than Australia or Canada, and the presumption of a life sentence is rarely overturned (Sheehy et al., 2012).

In her recent book, Liz Sheehy begins by reflecting on the current position in Canada with this question: '*Lavallee* changed the law of self-defence in 1990, thereby resolving the unfairness that had confronted battered women on trial for murder. Or did it?' (Sheehy, 2014: 7). The initial optimism following *Lavallee* has not been borne out, and there are reasons for ongoing concern. An en bloc review of cases in which women had killed abusive partners and claimed to have done so in self-defence conducted subsequent to *Lavallee* by Ratushny J considered ninety-eight applications; all but fourteen were rejected; and recommendations were made on behalf of seven but only accepted by government for five, none of whom were released from prison (Sheehy, 2014: 8). Sheehy (2014: 8–9) concludes: '*Lavallee* . . . facilitated plea bargains for manslaughter and compassionate sentences for battered women in circumstances in which they might have achieved acquittal based on self-defence had they gone to trial.' In the Australian context, Rebecca Bradfield had questioned whether such outcomes constituted 'mercy but not justice' (as cited by Sheehy, 2014: 9).

A recent review of battered women's homicide cases in Australia, Canada and New Zealand notes some positive developments. While in all three countries women were usually indicted for murder, in Australia and Canada there were few murder convictions – most commonly the women pleaded guilty to manslaughter, and in Australia these were commonly based on provocation or excessive self-defence where those partial defences still exist in some jurisdictions. However, almost one-third of cases in Canada and one in five cases in Australia did not proceed or resulted in an acquittal, as compared with only 10 percent in New Zealand. Australia was the only country in which acquittals were achieved in non-confrontational circumstances, and there were three cases; all other acquittals involved direct confrontations more consistent with traditional constructions of self-defence.

The proportion of acquittals was not aligned in any direct way with the substantive requirements of self-defence. For instance, the acquittal in *Falls* (unreported, Supreme Court of Queensland, per Applegarth J: 2–3 June 2010), which involved a non-confrontational form of self-defence, occurred in Queensland, which has one of the strictest formulations of self-defence. However, in that case, witness testimony and expert evidence was effective and gave a context to the accused woman's actions and to her fear, as well as to domestic violence and its effects. The judge (ibid., para 12–54–55) clearly explained that:

> it doesn't matter that at the moment she shot Mr Falls in the head he didn't at that moment offer or pose any threat to her. He had assaulted her. There was the threat that there would be another one and another one and another one after that until one day something terrible happened. It might have been the next day, it might have been the next week, but the risk of death or serious injury to her was ever present.

This provides a reminder that outcomes in such cases are not simply determined by substantive law, but *inter alia* also reflect aspects of defence lawyering, an understanding of the complexities of domestic violence and the presentation and reception of relevant social context evidence.

Sentencing remains a concern. In previous work with Julia Tolmie we found that sentencing did not always give recognition to the context of the offending when determining the objective seriousness of the offence and the extent of the offender's culpability, and where social context was considered it was commonly transformed into individual deficit or pathology. The sentencing process also provided limited recognition of the gendered and/or raced inequalities that provide the context for offending (Stubbs and Tolmie, 2015: 203). We also raised concerns that the link between the defendant's actions and the prior violence of her abusive partner is not always given full attention at sentencing. This is especially a concern where there has not been a trial involving a formal defence like self-defence or provocation which would require consideration of the behaviour of the deceased (Stubbs and Tolmie, 2005: 204). This is the inverse of the sentencing problem that presents in jurisdictions where provocation has been abolished, and reformers try to guard against the kinds of damaging, victim-blaming narratives formerly used by abusive men when raising provocation at trial that may creep in at sentencing (Freiberg et al., 2015). We also found that domestic violence was frequently presented in sentencing remarks as mutual.

More recent NSW data indicate that 100 percent of offenders convicted of murder from October 2004 to September 2011 received a custodial sentence and 91 percent of sentences were for eighteen years or longer. This contrasts with offenders sentenced for manslaughter, 90 percent of whom received custodial sentences and 70 percent of these were in the range of five to nine years (Select Committee on the Partial Defence of Provocation, 2013: 22). Previous research on sentences for battered women convicted of manslaughter in Australia during the period 1991–2007 identified fifteen cases where women received suspended sentences or non-custodial sentences (Stubbs and Tolmie, 2008). These comparisons provide some indication of the risks of going to trial for murder and the substantial role that partial defences appear to play in plea bargaining to manslaughter.

Conclusion

This chapter began with the recognition that the boundary between murder and manslaughter is shifting in response to ongoing debates about the lack of moral equivalence among different types of killings. With no agreed legal principles on which to settle these debates about the moral distinctions between murder and manslaughter, the task remains a contested, political and politicised one.

Heightened public attention to homicides in the context of domestic violence demands a response, and legislative reforms, whatever else they may achieve, signal political concern. However, it is hardly novel to recognise that the outcomes of law reform are likely to be uncertain and insufficient to achieve the desired change. However, both the femicides and homicides that have been the focus of this chapter reflect not just individual actions by those people accused or the outcomes of the relationships within which they occur, but are associated with complex gender relations that have structural underpinnings. Finding just outcomes in individual cases remains important and requires shifts not just in legal rules but in legal practice and legal cultures, but preventing such homicides requires much more. In settler nations such as Australia, the substantial overrepresentation of Indigenous people as victims and offenders in homicide should be kept in sight in developing strategies to reduce homicide that do not rely only on the criminal law.

Cases

Australia

Falls (Unreported, SC of Qld, Applegarth J, 2–3 June 2010)
Zecevic v DPP (Vic) ((1987) 162 CLR 645)

Canada

Lavallee (1990) 76 CR (3d) 329

Notes

1   A subsequent amendment in 1989 gave judges discretion to determine sentences in all cases.
2   For instance, while the previous law required that the provocation would cause an ordinary person *in the position of the accused* to lose self-control, the new formulation of provocation omits those key words 'in the position of the accused' and thus may work against trying to educate judges and juries about the effects of domestic violence.

References

Allard, S. (1991) Rethinking battered woman syndrome: A black feminist perspective. *UCLA Women's Law Journal*, 1: 191–207.

Belknap, J., Larson, D-L., Abrams, M. L., Garcia, C. and Anderson-Block, K. (2012) Types of intimate partner homicides committed by women: Self-defense, proxy/retaliation, and sexual proprietariness. *Homicide Studies,* 16(4): 359–379.

Brown, D., Farrier, D., McNamara, L., Steel, A., Grewcock, M., Quilter, J. and Schwartz M., (2015) *Criminal Laws*, 6th ed. Annandale: Federation Press.

Bryant, W. and Cussen, T. (2015) *Homicide in Australia: 2010–11 to 2011–12.* Canberra: Australian Institute of Criminology.

Bugeja, L., Butler, A., Buxton, E., Ehrat, H., Hayes, M., Mcintyre, S. J. and Walsh, C. (2013) The implementation of domestic violence death reviews in Australia. *Homicide Studies*, 17(4): 353–374.

Cho, S., Crenshaw, K. and McCall, L. (2013) Toward a field of intersectionality studies: Theory, applications, and praxis. *Signs*, 38(4): 785–810.

Collins, P. H. (2000) *Black Feminist Thought: Knowledge, Consciousness, and the Politics of Empowerment* (2nd ed.). New York: Routledge.

Coss, G. (2006) The defence of provocation: An acrimonious divorce from reality. *Current Issues in Criminal Justice*, 18(1): 51–78.

Crenshaw, K. (1991) Mapping the margins: Identity politics, intersectionality, and violence against women. *Stanford Law Review*, 43: 1241–1299.

Crofts, T. (2007) Wilful murder, murder – what's in a name? *Current Issues in Criminal Justice*, 19(1): 49–63.

Crofts, T. and Loughnan, A. (2013) Provocation: The good, the bad and the ugly. *Criminal Law Journal,* 37(1): 23–37.

Cunneen, C. and Stubbs, J. (2004) Cultural criminology: Engaging with race, gender and post-colonial identities. In Ferrell, J., Hayward, K., Morrison, W. and Presdee, M. (eds.) *Cultural Criminology Unleashed.* London: Glasshouse Press, pp. 97–108.

Cussen, T. and Bryant, W. (2015) *Indigenous and Non-Indigenous Homicide in Australia.* Research in Practice No. 37. Canberra: Australian Institute of Criminology.

Davis, K. (2008) Intersectionality as a buzzword: A sociology of science perspective on what makes a feminist theory successful. *Feminist Theory,* 9(1): 67–85.

Department of Justice. (2013) *Defensive Homicide: Proposals for Reform – Consultation Paper*. Victoria.

Dobash, R. E. and Dobash, R. P. (2015) *When Men Murder Women.* New York: Oxford University Press.

Douglas, H. (2012) A consideration of the merits of specialized homicide offences and defences for battered women. *Australian and New Zealand Journal of Criminology*, 45(3): 367–382.

DVDRT (Domestic Violence Death Review Team NSW) (2015) *Annual Report 2012–13.* NSW Domestic Violence Death Review Team, Sydney.

Easteal, P. and Hopkins, A. (2010) Walking in her shoes: Battered women who kill in Victoria, Western Australia and Queensland. *Alternative Law Journal*, 35(3): 132–137.

Edgely, M. and Marchetti, E. (2011) Women who kill their abusers: How Queensland's new abusive domestic relationships defence continues to ignore reality. *Flinders Law Journal*, 13: 125–2176.

Eriksson, L. and Mazerolle, P. (2013) A general strain theory of intimate partner homicide. *Aggression and Violent Behavior*, 18: 462–470.

Fitz-Gibbon, K. (2014) *Homicide Law Reform, Gender and the Provocation Defence: A Comparative Perspective.* Hampshire: Palgrave Macmillan.

Fitz-Gibbon, K. and Stubbs, J. (2012) Divergent directions in reforming legal responses to lethal violence. *Australian and New Zealand Journal of Criminology*, 45(3): 318–336.

Freiberg, A., Gelb, K. and Stewart, F. (2015) Homicide law reform, provocation and sentencing. In Fitz-Gibbon, K. and Freiberg, A. (eds.) *Homicide Law Reform in Victoria.* Sydney: The Federation Press, pp. 57–75.

Graycar, R. and Morgan, J. (2002) *The Hidden Gender of Law* (2nd ed.). Sydney: The Federation Press.

Hazzard, B. The Hon. (2014) Second reading speech, crimes amendment (provocation) bill 2014. NSW Parliament: Legislative Assembly (proof copy, no page numbers). Available from: www.parliament.nsw.gov.au/prod/parlment/nswbills.nsf/0/968c677044f30063ca2 57c910019ee05/$FILE/2R%20Provocation.pdf

Howe, A. (1997) More folk provoke their own demise: Revisiting the provocation defence courtesy of the homosexual advance defence. *Sydney Law Review*, 19(3): 366–384.

Human Rights & Equal Opportunity Commission. (2005) Aboriginal & Torres Strait Islander Social Justice Commissioner. *Social Justice Report 2004.* Sydney: HREOC.

Johnston, H. and Hotton, T. (2003) Losing control: Homicide risk in estranged and intact intimate relationships. *Homicide Studies*, 7(1): 58–84.

Kelly, L. (1988) *Surviving Sexual Violence.* Minneapolis: University of Minnesota Press.

Kelly, L. (2005) Inside outsiders: Mainstreaming violence against women into human rights discourse and practice. *International Feminist Journal of Politics*, 7(4): 471–495.

Leader-Elliott, I. (2015) Reform and the codification of the law of homicide: Reflection on the Victorian experience. In Fitz-Gibbon, K. and Freiberg, A. (eds.) *Homicide Law Reform in Victoria.* Sydney: The Federation Press, pp. 158–172.

Mahoney, R. (1991) Legal images of battered women: Redefining the issue of separation. *Michigan Law Review*, 90(1): 1–94.

Merry, S. E. (2003) Rights talk and the experience of law: Implementing women's human rights to protection from violence. *Human Rights Quarterly*, 25(2): 343–381.

Naffine, N. (2009) Moral uncertainties of rape and murder: Problems at the core of criminal law theory. In McSherry, B., Norrie, A. W. and Bronitt, S. (eds.) *Regulating Deviance: The Redirection of Criminalisation and the Futures of Criminal Law.* Oxford: Hart Publishing, pp. 213–232.

Norrie, A. (2005) *Law the Beautiful Soul.* London: Glasshouse Press.

Polk, K. (1994) *When Men Kill: Scenarios of Masculine Violence.* Cambridge: Cambridge University Press.

Polk, K. and Ranson, D. (1991) The role of gender in intimate homicide. *Australian and New Zealand Journal of Criminology*, 24(1): 15–24.

Quick, O. and Wells, C. (2012) Partial reform of partial defences: Developments in England and Wales. *Australian and New Zealand Journal of Criminology*, 45(3): 337–350.

Quilter, J. (2014) The Thomas Kelly case: Why a 'one punch' law is not the answer. *Criminal Law Journal*, 38: 16–37.

Radford, J. (1992) Introduction. In Radford, J. and Russell, D.E.H. (eds.) *Femicide: The Politics of Woman Killing*. New York: Twayne Publishers, pp. 3–12.

Ratushny, Judge L. (1997) *Self-Defence Review: Final Report*. Submitted to the Minister of Justice of Canada and to the Solicitor General of Canada. Available from: http://canada.justice.gc.ca/Publications/defence/rtush_en.html

Schneider, E. (2000) *Battered Women and Feminist Lawmaking*. New Haven, CT: Yale University Press.

Select Committee on the Partial Defence of Provocation. (2013) *The Partial Defence of Provocation*. New South Wales: Legislative Council, New South Wales Parliament.

Sheehy, E. (2014) *Defending Battered Women on Trial: Lessons from the Transcripts*. Vancouver, BC: UBC Press.

Sheehy, E., Stubbs, J. and Tolmie, T. (2012) Defences to homicide for battered women: A comparative analysis of laws in Australia, Canada and New Zealand. *Sydney Law Review*, 34(3): 467–492.

Sokoloff, N. and Dupont, I. (2005) Domestic violence at the intersections of race, class, and gender. *Violence Against Women*, 11(1): 38–64.

Stark, E. (2007) *Coercive Control: How Men Entrap Battered Women in Personal Life*. New York: Oxford University Press.

Stöckl, H., Devries, K., Rotstein, A., Abrahams, N., Campbell, J., Watts, C. and Moreno, C. G. (2013) The global prevalence of intimate partner homicide: a systematic review. *Lancet* 382(9895): 859–865.

Stubbs, J. and Tolmie, J. (1995) Race, gender and the battered woman syndrome: An Australian case study. *Canadian Journal of Women and Law*, 8(1): 122–158.

Stubbs, J. and Tolmie, J. (2005) Defending battered women on charges of homicide: The structural and systemic versus the personal and particular. In Chan, W., Chunn, D. E. and Menzies, R. (eds.) *Women, Mental Disorder and the Law*. London: Glasshouse Press, pp. 191–210.

Stubbs, J. and Tolmie, J. (2008) Battered women charged with homicide: Advancing the interests of Indigenous women. *Australian and New Zealand Journal of Criminology*, 41(1): 138–161.

US Department of Justice and US Department of Health and Human Services. (1996) *The Validity and Use of Evidence Concerning Battering and Its Effects in Criminal Trials: Report Responding to Section 40507 of the Violence Against Women Act*. Available from: www.ncjrs.gov/pdffiles/batter.pdf

Victorian Law Reform Commission. (2004) *Defences to Homicide- Final Report*. Melbourne.

Wallace, A. (1986) *Homicide: The Social Reality*. Sydney: NSW Bureau of Crime Statistics and Research.

Websdale, N. (1999) *Understanding Domestic Homicide*. Boston: Northeastern University Press.

Wilson, M. and Daly, M. (1998) Lethal and non-lethal violence against wives and the evolutionary psychology of male sexual proprietariness. In Dobash, R. E. and Dobash, R. P. (eds.) *Rethinking Violence Against Women*. Thousand Oaks, CA: Sage, pp. 199–230.

3 Representing intimacy, gender and homicide

The validity and utility of common stereotypes in law

Myrna Dawson

Two offenders are charged and convicted of homicide-related offences in separate killings. Each offender shot a female victim during a struggle and, as such, both scenarios involve the same set of basic facts – a man, a woman, a struggle, a shooting and a death. One characteristic does distinguish the two cases – the relationship that existed between the victim and her killer – a fact that has long been seen as a crucial element in violent incidents. In the first case, the offender was a stranger to the female victim. In the second case, the offender was the female's intimate partner. Numerous stereotypes exist that could be, and have been, used to justify the more lenient treatment of the offender who killed his intimate partner compared with the offender who killed a stranger. Furthermore, historically and still today, the common assumption is that intimacy serves to mitigate rather than aggravate violence and perhaps should do so if stereotypes about intimacy and violence are valid. This arguably occurs because the relationship between victims and their killers brings to the public (and legal) mind specific contexts in which these killings are thought to occur that may, in turn, determine the level of responsibility attributed to those involved. What is largely absent from these discussions and related research, however, is the systematic examination of the *actual* role that intimacy does play in determining responsibility and the punishment outcomes that result, as well as the validity of common stereotypes and their role in criminal justice decision making.

This chapter argues that this situation has arisen because stereotypes about intimacy and violence and the perceived leniency of the criminal justice system are so common in our everyday world that they have become part of both conventional and sociological wisdom, similar to what Hagan and O'Donnel (1978) argued about gender and sentencing more than three decades ago. That is, even without a solid base of consistent empirical evidence, sociologists and the public (including court actors) have come to assume that offenders who kill intimate partners are less culpable and less dangerous than those who kill victims with whom they shared more distant relationships (Auerhahn, 2007; Dawson, 2006; Miethe, 1987). It is also assumed that the courts respond accordingly despite what appear to be contradictory findings from the limited and somewhat dated research that has focused specifically on this question (Auerhahn, 2007; Bonds and Jeffries, 2014; Dawson, 2012). The chapter further argues that the way in which intimacy and gender are intricately linked in crimes of violence is so ingrained in conventional and sociological wisdom that their combined influence on law when determining offender (or victim) responsibility when violence occurs has largely been ignored (see recent exception, Gillespie et al., 2013). This has precluded the recognition that the majority of stereotypes about intimacy and violence are actually stereotypes about men's violence against female partners.

To begin to challenge conventional wisdom, this chapter reviews dominant stereotypes about intimacy and violence that are found in the literature, linking them to explanations for criminal justice leniency. Next, findings about the validity of one of the most common stereotypes about Intimate partner homicide (IPH) – that such acts largely arise as spontaneous 'crimes of passion' – are examined, providing preliminary evidence that at least one of these stereotypes may be more conventional wisdom than empirical fact. To understand the role such stereotypes might play in law, an exploratory analysis of sentencing transcripts in cases of intimate partner homicide is examined to determine whether these or other stereotypes can be identified. An emerging theme that focuses on Intimate partner violence (IPV) as a serious social issue is discussed in detail to contribute to our understanding of how judges speak about intimacy and violence. The chapter concludes with a brief discussion about some of the challenges faced when examining the validity of stereotypes and their role in determining punishments. The importance of doing so, however, is underscored as a first step in achieving a reliable and valid understanding of the role played by intimacy in law, particularly when allocating responsibility for violent crime and, in particular, homicide.

This examination is timely given that, in the last several decades, the social construction of interpersonal relationships in law has undergone fundamental changes. Family violence – historically perceived as private violence and not appropriate for legal intervention – has increasingly been labeled as criminal. Controversy continues to reign, however, over the extent to which family violence – also referred to as domestic or intimate partner violence – is gendered violence, although it is most commonly recognized as such (Grant, 2010; Johnson and Dawson, 2011; World Health Organization, 2002). National and international debates also continue over the degree to which this type of violence should be treated as criminal and, if so, what punishments are most appropriate. For example, much discussion has centred upon the appropriate legal responses to various types of homicide, particularly those that occur between intimate partners (Fitz-Gibbon and Stubbs, 2012; Johnson and Dawson, 2011). Historically and still today, the provocation defence has been the subject of much controversy internationally (Fitz-Gibbons and Pickering, 2012). Some jurisdictions (e.g. Australia, the United Kingdom) have abolished or reformed the partial defence of provocation (see Fitz-Gibbon and Pickering, 2012), whereas others have sought to make punishments more appropriate through sentencing reforms (Dawson, 2012). In Canada, for example, at one time our penal laws made no mention of the relationship between a victim and a defendant and its meaning in the criminal process (Grant et al., 1998). Today, however, the sentencing principles in the Canadian Criminal Code stipulate that the relationships that offenders have (or had) with their victims may act as an aggravating factor at sentencing, so an offender who abuses a spouse or child may now be subject to harsher penalties.

Regardless of legislative and policy changes, many argue that crimes between intimates continue to be treated more leniently than crimes between those who share more distant relationships (Black, 1976, 1993; Dawson, 2006). Some remain skeptical about the willingness of criminal justice actors to seriously address the problem of IPV despite the number of legal transformations, particularly in recent decades (Fineman, 1994; Sheehy, 2014). More specifically, traditional ideological rationales or stereotypes may continue to operate that see the severity of some violence consistently downplayed (Bond and Jeffries, 2014; Rapaport, 1991, 1994). Returning to the hypothetical cases above, it is acknowledged that no two cases are exactly alike once one gets beyond these basic facts. In fact, it is a certainty that there are variations in the circumstances leading up to these two crimes, stemming, in part, from the different relationships shared by the victims and offenders. However, the contention of this chapter is that research has yet to systematically examine in any meaningful way whether and what these differences actually are or what impact any perceived or actual differences have (or should have) on punishment outcomes. The central objective of this chapter, then, is to begin to explore what some of those perceived differences might be and how they might enter into more nuanced discussions about appropriate punishments when responding to IPH.

Stereotypes about intimacy and violence

During the past several decades, a large body of research has developed around the role of criminal stereotypes when determining punishments for various crimes, including homicide (Auerhahn, 2007; Farrell and Holmes, 1991; Farrell and Swigert, 1986; Johnson, 2003; Miethe, 1987; Steen et al., 2005; Swigert and Farrell, 1977). It is not the goal to review this literature in detail here, but rather to highlight that the majority of studies have focused on stereotypes related to an offender's gender or race/ethnicity, linking these characteristics to varying perceptions of crimes or criminals (e.g. males and/ or black offenders) as more dangerous, more threatening and more culpable than other crimes or criminals (e.g. females and/or white offenders; Albonetti, 1991; Daly, 1994; Daly and Tonry, 1997; Johnson, 2003; Steen et al., 2005; Steffensmeier et al., 1998). Largely ignored by the criminal stereotype literature is what has long been argued to be a key element in determining the nature of and response to crime (Black, 1976, 1993; Waegel, 1981) – the degree of intimacy that exists (or existed) between victims and offenders (for an exception, see Miethe, 1987). To address this gap, traditional stereotypes about intimacy and violence were identified and conceptually linked to court outcomes (see full discussion in Dawson, 2006). These stereotypes are briefly described below, organized around the focal-concerns framework emphasizing three concerns of court actors when determining punishments: (1) defendant culpability/blameworthiness, (2) public protection and (3) practical constraints of the system (Johnson, 2003; Steffensmeier et al., 1998). While not an exhaustive list, Table 3.1 shows the dominant stereotypes that can be found in the literature about intimacy and violence.

Table 3.1 Stereotypes associated with intimacy and violence and related hypotheses about impact on criminal justice outcomes

Focal Concern	
Offender culpability	***Mitigating emotions.*** Intimate violence is treated more leniently because such acts are perceived to be motivated by strong emotions that criminal justice actors believe reduce the defendant's culpability. ***Victim participation.*** Intimate violence may be treated more leniently because such acts are assumed to involve some degree of victim involvement which is perceived by criminal justice officials to mitigate the defendant's culpability for his/her crime.
Protection of the public	***Deterring future crime.*** Intimate violence may be treated more leniently because such defendants are believed to be beyond the deterrent message of criminal law. ***Future dangerousness.*** Intimate violence may be treated more leniently because criminal justice officials believe such offenders pose little future dangerousness to the public at large. ***Horizontal crimes.*** Intimate violence may be treated more leniently because victims and defendants in these cases often share similar social ranks and, thus, are not perceived to pose a threat to the maintenance of the social order. ***Private crimes.*** Intimate violence may be treated more leniently because these crimes are assumed to be more private acts and, thus, are perceived to pose little threat to maintenance of the social order.
Practicality	***Preservation of the family.*** Intimate violence is treated more leniently because criminal justice officials believe they are preventing further disruption of intimate or familial relationships. ***Frequent crimes.*** Intimate violence may be treated more leniently because these cases are encountered more frequently by the courts, leading to their classification as 'normal' incidents that are 'less serious', allowing for more expedient processing of these cases. ***Informal vs. formal controls.*** Intimate violence may be treated more leniently because criminal justice officials perceive informal controls to be more available in such disputes; and because there is an inverse relationship between informal and formal controls, the latter should be less visible. ***Legacy of patriarchal norms.*** Intimate violence may be treated more leniently because of the legacy of patriarchal legal doctrines that reflect the belief that intimate violence is inappropriate for legal intervention.

Source: Dawson, M. (2006) Intimacy, violence and the law: Exploring stereotypes about victim–defendant relationship and violent crime. *Journal of Criminal Law and Criminology*, 96(4): 1417–1450.

Focal concern: defendant culpability

The first focal concern, often associated with the retributive principle of punishment, emphasizes that punishment should increase with the degree of defendant culpability. In addition to the harm caused by his/her offence (e.g. Gottfredson and Gottfredson, 1988; Huang et al., 1996), other factors can contribute to assessments of culpability or blameworthiness, including: (1) biographical factors (e.g. criminal history) which typically increase blameworthiness; (2) prior victimization of the defendant which can mitigate blameworthiness; and (3) the defendant's role in the crime (e.g. leader, organizer, follower). Two stereotypes about intimacy and violence may be linked to culpability or blameworthiness.

Mitigating emotions

One explanation for the role of intimacy in law draws from the theory of relative culpability inherent in the law of homicide that distinguishes between 'hot-blooded' and 'cold-blooded' crimes. Killing out of anger or other strong emotion can decrease defendant culpability because strong emotion undermines one's capacity to deliberate and plan one's actions or reduces agency and self-restraint (Grant, 2010; Rapaport, 1994). Cold-blooded violence, often referred to as instrumental violence, is most often associated with offenders motivated by rational calculation, risk minimization, or some type of gain (e.g. robbery). In contrast, hot-blooded or expressive violence typically lacks rational consideration (Miethe and Regoeczi, 2004), stemming instead from 'character contests' (Luckenbill, 1977), a desire to retaliate (Felson, 1978; Rapaport, 1994) or 'righteous slaughter' (Katz, 1988).

Intimate partner homicides, and particularly male-on-female killings, have been traditionally viewed as the archetype of expressive, hot-blooded acts because of the intensity of intimate partner relationships (Loftin, 1986; Maxfield, 1989; Messner and Tardiff, 1985; Parker and Smith, 1979; Rojek and Williams, 1993; Sampson, 1987; Smith and Parker, 1980). Killings between strangers or non-intimates are more often viewed as instrumental in that violence is often committed for gain (Block, 1981; Riedel, 1987; Rojek and Williams, 1993). While some research questions the validity of these typologies (Dawson, 2006; Felson and Messner, 1996; Miethe and Drass, 1998; Miethe and Regoeczi, 2004; Polk and Ranson, 1991), expressive violence continues to be linked with intimacy and instrumental violence with more distant relationships. Therefore, because instrumental violence is believed to occur most often among strangers, such acts will be (and should be) treated more seriously by the courts than other types of crimes (e.g. IPV).

Victim participation

Research has shown that crimes between individuals known to each other are also more likely to generate images of victim participation, including provocation, compared with crimes involving strangers (Hessick, 2007; Kern et al., 2007; McCormick et al., 1998; Riedel, 1987), particularly in cases of intimate partner killings. Judgments about victim provocation have been shown to affect decisions about charges, dismissals and sentences (Grant, 2010; Miethe, 1985; Sheehy, 2014; Williams, 1976; Wolfgang, 1957, 1958). Court actors have also been shown to consider broader contributory actions by the victim even if provocation is absent (Kalven and Zeisel, 1971; Williams, 1976). For example, in cases of IPH, Rapaport (1991: 380) states:

> If acquaintances, friends, and most especially family members quarrel and a homicide ensues, we are disposed to view the victim as sharing some responsibility with his or her killer for the killing – whether or not the provocation would be considered legally sufficient to reduce the charge from murder to manslaughter. The victim is regarded as having assumed a measure of the risk of victimization simply by remaining in an intimate relationship with the killer whom he or she may have known to be disposed to violence. We assume that the victim possessed some degree of control over the circumstances of his or her victimization, which puts the homicide in a less frightening light and diminishes the degree of punishment that appears appropriate.

Based on the above, the *victim participation* stereotype also leads to the expectation that cases involving intimate partners will attract less serious responses than those involving strangers. However, among intimate partner homicides, estranged victims and defendants will attract more severe responses than cases involving those still in a relationship because estranged victims tried to diminish their risk by exiting the relationship, and thus participation in their own victimization may be perceived as minimal or absent, which has been supported by research (Dawson, 2003; Rapaport, 1994).

Focal concern: public protection

A second concern for court actors is public protection, which includes decisions about imprisonment to deter offenders themselves or would-be offenders, as well as related considerations of future danger and risk of recidivism. The following four stereotypes demonstrate how notions of dangerousness and recidivism may differ, depending on degree of intimacy.

Deterring future crime

The law is concerned with two types of deterrence: general deterrence and specific deterrence. General deterrence is the symbolic effect of punishment resulting in individuals avoiding future crime when they see others punished. Specific deterrence is the effect of punishment on the individual offender achieved through his/her own experience. Chambliss (1984) argues that the deterrent effect of punishment depends on: (1) whether crimes are expressive or instrumental and (2) whether offenders have high or low commitment to crime. The threat of sanctions should be most effective in deterring instrumental crimes by persons with low commitment (see also Parker and Smith, 1979; Thomas and Williams, 1977). Expressive crimes are often viewed as beyond deterrence, in part because of their perceived spontaneity.

The two stereotypical images about offenders who kill intimate partners discussed above are relevant when considering deterrence (Rapaport, 1994). The first is that of out-of-control killers whose emotions undermine their ability to act rationally (see *mitigating emotions*). The second is that of otherwise peaceful, non-violent individuals who, having killed in response to some provocation, are unlikely to re-offend (see *victim participation*). These images underscore a perception of offenders who kill intimates as expressive actors with low intent and little commitment to crime. As a result, court actors may believe that they are relatively powerless to deter intimate partner violence, in contrast to forms of instrumental violence, as discussed further below (Lundsgaarde, 1977).

Future dangerousness

Events perceived to be isolated 'crimes of passion' with little probability of reoccurrence may not be considered deserving of severe sanctions because there is also little perceived risk of future danger (Lundsgaarde, 1977). As noted, offenders in these cases may often be perceived as otherwise peaceful individuals and unlikely to re-offend. In contrast, offenders who prey on strangers are feared most by society (Miller et al., 1991) and, thus, tend to attract more severe sanctions because of their perceived greater risk of future danger to the public (Davis and Smith, 1981). Consistent with this stereotype, Miethe (1987) found that the source of differential treatment of intimates and non-intimates stemmed from differential conceptions of 'dangerousness'. He found that factors indicative of 'dangerousness' (e.g. being male, black, using a weapon) were important when sentencing offenders who victimized strangers but had no effect on sentences for offenders who knew their victims. Miethe (1987) concluded that it is not images of provocation and culpability that lead to varying outcomes for intimate and non-intimate offenders, but rather varying conceptions of 'dangerousness'.

Private crimes

Where violence falls on the public-private continuum is seen to be associated with the degree of threat to the social order (Lundsgaarde, 1977). The killing of a police officer, for example, symbolically threatens the social order, and as a result, sanctions against these killers are often severe. The location of a crime on the public-private continuum also depends, in part, on the social distance or degree of intimacy between victims and offenders. Violence between intimates is more often seen to fall within the private domain and killings among strangers in the public domain (Cretney and Davis, 1997; Hartman and Belknap, 2003; Mills, 1998). Lundsgaarde (1977: 141) states:

> Thus, killings among intimates are generally viewed by society at large as less problematic than are killings that involve strangers. This is true in part because intimates form symmetrical social relationships that insulate them within a series of obligations subject to enforcement by social and psychological sanctions. The robber, rapist, killer or even the self-styled terrorist is not restrained in his behavior by anything other than criminal sanctions.

As such, the *private crimes* stereotype argues that violence arising from unsatisfactory relationships is not often viewed as a threat to social order. Rather, such acts, which often take place in the privacy of one's home, are commonly believed to arise from life's stressful events and, as such, will attract more lenient responses than will public crimes.

Horizontal crimes

It is also argued that crimes committed among victims and defendants who share similar social ranks (i.e. horizontal crimes) are not viewed as seriously by court actors as those acts that occur between defendants of lower social rank than their victims (i.e. upward crimes) (Black, 1976; Turk, 1969). Violence between intimates is often perceived as horizontal because intimate relationships tend to develop among people of similar social and cultural backgrounds. Ferraro and Boychuk (1992) argue that it is these similar social ranks more than the degree of intimacy that leads to lenient treatment of some crimes. That is, the law's patriarchal authority has distinct race and class boundaries such that violence which does not threaten these boundaries is viewed as less threatening to the social order than violence that crosses boundaries. Arguably, then, the state will be more concerned with stranger violence because this type of victimization is more often upward in nature and feared most by the public (Conklin, 1972; McIntyre, 1967; Ouimet and Coyle, 1991; Riedel, 1993).

Focal concern: practical constraints

The constraints of the criminal justice system also come into play in criminal justice decision making. For example, organizational concerns relate to ensuring the stable flow of cases, maintaining work relationships and remaining sensitive to local concerns (Dixon, 1995; Flemming et al., 1992; Steffensmeier et al., 1993; Ulmer, 1995; Ulmer and Kramer, 1996). Legal actors also have individual concerns about disrupting family ties and the ability of an offender to do time (Daly, 1987; Hogarth, 1971; Steffensmeier, 1980; Steffensmeier et al., 1995). The final four perspectives highlight how stereotypes about intimacy and violence may be related to practical concerns leading to the more lenient treatment of some offenders.

Frequent crimes

Assessments of case seriousness are often made in relation to the kinds of cases regularly encountered, and the decision to treat a case as serious depends, in part, on the overall range and character of cases processed by those responding. This composition of the total collection of cases, or the "contextual gestalt" (Emerson, 1983: 429), produces a "sliding scale of severity" (Friedson, 1970: 257) which is used by decision makers to respond to individual cases. In routinely interacting with offenders, court actors accumulate knowledge "of the typical manner in which offences of given classes are committed, the social characteristics of the persons who commit them, the features of the settings in which they occur, the types of victims often involved and the like" (Sudnow, 1965: 259). This process results in the construction of a 'normal crimes' lens through which future cases are assessed (Sudnow, 1965). For example, agencies that deal regularly with homicide may make finer, more varied distinctions among 'serious' or 'normal' homicides.

One characteristic commonly used to classify crimes is the victim–offender relationship. Waegel (1981) found this to be the earliest piece of information sought and given the greatest significance, arguing that a key reason for this is that the victim–offender relationship is a core feature of the routine offence pattern in crimes. For example, a prior relationship between those involved might cue stereotypes about acts without clearly defined victims and offenders, particularly when alcohol or drugs are involved. Violence most often occurs among defendants and victims who know each other (Block and Christakos, 1995; Moyer, 1992). Defendants who are known to their victims are also more likely to be arrested than strangers (Cotter, 2014; Davis and Smith, 1981). Therefore, the proportion of cases involving those known to each other is far higher than cases among strangers. As such, the *frequent crimes* stereotype argues that cases involving intimate partners will be treated more leniently because court actors encounter these cases more often than crimes between non-intimates and see the former as more 'normal' (hence, less serious) than the latter.

Informal controls

The law is only one form of social control, which operates alongside more informal controls provided by families, friendships, neighborhoods and other groups (Black, 1976, 1993; Horwitz, 1990). When informal controls are more visible, formal controls will likely be less visible and determined by various social structural characteristics (for a review, see Black, 1976, 1993). When considering intimacy, the key social structural factor is morphology, defined as 'the distribution of people in relation to one another' depending upon one's interactional networks, relational intimacy and integration with others (Black, 1976: 37). The law will be most visible where there is little interaction, intimacy or integration; that is, where informal social controls are weakest. Despite the growing presence of the law among intimates, they are still subject to less legal control than non-intimates. For strangers, the law should reach its highest level because informal social controls are absent, whereas minimal law should enter the family domain, where informal controls are seen as more dominant. When intimate disputes do enter the courts, the outcome may depend upon the degree of intimacy that exists between those involved. For example, the longer the marriage, the less serious IPV may be sanctioned.

Legacy of patriarchal norms

Early feminist researchers argued that the law's presence (or absence) in the domestic sphere stemmed from traditional beliefs about the nuclear family and its function in society (Fineman, 1994). Within this environment, nineteenth-century legal doctrines subordinated a wife to her husband, whose responsibility it was to keep the family in order. Historically, under common law, the legal existence of a woman was suspended when she married, and she could not use the law for protection from acts by her husband that would otherwise be criminal. In the nineteenth century, the Married Women's Property Act was meant to improve the civil status of women, but criminal law continued to defer to male authority in the home. Therefore, the *legacy of patriarchal norms* stereotype suggests that the 'constraints' of the system when responding to IPV are not actual but *perceived* by actors because of this patriarchal legacy. Today, feminists argue that the rhetoric of marital equality conceals how similar attitudes continue to operate (Fineman, 1994; Marcus, 1994). Specifically, assumptions about hierarchy and control continue to reinforce ingrained cultural notions, which are in turn perpetuated through the language of law, particularly with respect to violence by men against female partners (Fineman, 1994; Pleck, 1989; Rapaport, 1991).

Preservation of the family

A final stereotype highlights the courts' concern for preserving the family when responding to IPV, particularly when children are involved. While research examining this issue is limited, early interviews found that criminal justice officials were reluctant to proceed with cases stemming from arguments between family members (Gottfredson and Gottfredson, 1988; Vera Institute of Justice, 1977). Some judges indicated that they often felt that imprisonment would serve no purpose and might, in fact, disrupt relationships further as a result of an overreaction to personal or intimate grievances. This stereotype argues, then, that IPV is treated more leniently because legal actors do not want to disrupt family units further by responding to disputes not appropriate for legal intervention. In fact, it has been argued that the traditional pattern of responses to crimes between victims and defendants was a preference to keep such cases out of the legal system, with decision makers seeking other ways to deal with crimes between relatives, friends and acquaintances (Gottfredson and Gottfredson, 1988). It is not clear whether or not such responses or attitudes have changed significantly in actual practice today despite legislative and policy reform.

The above stereotypes are part of historical and still often contemporary views of violence that occurs between victims and offenders who share relationships of varying degrees. Despite these traditional understandings of how such violence is thought to occur and the characteristics of those involved, there has been little research that has empirically examined their validity, an issue discussed next.

Challenging the validity of common stereotypes: the case of 'mitigating emotions'

In contrast to the view of an act that involves 'mitigating emotions' – the first stereotype discussed – is the view of an act that involves premeditation, or at the very least intent, which is a factor that can make homicides more serious (Grant et al., 1998). The meanings of the terms 'premeditation' and 'intent' have been discussed extensively in case law, but have yet to be discussed to any degree in social science research. In Canada, if premeditation or pre-planning is proven, the most serious charge of first-degree murder typically applies. Inherent in the notion of premeditation is intent (or *mens rea*), which typically distinguishes between murder and manslaughter. If IPH more often involves mitigating emotions, the role of premeditation or intent should be documented less often in these cases. Some earlier research found this to be the case (Dawson, 2006). In this study, to capture premeditation/intent, drawing from work by Wallace (1986), a modified version of indicators to capture degrees of premeditation/intent was used: (1) defendant purchased a weapon prior to the killing; (2) defendant brought a weapon to the scene of the homicide; (3) victim was sleeping when killed; (4) defendant previously threatened to kill the victim; (5) defendant contracted out the killing; (6) victim abducted/lured to his/her death; (7) defendant followed/laid in wait to kill victim; (8) defendant made previous attempt(s); and, finally, (9) evidence documents that the defendant intended to kill the victim (e.g. letters, wills).

Using 108 matched cases (54 pairs), evidence of premeditation/intent was coded and compared between the two types of homicides. Contrary to the stereotype of IPH as the archetypal 'crime of passion', evidence of premeditation and/or intent was more frequent among those cases that involved intimate partners (22/54 cases; 41 percent) than among non-IPHs (17/54 cases; 31 percent). While not conclusive, the finding does challenge the stereotype that IPHs are primarily spontaneous events involving mitigating emotions. Of more concern, perhaps, is that this study also showed that despite the greater evidence of premeditation/intent and similar case characteristics, IPH cases received shorter sentences in the majority of comparisons (44 percent).

To summarize this section, various stereotypes about intimacy and violence can be found in the literature, highlighting what appear to be common beliefs about the way in which IPV occurs and those involved. What is absent from the literature is how valid such stereotypes are in representing the reality of these crimes. As such, it is unclear whether there are any empirical bases for what appears to be conventional and sociological wisdom about intimacy and violence upon which its role in law may be based. Supporting this argument, the accuracy of the 'mitigating emotions' stereotype was called into question, suggesting that it is time to systematically assess what we *think* we currently know about intimacy and violence. How concerned we should be about the validity of such stereotypes, however, is related, in part, to their perceived or actual role in criminal justice decision making. The next section examines the presence of these stereotypes in judicial sentencing remarks and, in doing so, identifies some of the challenges researchers will face when trying to further our understanding of the law's response to intimacy and violence. The goal of this analysis is not to determine the validity of these stereotypes because we are not comparing their legal portrayals to all the actual facts for each case (if those are ever known). Rather, the purpose is to identify whether themes related to the stereotypes discussed above (or others yet to be identified) appear in judicial comments and what the challenges are to understanding the role of such stereotypes in punishment outcomes.

Exploratory analysis

Data

In Canada, first-degree murder convictions come with a mandatory life sentence with a twenty-five-year period of imprisonment before parole eligibility; as such, judicial discretion in these cases and sentencing remarks are minimal. A life sentence is also mandatory for second-degree murder, but parole eligibility can range from ten to twenty-five years. For manslaughter convictions, there is no mandatory minimum period of imprisonment. As such, sentencing remarks are more often available for the latter two types of convictions, so a sample of cases was drawn from a research project examining the court processing of homicides in one Canadian province over a period of four decades. Because sentencing remarks are not always reported, however, sample selection began by identifying IPH cases for which sentencing transcripts were available by searching the LawSource and CanLII databases. There were 135 transcripts located pertaining to initial sentencing decisions from which the sample was drawn.

The primary focus of the analysis was intimacy, but a secondary interest was how discussions might vary by offender gender. Therefore, groups of cases were identified with at least one female and one male offender. Given that cases spanned four decades – a period of time during which significant transformations occurred in formal responses to IPV – cases were also matched by time period. Of particular interest were cases disposed of before and after 1996, when sentencing amendments in Canada stipulated that spousal relationships could be considered an aggravating factor at sentencing. The final sample comprised forty cases: seventeen female and twenty-three male offenders. Slightly more than half the cases (55 percent) were disposed of after 1996 and the remaining cases prior to 1996.

Analysis

The analysis began deductively using a coding protocol that captured themes that related to each of the stereotypes discussed, but was also approached inductively allowing for other themes/stereotypes to emerge. Each transcript was coded separately by three researchers. Discussions were held throughout the coding and analytic process to determine whether identified themes supported particular stereotypes and, if so, whether evidence was valid and consistent. It is important to reiterate that the goal of this exploratory analysis is not to provide definitive conclusions about the presence of related stereotypes. Rather, the findings are to serve as an impetus for more nuanced, and arguably long overdue, discussions about the validity of such stereotypes and their perceived or actual impact on punishments.

Results

Table 3.2 shows frequencies for each of the deductive and inductive codes identified in the total sample and by female and male offenders. The two most common themes identified emerged inductively. The first was *IPV as a serious social issue*, which was found in close to half of the IPH cases (48 percent). This was the most common theme identified for male offenders (52 percent) and, while not the most common for female offenders, it was present in a significant proportion of cases (41 percent). Tied for the most common theme overall was the *presence/role of alcohol*, identified in close to half the cases (48 percent) and the second most common theme for both female and male offenders (53 percent and 44 percent, respectively). *Victim participation* was mentioned in 38 percent of the cases but was more frequently discussed in cases involving female offenders (53 percent) compared with male offenders (26 percent). The theme of *future dangerousness* was present in the sentencing remarks in two categories – those who posed no future danger (38 percent) and those who posed some future danger to the public (10 percent). Most commonly for both female and male offenders, it was their lack of future danger that was discussed, although more often for female (59 percent) than for male offenders (22 percent). Finally, themes related to *mitigating emotions* were present in one-third of the sample – more often for female offenders (41 percent) than for male offenders (26 percent).

Table 3.3 shows whether and how the presence of stereotypes varied pre- and post-amendments in 1996; while small numbers preclude definitive conclusions, some interesting patterns were documented. As would be expected, the theme *IPV as a serious social issue* appeared more often in the post-1996 time period (twelve cases, 55 percent) compared with the pre-1996 time period (six cases, 33 percent). *Mitigating emotions* was also more evident in the post-1996 period (nine cases, 41 percent) than in the earlier period (four cases, 22 percent). Furthermore, it appears that judges were less likely to view IPH as a focal crime for general deterrence in recent years, as its presence diminished post-1996 (from 28 percent to 9 percent). Again, because of small numbers, percentages are unstable as indicators of change; however, descriptive patterns are offered as particular avenues to pursue in future research, as discussed below.

Intimate partner violence as a serious social issue

Given its dominance as a theme that emerged inductively, *IPV as a serious social issue* is examined in further detail. Six of the nine cases involving female offenders

Table 3.2 Frequency of themes related to stereotypes about intimacy and violence for total sample, female offenders and male offenders

Themes	Total		Female Offenders		Male Offenders	
	(N = 40)		(n = 17)		(n = 23)	
	N	%	n	%	n	%
IPV as a serious issue	19	48	7	41	12	52
Presence/role of alcohol	19	48	9	53	10	44
Victim participation	15	38	9	53	6	26
No future danger	15	38	10	59	5	22
Mitigating emotions	13	33	7	41	6	26
General deterrence	7	18	2	12	5	22
Premeditation/intent	7	18	4	24	3	13
Future dangerousness	4	10	2	12	2	9

Table 3.3 Frequency of themes related to stereotypes about intimacy and violence for study period as well as for the period prior to and after the 1996 sentencing amendments

Themes	Total		Pre-amendments		Post-amendments	
	(N = 40)		(n = 18)		(n = 22)	
	N	%	n	%	n	%
IPV as a serious issue	19	48	6	33	12	55
Presence/role of alcohol	19	48	10	56	9	41
Victim participation	15	38	7	39	8	36
No future danger	15	38	8	44	2	32
Mitigating emotions	13	33	4	22	9	41
General deterrence	7	18	5	28	2	9
Premeditation/intent	7	18	3	17	4	18
Future dangerousness	4	10	2	11	2	9

disposed of post-1996 included this theme (67 percent), as did six of the thirteen cases involving male offenders (46 percent). This shows that intimacy is a factor in criminal justice decision making, and while more common since sentencing amendments, similar concerns were present in the earlier time period, at least in this sample of cases. The way in which intimacy is portrayed by judges in discussing their sentencing decisions varied between the two time periods, however. In sentencing remarks prior to 1996, judges appear to emphasize the sentencing principle of deterrence as their primary goal (see also Table 3.3, 'General deterrence'). The following cases illustrate this point:

Those who would solve their domestic disputes by violence must clearly know that these disputes must be solved through the courts and not through the barrel of a gun.

(Female offender; *R v. Giesecke* [1994])

I don't think there can be any doubt that there is a high incidence of wife beating, not only in this province but throughout the country, and it is necessary that the Courts act promptly and, I think, severely in whatever efforts they can to reduce this incidence of violence. . . . [T]he prevalence and the nature of this type of crime, and the fact that it seems to be increasing, requires, I think, a fairly substantial sentence. . . . The crime rate of domestic homicides and domestic beatings can be reduced only by increasing the certainty of punishment provided that the crime itself receives strong moral condemnation of society.

(Male offender; *R. v. Tippett* [1987])

There can be no circumstances in which a man can be entitled to use violence against his wife. It is simply intolerable and the sentences of the courts must indicate that such conduct cannot be tolerated.

(Male offender; *R. v. Mullen* [1988])

I must of course take into account that there is a large, large number of domestic disputes in our present-day society. . . . In my opinion however this case ranks among the worst conceivable cases of manslaughter and calls for a very lengthy sentence that is strongly denunciatory of this vicious and horrible crime, and one that will serve as a warning that the use of violence to resolve domestic disputes will not be tolerated by society or by the courts. . . . The overriding principle that guides me in this case is that enunciated by Howland, C.J.O., in R. v. Glen. He said: The prime consideration in imposing the proper sentence for this offence is the protection of the public by general and individual deterrence. This Court has a duty to make it clear that however unhappy a spouse may be about his or her marital life, and however great the marital stress may become, resorting to violence is not the answer.

(Male offender; *R. v. Toye* [1987])

In contrast, judicial comments in more recent years appear to support the sentencing principle of denunciation as the primary goal, emphasizing the need to express moral outrage at the way in which the IPH violated the expectation of trust, protection, and safety in an intimate relationship. The following excerpts illustrate this context further:

The aggravating circumstances here arise out of the domestic relationship between [the female offender and the male victim] as common law spouses, the singularly disproportionate acceleration of the level of violence toward her spouse, the abuse of her position of trust toward her partner.

(Female offender; *R. v. Fisher* [2004])

This relationship was meant to foster a mutual dependence and trust between the parties. [The offender] breached that trust. . . . I cannot say it any better than a judge did in another case. In that case the judge said this: "An intimate spousal relationship is based upon trust, mutual respect and love. These are the pillars upon which a nurturing relationship is built and maintained. These are the values that define who we are and what we want to be as a people, as society and as a nation." Violence damages the core values that are the underpinnings of any domestic union. Violence destroys the trust that is integral to a nurturing relationship. Violence demonstrates profound disrespect for the other partner's physical and emotional integrity. It is a denial of everything that a relationship is intended to provide. It is a betrayal of love itself. The emotional harm caused by such a breach of trust runs deep. The consequences to all its victims are as serious as they are longstanding. The intimate relationship is intended to provide comfort and security to those within it. It is intended to be a safe haven, a refuge from the storms of life. If the deliberate infliction of harm upon a spouse is a breach of trust, then the taking of life becomes particularly egregious in circumstances where there is an expectation of both protection and safety. There is a moral and legal duty to protect one's spouse from harm. This is a feature common to any spousal relationship in every civilized society. It is a social value that the law seeks to protect. It is a social value that is worth protecting. To cause harm, to take life where there is a duty to protect can only be described as a profound breach of this duty and of a trust that the law regards as sacred. . . . Spousal violence is all too prevalent in our society. Studies have shown that spousal violence deeply affect[s] the institution of a strong family fabric which is and must remain the core of a Canadian Just Society. There is need to denounce family violence and to deter it wherever it occurs.

(Female offender; *R. v. Jeffries* [2010])

It is an aggravating factor that this offence arose out of spousal violence. Perpetrators of spousal violence are consistently condemned by the courts for having violated one of the core principles of our society. Denunciation and deterrence remain at the heart of sentencing for cases of domestic violence. . . . Domestic violence will not be tolerated by our society. The courts are expected to deal severely with offenders who repeatedly breach court orders and those who persist in perpetrating domestic violence. Mr. Jamieson falls squarely into both categories. The unlawful taking of another life, as Mr. Jamieson did, is the most serious of crimes. Spousal and family relationships are intended to be a safe place because implicit in the spousal relationship is an obligation for each to protect the other from harm. That is why spousal violence is so abhorrent. Violence is the antithesis of the duty of the parties to each other. It represents a breach of this most sacred trust. That is why the courts treat spousal violence differently. Additionally, there is an implicit duty on each party that in the event either one suffers harm, there is a duty to protect the other against further harm, and an affirmative duty to ameliorate whatever harm has been caused. Those are the characteristics of a family which we as a society hold dear and why the courts treat violence in a family so seriously.

(Male offender; *R. v. Jamieson* [2012])

The killing is yet another instance of domestic violence in our community perpetrated by a male against a female partner. It was a clear breach of trust.

As [named removed] observed in her Victim Impact Statement, [the victim] was killed by a man she had known intimately for 28 years. Domestic violence is of sufficient concern to Parliament, that its presence is expressly identified as an aggravating factor in s. 718.2(a)(ii) of the Criminal Code. [The victim] was killed in her home, indeed in her own bedroom, a location that should have been a place of safety and security. Domestic assault is a blight on our society. I am hardly the first judge to recognize this.

(Male offender; *R. v. Klimovich* [2013])

Regardless of the sentencing principle emphasized, the emphasis on IPV as a serious social issue should be encouraging on the surface; however, the fact that this theme is present in a greater proportion of cases involving female offenders post-1996 compared with male offenders is a pattern that should be explored in future research. It is well documented that females are more likely to kill family members, including spouses, compared with other victims, but males continue to far outnumber females in perpetration of IPH. Are women being treated as 'doubly deviant', as argued decades ago, because their violence not only contradicts their perceived and valued feminine gender role, but also because they have perpetrated the violence against their male partner, the patriarchal head of the household?

Furthermore, discussing IPV as a serious social issue remains rhetoric unless followed by punishments that reflect the severity portrayed. In the total sample, a comparison of cases in which this theme was present showed an average sentence of 9 years compared with 7.5 years in cases where this theme was not present, suggesting that punishments are somewhat higher. Looking at female offenders only, cases in which this theme was present had an average sentence length of 8 years ($N = 7$) compared with 2.5 years ($N = 10$) in cases in which it was not present. For male offenders, cases with this theme had an average sentence length of 12 years compared to 9.5 years for cases in which this theme was not noted. Again, while the sample is small and not representative, at first glance, it appears that when judges do discuss IPV as a serious social issue, the incremental increase in punishment severity is greater for female (an increase of 5.5 years) than male offenders (an increase of 2.5 years). As such, future research needs to examine the way in which intimacy is used to justify more lenient or more serious sentences for female and male offenders and whether the subsequent actions in the form of actual sentences match judicial commentary.

Discussion and conclusion

This chapter has argued that the role of intimacy in law when responding to violence may be based on stereotypes that have become entrenched in conventional and sociological wisdom but have yet to be empirically validated. Some initial support was provided for this argument by examining the presence of premeditation/intent in cases of IPH and non-IPH. It was further argued that despite the dominance of these stereotypes, and regardless of their validity, little is actually known about the role they may (or may not) play in determining punishments for violent crime. An exploratory analysis demonstrated that some stereotypes are present in the legal portrayals of these cases, and their presence varies by gender of the offender. Variations in the presence of stereotypes overall and by gender require further research before anything but speculation can be offered, and the goal of this chapter is to serve as the impetus for such examinations. Our lack of knowledge about the validity of stereotypes related to intimacy and violence as well as their subsequent role in criminal justice decision making arguably stem from the same source – a lack of systematic, detailed information about the characteristics of these crimes and how courts respond to them. In this last section, then, some challenges in moving forward with such research and some future priorities are identified by identifying some limitations of the research findings presented above.

Identifying indicators for stereotypes about intimacy and violence

One of the obstacles when examining the role of criminal stereotypes is identifying reliable and valid indicators recognized in the social sciences and in law. For example, provocation is a recognized legal concept, but what social science indicators capture provocation that would also be recognized in law or by court actors? What measures can capture other forms of victim precipitation or, more broadly, victim participation (as conceptualized in this chapter) that might lead court actors to perceive reduced offender culpability? For example, in the above analysis, results showed that victim participation was more often portrayed for male victims; that is, they were constructed by the courts as having some responsibility for the events leading to their deaths, more often than female victims (53 percent compared with 26 percent, respectively). But what types of actions by victims were coded as being perceived by judges as representing some form of victim participation? How much can be inferred? What are the challenges posed by the data sources available?

In addressing these questions, looking at cases involving male offenders and female victims, judges noted the following:

> [The offender] threatened to take the knife to his pregnant daughter.
>
> (R v. Jamieson)

> The attack occurred in the course of a heated argument between [the couple] during which she made provocative utterances.
>   (*R v. Klimovich*; although what those utterances were was not discussed)

> I am satisfied beyond a reasonable doubt that the accused intended to kill his wife, but that he did so in the heat of passion under legal provocation.
>   (*R v. Li*; the type of provocation is not described)

> [The victim's] lifestyle may not have been particularly exemplary, but she had a right to live it as she saw fit.
>
> (R. v. Pepin)

[The victim] struck him forcibly on the back of the head from behind with a bottle of beer.

(R. v. Strong)

In cases involving male victims, judges noted that:

[The victim] struck the boy [the offender's child], the boy cried and [the offender] struck [the victim] with the knife.

(R. v. Brohart)

He had been imploring her to do something but in the course of the conversation he told her that he would just like to go to sleep and not wake up again.

(R. v. Brush)

The accused [was] a victim of serious domestic abuse.

(R v. Cabrera)

[The accused] was exposed to a longstanding history of emotional and physical abuse at the hands of [the victim]. . . . she was in fact protecting herself from having another beating inflicted upon her.

(R. v. Cowley)

[They] had been involved in a relationship that was described as volatile and on-again off-again. . . . I find that the relationship was volatile and that both had angry and occasionally abusive outburst[s].

(R v. Dupuis)

You were continually harassed – if one might use that term – bothered by the fact that money was always in short supply and that you were being put down by your husband. There is some evidence that on occasions he was violent with you and struck you, resulting in bruises. These injuries were witnessed by your children and it is claimed that in the last two years he would slap you about once a month. You were not in a position to fight back and it was plain to those who knew you that your health was deteriorating in proportion to the duration of your marriage.

(R. v. Fors)

But most of all, they fought together, and used drugs together. . . . [The victim's] convictions arose out of his conduct towards [the accused], threatening death, assault with a weapon, assault. . . . [T]hat is not to say that she was only a recipient of violence, she too had made threats and used weapons, but [the accused] either recanted his allegations or didn't show up to give evidence about them.

(R. v. Foy)

As can be seen from the above, there is much variation in the amount of time that passes between what might be perceived as the victim's contributory actions and the ultimate killing, particularly for male victims whose responsibility often was found in their long-term abuse of their female killer. However, the theme is 'victim participation' more broadly and not provocation, which would require some more immediacy. In particular, one might also argue that the victim's actions are somewhat more contributory in cases involving female offenders, again prior and long-term abuse in some cases, compared with cases involving male offenders. However, as noted, in some cases, judges only acknowledged the role of provocation, failing to indicate what constituted the provocation (e.g. provocative utterances). However, if we are to understand how judges discuss these cases, barring sit-down interviews with those involved in each case (which is unlikely), sentencing transcripts are the most appropriate data source, even with their limitations, not the least of which is that not all cases get reported and not all facts are covered when they are reported.

A second short example pertains to the stereotypic theme of 'mitigating emotions'. What threshold must be reached in judges' comments to conclude that strong emotion or loss of control was perceived to be a mitigating factor, particularly if it was not directly stated that it rarely occurred? For example, is it enough that the couple were arguing, as in the cases below?

> At some point during the argument, [the offender], enraged and provoked by things said by [the victim], obtained two knives from the kitchen and attacked his wife in a frenzied way, killing her.

> I am satisfied beyond a reasonable doubt that Ms. Dupuis stabbed Mr. Paglia in the course of an angry argument.

> The night of the incident, the failure of yet another relationship on a background of such failures, the insecurity engendered by that failure, the apparent callousness of the victim in rejecting gifts from her daughters when she was trying to effect a reconciliation, her physical and mental exhaustion, all these caused her to snap and to do that which she immediately regretted doing, and which she had not intended to do.

The first and third quotes seem more straightforward – 'enraged and provoked', 'in a frenzied way' and 'all these caused her to snap', but the second quote is less clear ('in the course of an angry argument'), so ambiguity prevents a straightforward decision as to its relevance for this theme. When themes overlap with each other, the complexities are increased, as discussed next.

Untangling overlapping stereotypes to isolate their roles in determining punishment

When discussing the dominant stereotypes described at the beginning of the chapter, it was noted that they are not mutually exclusive, although each was tied to particular explanations or concerns for criminal justice decision makers. They can overlap with each other, or with newly emerging themes in judicial commentary, making it difficult to determine whether the judge was discussing a particular thematic stereotype or some other theme or situational characteristic. Nowhere was this more evident than when examining cases that involved the theme of 'presence/role of alcohol' and 'mitigating emotions', as shown in the following example:

> In my view, the proximate cause of attack on [the female victim] was that he was blind drunk at the time. No more and no less. He says he does not remember anything that happened and I believe him. He had been drinking all day. When he came home he did not like something that she said. Then, as he said, something clicked in his head. In a drunken stupor he foolishly grabbed a knife and stabbed her. It was alcohol, not her words, that fuelled his actions. . . . [I]t is also . . . very clear that he acted suddenly. His actions were not thought out. They were quick, and impulsive, and fuelled by alcohol.
>
> [R. v. Boutilier]

In the above quote, it is clear that the judge sees alcohol as playing a key role in the offender's actions, but the judge also acknowledges that 'something clicked in his head' and he 'acted suddenly . . . actions were not thought out. They were quick and impulsive.' But would they have been such if not for the alcohol? It is not clear.

To date, there has also been little systematic research examining the role of intimacy in law. Therefore, we lack consistent empirical evidence about whether and how intimacy affects criminal justice decision making in cases of violent crime. Moreover, few studies have focused exclusively on the victim–defendant relationship as the key variable of interest (see exceptions in Dawson, 2004, 2006, 2012; Miethe, 1987; Simon, 1996a, 1996b) or examined the way in which the gender of the offender might condition the effect of intimacy on criminal justice decision making. These are glaring gaps in research given that, as documented above, there are long-recognized and powerful stereotypes about intimacy and violence and those involved. Further, while various commonsense assumptions – conventional wisdom, so to speak – exist about intimacy and violence, little theoretical and empirical work has examined whether and how these assumptions may be associated with disparate treatment of these cases within the criminal justice system (for an exception, see Miethe, 1987). Until such time as that occurs, the role of intimacy and its impact on punishment (including its close relation to gender-based violence and society's response to it) will remain unknown, particularly in cases that involve the same set of basic facts – a man, a woman, a struggle, a shooting and a death – but vary in the relationship that existed between the victim and the offender.

References

Albonetti, C. A. (1991) An integration of theories to explain judicial discretion. *Social Problems*, 38(2): 247–266.

Auerhahn, K. (2007) Just another crime? Examining disparity in homicide sentencing. *The Sociological Quarterly*, 48: 277–313.

Black, D. (1976) *The Behavior of Law*. New York: Academic Press.

Black, D. (1993) *The Social Structure of Right and Wrong*. San Diego: Academic Press.

Block, R. (1981) Victim-offender dynamics in violent crime. *Journal of Criminal Law and Criminology*, 72(2): 743–761.

Block, C. R. and Christakos, A. (1995) Intimate partner homicide in Chicago over 29 years. *Crime and Delinquency*, 41(4): 496–526.

Bonds, C.E.W. and Jeffries, S. (2014) Similar punishment? Comparing sentencing outcomes in domestic and non-domestic violence cases. *British Journal of Criminology*, 54(5): 849–872.

Chambliss, W. (1984) Types of deviance and the effectiveness of legal sanctions. *Crime and Delinquency*, 41(4): 425–526.

Conklin, J. E. (1972) *Robbery and the Criminal Justice System*. Philadelphia: J.B. Lippincott.

Cotter, A. (2014) *Homicide in Canada, 2013. Juristat* (Catalogue no. 85–002-X). Ottawa: Statistics Canada.

Cretney, A. and Davis, G. (1997) Prosecuting domestic assault: Victims failing courts or courts failing victims. *The Howard Journal of Criminal Justice*, 36: 146–157.

Daly, K. (1987) Structure and practice of familial-based justice in a criminal court. *Law and Society Review*, 21(2): 267–290.

Daly, K. (1994) *Gender, Crime and Punishment*. London: Yale University Press.

Daly, K. and Tonry, M. (1997) Gender, race, and sentencing. In Tonry, M. (ed.) *Crime and Justice: A Review of Research*, Vol. 22. Chicago, IL: University of Chicago Press, pp. 201–252.

Davis, R. C. and Smith, B. E. (1981) Crimes between acquaintances: The response of criminal courts. *Victimology: An International Journal*, 6(1–4): 175–187.

Dawson, M. (2003) The cost of "lost" intimacy: The effect of relationship state on criminal justice decision-making. *British Journal of Criminology*, 43(4): 689–709.

Dawson, M. (2004) Rethinking the boundaries of intimacy at the end of the century: The role of victim-defendant relationship in criminal justice decision-making over time. *Law and Society Review*, 38(1): 105–138.

Dawson, M. (2006) Intimacy, violence and the law: Exploring stereotypes about victim-defendant relationship and violent crime. *Journal of Criminal Law and Criminology*, 96(4): 1417–1450.

Dawson, M. (2012) Intimacy, homicide, and punishment: Examining court outcomes over three decades. *Australian and New Zealand Journal of Criminology*, 45(3): 400–422.

Dixon, J. (1995) The organizational context of criminal sentencing. *American Journal of Sociology*, 100(5): 1157–1198.

Emerson, R. M. (1983) Holistic effects in social control decision-making. *Law and Society Review*, 17(3): 425–455.

Farrell, R. and Holmes, M. (1991) The social and cognitive structure of legal decision-making. S*ociological Quarterly*, 32: 529–542.

Farrell, R. A. and Swigert, V. (1986) Adjudication in homicide: An interpretive analysis of the effects of defendant and victim social characteristics. *Journal of Research in Crime and Delinquency*, 23(4): 349–369.

Felson, R. B. (1978) Aggression as impression management. *Social Psychology*, 41: 357–376.

Felson, R. B. and Messner, S. F. (1996) To kill or not to kill? Lethal outcomes in injurious attacks. *Criminology*, 34(4): 519–545.

Ferraro, K. J. and Boychuk, T. (1992) The court's response to interpersonal violence: A comparison of intimate and nonintimate assault. In Buzawa, E. S. and Buzawa, C. G.

(eds.) *Domestic Violence: The Changing Criminal Justice Response*. Westport, CT: Auburn House, pp. 209–225.

Fineman, M. A. (1994) *Preface in the Public Nature of Private Violence*. New York: Routledge.

Fitz-Gibbon, K. and Pickering, S. (2012) Homicide law reform in Victoria, Australia: From provocation to defensive homicide and beyond. *British Journal of Criminology*, 52: 159–180.

Fitz-Gibbon, K. and Stubbs, J. (2012) Editorial in special issue: Legal responses to lethal violence. *Australian and New Zealand Journal of Criminology*, 45(3): 316–317.

Flemming, R., Nardulli, P. and Eisenstein, J. (1992) *The Craft of Justice: Work and Politics in Criminal Court Communities*. Philadelphia: University of Pennsylvania Press.

Friedson, E. (1970) *Profession of Medicine: A Study of the Sociology of Applied Knowledge*. New York: Harper and Row.

Gillespie, L. K., Loughran, T. A., Smith, M. D., Fogel, S. J. and Bjerregaard, B. (2013) Exploring the role of victim sex, victim conduct, and victim-defendant relationship in capital punishment sentencing. *Homicide Studies*, 18(2): 175–195.

Gottfredson, M. R. and Gottfredson, D. M. (1988) *Decision Making in Criminal Justice: Towards a Rational Exercise of Discretion* (2nd ed.). New York: Plenum.

Grant, I. (2010) Intimate femicide: A study of sentencing trends for men who kill their intimate partners. *Alberta Law Review*, 47: 779–822.

Grant, I., Chunn, D. and Boyle, C. (1998) *The Law of Homicide*. Scarborough, ON: Carswell.

Hagan, J. and O'Donnel, N. (1978) Sexual stereotyping and judicial sentencing. A legal test of the sociological wisdom. *Canadian Journal of Sociology*, 3(3): 309–319.

Hartman, J. L. and Belknap, J. (2003) Beyond the gatekeepers: Court professionals' self-reported attitudes about and experiences with misdemeanor domestic violence cases. *Criminal Justice and Behavior*, 30: 349–373.

Hessick, C. B. (2007) Violence between lovers, strangers and friends. *Washington Law Review*, 85: 344–402.

Hogarth, J. (1971) *Sentencing as a Human Process*. Toronto: University of Toronto Press.

Horwitz, A. (1990) *The Logic of Social Control*. New York: Plenum Press.

Huang, W.S.W., Finn, M. A., Ruback, R. B. and Friedman, R. R. (1996) Individual and contextual influences on sentence lengths: Examining political conservatism. *Prison Journal*, 76(4): 398–419.

Johnson, B. D. (2003) Racial and ethnic disparities in sentencing departures across modes of conviction. *Criminology*, 41(2): 449–489.

Johnson, H. and Dawson, M. (2011) *Violence Against Women in Canada: Research and Policy Perspectives*. Toronto: Oxford University Press.

Kalven, H. J. and Zeisel, H. (1971) *The American Jury*. Boston: Little, Brown.

Katz, J. (1988) *Seductions of Crime*. New York: Basic Books.

Kern, R., Libkuman, T. M. and Temple, S. L. (2007) Perceptions of domestic violence and mock jurors' sentencing decisions. *Journal of Interpersonal Violence*, 22: 1515–1535.

Loftin, C. (1986) Assaultive violence as a contagious social process. *Bulletin of the New York Academy of Medicine*, 62: 550–555.

Luckenbill, D. (1977) Criminal homicide as situated transaction. *Social Problems*, 25: 176–186.

Lundsgaarde, H. P. (1977) *Murder in Space City: A Cultural Analysis of Houston Homicide Patterns*. New York: Oxford University Press.

Marcus, I. (1994) Reframing domestic violence: Terrorism in the home. In Fineman, M. A. and Mykituik, R. (eds.) *The Public Nature of Private Violence*. New York: Routledge, pp. 11–35.

Maxfield, M. (1989) Circumstances in supplementary homicide reports: Variety and validity. *Criminology,* 27: 671–695.

McCormick, J. S., Maric, A., Seto, M. C. and Barbaree, H. E. (1998) Relationship to victim predicts sentence length in sexual assault cases. *Journal of Interpersonal Violence,* 13: 413–420.

McIntyre, J. (1967) Public attitudes toward crime and law enforcement. *Annals of the American Academy of Political and Social Science,* 374(November): 34–46.

Messner, S. F. and Tardiff, K. (1985) The social ecology of urban homicide: An application of the routine activities approach. *Criminology,* 23: 241–267.

Miethe, T. D. (1985) Socioeconomic disparities under determinate sentencing systems: A comparison of pre-guideline and post-guideline practices in Minnesota. *Criminology,* 23: 337–363.

Miethe, T. D. (1987) Stereotypical conceptions and criminal processing: The case of the victim-offender relationship. *Justice Quarterly,* 4(4): 571–593.

Miethe, T. D. and Drass, K. A. (1998) Exploring the social context of instrumental and expressive homicides: An application of qualitative comparative analysis. *Journal of Quantitative Criminology,* 15(1): 1–21.

Miethe, T. D. and Regoeczi, W. C. (2004) *Rethinking Homicide: Exploring the Structure and Process Underlying Deadly Situations.* New York: Cambridge University Press.

Miller, J. L., Rossi, P. H. and Simpson, J. E. (1991) Felony punishments: A factorial survey of perceived justice in criminal sentencing. *Journal of Criminal Law and Criminology,* 82(2): 396–420.

Mills, L. G. (1998) Mandatory arrest and prosecution policies for domestic violence: A critical review and case for more research to test victim empowerment approaches. *Criminal Justice and Behavior,* 25: 306–318.

Moyer, S. (1992) Race, gender and homicide: Comparisons between aboriginals and other Canadians. *Canadian Journal of Criminology,* July–October, 387–391.

Ouimet, M. and Coyle, E. J. (1991) Fear of crime and sentencing punitiveness: Comparing the general public and court practitioners. *Canadian Journal of Criminology,* 33: 149–162.

Parker, R. N. and Smith, D. W. (1979) Deterrence, poverty and type of homicide. *American Journal of Sociology,* 85(3): 614–624.

Pleck, E. (1989) *Domestic Tyranny: The Making of American Social Policy Against Family Violence from Colonial Times to the Present.* New York: Oxford University Press.

Polk, K. and Ranson, D. (1991) Patterns of homicide in Victoria. In Chappell, D. and Strang, H. (eds.) *Australian Violence: Contemporary Perspectives.* Canberra: Australian Institute of Criminology, pp. 53–119.

Rapaport, E. (1991) The death penalty and gender discrimination. *Law and Society Review,* 25(2): 367–383.

Rapaport, E. (1994) The death penalty and the domestic discount. In Fineman, M. A. and Mykitiuk, R. (eds.) *The Public Nature of Private Violence.* New York: Routledge, pp. 224–251.Riedel, M. (1987) Stranger violence: Perspectives, issues and problems. *Journal of Criminal Law and Criminology,* 78(2): 223–258.

Riedel, M. (1993) *Stranger Violence: A Theoretical Inquiry.* New York: Garland.

Rojek, D. and Williams, J. (1993) Interracial vs. intraracial offences in terms of the victim/offender relationship. In Wilson, A. V. (ed.) *Homicide: The Victim/Offender Connection.* Cincinnati, OH: Anderson, pp. 249–266.

Sampson, R. J. (1987) Personal violence by strangers: An extension and test of the opportunity model of predatory victimization. *Journal of Criminal Law and Criminology,* 78(2): 327–356.

Sheehy, E. A. (2014) *Defending Battered Women on Trial: Lessons from Transcripts*. Vancouver, BC: UBC Press.

Simon, L. M. (1996a) Legal treatment of the victim-offender relationship in crimes of violence. *Journal of Interpersonal Violence*, 11: 94–106.

Simon, L. M. (1996b) The effect of the victim-offender relationship on the sentence length of violent offenders. *Journal of Crime and Justice*, XIX(1): 129–148.

Smith, M. D. and Parker, R. N. (1980) Type of homicide and variation in regional rates. *Social Forces*, 59(1): 136–147.

Steen, S., Engen, R. L. and Gainey, R. R. (2005) Images of danger and culpability: Racial stereotyping, case processing, and criminal sentencing. *Criminology*, 43(2): 435–468.

Steffensmeier, D. (1980) Assessing the impact of the women's movement on sex-based differences in the handling of adult criminal defendants. *Crime and Delinquency*, 23: 344–356.

Steffensmeier, D., Kramer, J. H. and Streifel, C. (1993) Gender and imprisonment decisions. *Criminology*, 31: 411–446.

Steffensmeier, D., Kramer, J. H. and Ulmer, J. (1995) Age differences in sentencing. *Justice Quarterly*, 12(3): 701–719.

Steffensmeier, D., Ulmer, J. and Kramer, J. (1998) The interaction of race, gender, and age in criminal sentencing: The punishment cost of being young, black, and male. *Criminology*, 36(4): 763–798.

Sudnow, D. (1965) Normal crimes: Sociological features of the penal code in a public defender office. *Social Problems*, 12: 255–279.

Swigert, V. L. and Farrell, R. A. (1977) Normal homicides and the law. *American Sociological Review*, 42(1): 16–32.

Thomas, C. W. and Williams, J. S. (1977) Actors, actions, and deterrence: A reformulation of Chambliss's typology of deterrence. In Riedel, M. and Vales, P. A. (eds.) *Treating the Offender: Problems and Issues*. New York: Praeger.

Turk, A. T. (1969) *Criminality and Legal Order*. Chicago: Rand McNally.

Ulmer, J. (1995) The organization and consequences of social pasts in criminal courts. *Sociological Quarterly*, 35(3): 14–33.

Ulmer, J. and Kramer, J. (1996) Court communities under sentencing guidelines: Dilemmas of formal rationality and sentencing disparity. *Criminology*, 34(3): 383–408.

Vera Institute of Justice. (1977) *Felony Arrests. Their Prosecution and Disposition in New York City's Courts*. New York: Vera Institute of Justice.

Waegel, W. B. (1981) Case routinization in investigative police work. *Social Problems*, 28(3): 263–275.

Wallace, A. (1986) *Homicide: The Social Reality*. New South Wales: New South Wales Bureau of Crime Statistics and Research.

Williams, K. M. (1976) The effects of victim characteristics on judicial decision-making. In McDonald, W. F. (ed.) *Criminal Justice and the Victim*. Beverly Hills: Sage, pp. 177–214.

Wolfgang, M. (1957) Victim-precipitated criminal homicide. *Journal of Criminal Law, Criminology and Police Science*, 48: 1–11.

Wolfgang, M. (1958) *Patterns in Criminal Homicide*. Philadelphia: University of Pennsylvania Press.

World Health Organization. (2002) *World Report on Violence and Health*. Geneva: WHO.

4 Constructions of masculinity and responsibility in the sentencing of children who commit lethal violence

Kate Fitz-Gibbon

In 1993 the killing of two-year-old James Bulger by two ten-year-old boys in Liverpool (UK) and the subsequent trials of John Venables and Robert Thompson captured worldwide attention and animated debate surrounding the perpetration of violence by children (Franklin and Petley, 2006; James and Jenks, 1996). Despite their youth, both boys were charged with murder, tried as adults, convicted by jury and sentenced to a minimum of eight years detention for their role in a crime that was described by the judge as 'an act of unparalleled evil and barbarity' (cited in *R v Home Secretary, ex p Venables and Thompson* [1998] AC 407, per Morland J). In attempting to understand what drove the actions of the two boys involved, the case prompted debate surrounding the loss of childhood innocence, the 'born' evil of children who commit crime and the role of environmental factors in moral development (James and Jenks, 1996).

The case also revealed shortcomings in the way that traditional frameworks of the criminal law are used to respond to children who commit lethal violence and the limits of the adult criminal court system to adequately accommodate the needs of young offenders. Despite this, in over twenty years since *Bulger* the English courts have continued to adopt an inherently punitive response to children in trouble with the law. In contrast, Scandinavian jurisdictions, such as Norway, have been noted for their youth welfare approach to child homicide perpetrators (Asquith, 1996; Green, 2007, 2012), and other UK jurisdictions, such as Scotland, have increased the age of criminal prosecution to better align with the UN recommended standard of twelve years old (McCallum, 2011). The punitive nature of the English response is, however, mirrored by the approach adopted across Australian jurisdictions, where the age of criminal responsibility remains at ten years old and recent legislation introduced at the state level has adopted an increasingly punishment-focused stance towards young offenders. However, unlike England and Wales, where the law's response to child homicide offenders has been the focus of numerous scholarly reviews, there is a relative paucity of research from Australia on the contexts within which children commit lethal violence and the ways in which such violence is understood and responded to by the Australian criminal justice system. This gap in scholarship is concerning due to the significant political and media attention that has been given to the notion of 'youth out of control' in recent years, including through policy and media campaigns targeting alcohol-fuelled violence and the carrying of knives by young persons in the community.[1] In casting an insight into the contexts within which young people perpetrate homicide and the discourses mobilised at sentencing, this chapter seeks to partially address this gap in current Australian criminological scholarship.

Nationally in Australia between July 2007 and June 2012 there were 84 homicides committed by an offender under the age of seventeen years (Bryant and Cussen, 2015; Chan and Payne, 2013; Virueda and Payne, 2010). This accounts for 6.7 per cent of the 1,249 homicides that occurred in Australia over this five-year period. Such cases overwhelmingly involve male perpetrators and male victims. Reflecting this gendered profile, in examining the sentencing of child homicide offenders in Australia this chapter draws from research examining the perpetration of non-lethal violence by young males (Cunneen and White, 2007; Richards, 2011; White and Mason, 2006), as well as the significant body of research that has examined cultures of masculinity and the propensity for violence among young men.

Heavily influenced by the work of feminist scholars and in particular the conceptualisation by sociologist Raewyn Connell (1987, 2000, 2005) of hegemonic and subordinate masculinities, as well as Messerschmidt's (1993, 1994) exploration of men and crime, this body of research has considered how masculinity intersects with race, social class, employment, contexts of power and the subordination of women to explain the construction of the male identity as well as men's engagement in anti-social and criminal behaviour.[2] While Connell's hegemonic masculinity was conceptualised as the 'most honoured way of being a man' (Connell and Messerschmidt, 2005: 832), to which all other forms of masculinity were subordinate, over the last three decades there has been an increasing recognition among scholars of multiple constructions of masculinity (Connell and Messerschmidt, 2005; Messerschmidt, 1993; Morgan, 1987; Walker, 1998). Specific to young persons, this has given rise to a body of research that examines the ways in which young persons construct, perform and protest their masculinity, and how this may come to be exhibited through the perpetration of violence (Harland and McCready, 2014; Messerschmidt, 1993; Tomsen, 1997; Treadwell and Garland, 2011; Walker, 1998).

In the introduction to the second edition of *Masculinities*, Connell (2005: xv–xvi) argues that greater knowledge of constructions of masculinity can be beneficial in gaining a better understanding of, among other things, the identity formation of youths, health and safety of men, men's relationship with children, and the prevention of male violence. This chapter builds on several of these focuses by examining the extent to which discourses of masculinity, and constructions of what it means to be a young man in contemporary Australia, are influential in the sentencing of children convicted of a homicide offence in Victoria (Australia). To do so, this chapter is structured in three parts. Part one provides an overview of the qualitative case analysis completed as part of this research. Part two examines scenarios of child-perpetrated lethal violence as analysed as part of a ten-year analysis of sentencing judgments for cases finalised in the Victorian Supreme Court (VSC) between January 2003 and December 2012. This analysis is used to frame the second half of the chapter, which examines how judicial constructions of masculinity in cases of child-perpetrated homicide are used to frame our understandings of the responsibility of the child offender. In doing so, part three explores four key themes that emerged from the sentencing case analysis – the judicial construction of dangerous and irresponsible masculinity, judicial responses to collective violence, judicial discourses of understanding and the emergence of judicial discourses of redemption and rehabilitation.

Research design: a ten-year qualitative case analysis

In light of recent political and media attention on youth violence across Australia, this research seeks to provide a more detailed understanding of the contexts within which children commit lethal violence and the discourses that are mobilised at sentencing to construct responsibility and culpability. To do so, a qualitative thematic analysis was conducted of all cases of child-perpetrated homicide ($N = 23$) finalised in the VSC between 1 January 2003 and 31 December 2012. This was undertaken using publicly accessible sentencing judgments which provide an overview of the factors (aggravating and mitigating) considered by the judge to be relevant at sentencing, the judge's retelling of the event of homicide and a discussion of the background of the child offender. All relevant cases were identified using a systematic search of the Australasian Legal Information Institute (AustLII) database for the ten-year period under study.[3] For the purpose of this chapter's focus, the case analysis was confined to homicides finalised during the period studied which involved an offender aged between ten and seventeen years. This mirrors the definition of 'child' adopted in current Victorian legislation and captures all child offenders over the age of criminal responsibility, which is set at ten years old in Victoria (Children, Youth and Families Act 2005).

Case analysis has been used within criminological and socio-legal research over the past three decades to provide insight into the contexts within which homicides occur and legal responses to lethal violence (see, e.g., Alder and Polk, 1996; Burman, 2010; Fitz-Gibbon, 2012, 2014; Polk, 1994; Sheehy, 2014). For this study, the case analysis was specifically concerned with identifying the context within which the lethal violence occurred, including an analysis of any precipitating factors, the role of persons beyond the child offender and the backgrounds of the perpetrators involved as well as an analysis of the discourses employed to construct culpability and responsibility by members of the judiciary during the sentencing process. This analysis was informed by an examination of the judicial retelling of the homicide event, the extent to which the event was framed in the context of the child's background and/or the role of any third parties, as well as consideration of the role of broader statements made in relation to community sentiment surrounding youth crime.

As presented in Table 4.1, between January 2003 and December 2012 there were twenty-three reported cases of child-perpetrated homicide finalised in Victoria, involving twenty-six child offenders. Several of the cases identified within this period involved multiple offenders with variable ages; however, due to the focus of this research, this chapter is concerned with only the child homicide offender(s). With this in mind, the age range of child offenders convicted of a homicide offence ranged between fourteen and seventeen years, while the age range of victims involved in these cases was significantly wider, ranging from seventeen to sixty-six years.

The offender(s) in all cases identified were male, and with one exception (see *R v SV* [2012] VSC 478), all cases involved a male victim. This is to be expected, given that males commit the vast majority of homicides in Australia (Bryant and Cussen, 2015; Chan and Payne, 2013); however, it does confirm the dominant focus on male offenders in scholarly, political and medial discourses of youth violence. The majority of cases also involved the perpetration of lethal violence on a stranger, with only six of the twenty-three cases involving a victim that was to some degree known to the offender(s) prior to the offence. There were no cases during this ten-year period where a child killed a family member or related person.

As shown in Table 4.1, in terms of culpability as legally defined by the courts, of the twenty-three cases analysed, six resulted in a conviction for murder and seventeen resulted in a conviction for manslaughter by unlawful and dangerous act.[4] In nine cases, secondary convictions were also recorded against the offender – these included convictions for armed robbery, affray, intentionally causing serious injury and recklessly causing injury. In a further twelve cases, the child offender had had some degree of prior interaction with the criminal justice system – in some cases this was relatively minor, such as a police warning or a fine. In other cases, it was relatively common for the young person to have previously been charged with offences in the Children's Court but, because of their young age at the time, not to have had a conviction recorded against them. In two of the more extreme examples of child offenders with prior criminal activity, a sixteen year old convicted of manslaughter already had twenty-three prior convictions, sustained on four different occasions (*DPP v Reynolds & Others* [2004] VSC 533), while there was also another case of a seventeen year old convicted of manslaughter who at the time of committing that offence had forty-three prior convictions for a range of offences, including for serious assault, threats to kill and robbery (*R v G.M.* [2006] VSC 473). The extent to which those secondary convictions were viewed as symbolic of a demonstrated propensity for violence is examined in the following section on dangerous and irresponsible masculinity.

Constructions of masculinity in the sentencing of children who commit lethal violence

The following four sections provide a detailed analysis of these case data, and in doing so illuminate the extent to which the relationship between masculinity and violence is influential in judicial constructions of responsibility at the sentencing stage of the criminal justice system. This analysis builds on a significant bank of prior criminological research that has explored the relationship between men (often young), masculinity and violence (see, e.g., Alder and Polk, 1996; Goodey, 1997; Harland and McCready, 2014; Polk, 1994; Tomsen, 1997, 2001; Treadwell

Table 4.1 Child-perpetrated homicide in Victoria: 1 January 2003 to 31 December 2012

Defendant Name (Year)	Homicide Conviction	Defendant Age/ Victim Age	Method	Relationship between Victim and Defendant
Nguyen (2003)	Manslaughter	17/19	Stabbed	Acquaintances
Perera (2003)	Manslaughter	17/17	Stabbed	Strangers
Tipas (2004)	Manslaughter	17/19	Stabbed	Acquaintances
WJR andGSJ[i] (2004)	Manslaughter	16 and 16/66	Arson causing death	Strangers
TY (2005/2007)	Murder	14/18	Struck in head with umbrella	Strangers
LMA (2005)	Manslaughter	16/20	Stabbed	Friends
Athuai (2005)	Murder	17/17	Stabbed	Strangers
DJE (2006)	Murder	17/18	Assaulted with axe	Friends (housemates)
BTP (2006)	Manslaughter	15/59	Stabbed	Family friends
GM (2006)	Manslaughter	17/ unknown	Stabbed	Strangers
HR[ii] (2008)	Manslaughter	17/20	Bashed	Strangers
MA[iii] (2008)	Manslaughter	17/42	Hit by car	Strangers
EJC (2008)	Manslaughter	17/17	Bashed	Acquaintances
MBA andWH(2008)	Manslaughter	17 and 17/41	Bashed	Strangers
AO (2009)	Manslaughter	16/45	Assaulted with glass bottle	Strangers
OJS (2009)	Manslaughter	15/21	Hit by car	Strangers
LK[iv] (2009)	Manslaughter	16/17	Assaulted with axe	Strangers
MM (2009)	Murder	16/41	Assault w/o weapon	Stranger
Smith (2010)	Murder	17/20	Stabbed	Strangers
JC[v] (2010)	Manslaughter	15/20	Stabbed	Strangers
RPJ (2011)	Manslaughter	17/17	Single punch	Strangers
SV (2012)	Manslaughter	14/40	Stabbed	Strangers
ZN (2012)	Murder	17/20	Assaulted with glass bottle	Acquaintances

Source: Developed by authors

[i] In this case there was a third offender, Reynolds, who was over eighteen years old at time of the offence (see *DPP v Reynolds & Ors* [2004] VSC 533).

[ii] In this case there was a second offender, Simpas, who was over eighteen years old at time of the offence (see *R v Simpas and HR* [2008] VSC 222).

[iii] In this case there were additional offenders who were over eighteen years old at time of the offence (see *R v Mohamed & Ors* [2008] VSC 299).

[iv] In this case there were four offenders sentenced for manslaughter, three of whom were over eighteen years old at time of the offence (see *R v Huynh & Ors* [2009] VSC 291).

[v] In this case there were additional offenders who were over eighteen years old at time of the offence (see *R v Andreevski & Ors* [2010] VSC 618).

and Garland, 2011; Walker, 1998; Whitehead, 2005), as well as research that has examined the construction of masculinity within the realm of law and legal institutions (Collier, 2010; Howe, 2008; Naffine, 1990). In relation to the latter, scholars have examined how legal practitioners 'talk about men' and the extent to which this encourages a 'discourse of masculinity' to emerge in law institutions, such as the courtroom (Collier, 2010: 31). In analysing how judges 'talk about' children convicted of a homicide offence, this chapter considers the proliferation of the traditional discourse of dangerous, irresponsible and collective masculinity alongside less explored judicial discourses of understanding, redemption and rehabilitation.

Dangerous and irresponsible masculinity

Over the last five years the public image of youth as 'out of control' has proliferated in Australia and the UK, encouraging an international Western discourse of dangerous and irresponsible masculinity. Both characteristics – dangerousness and irresponsibility – have been central tenets in constructions of deviant masculinity throughout criminological, sociological and feminist research. In the context of this research, dangerousness and irresponsibility are considered in relation to allocations of responsibility in cases where the act of lethal violence is understood to be a spontaneous and unprovoked expression of one's masculinity. These cases were largely defined by the level of attention paid throughout the judgment to one of two features: the premeditated carrying of knives and/or the negative impact of alcohol-fuelled collective violence. This dominant context of 'random', 'stranger' and 'unprovoked' violence observed in the case analysis is mirrored in prior Australian research examining the differences between juvenile and adult non-lethal offending (Cunneen and White, 2007).

The problematic acceptance of a culture of violence among young males was evident in at least eight of the twenty-three cases under examination where the child offender had armed himself with a weapon, typically a knife, prior to the perpetration of the homicide. This prevalence of knife carrying across the cases mirrors earlier Victorian research, which found that young persons aged fourteen to fifteen years old, from low socioeconomic backgrounds, were most likely to carry a knife of all persons aged under twenty-five years in Victoria (Bondy et al., 2005). In some of the homicide cases the offender described this as having been done out of a misguided sense of personal protection, but in sentencing, judges expressly condemned this conduct. Indeed, regardless of whether the knife was used in the latter commission of the fatal act, the premeditated carrying of a knife enhanced the individual responsibility of the child and encouraged an emphasis on punishment and the dangerousness of the offender. This broad level of disapproval expressed by judges towards the carrying of knives by young persons in the community is captured in the remarks made by the Honourable Justice Kaye:

> The use, particularly by youths, of knives and similar weapons is all too prevalent in recent times. There is a need in a case such as this for the Court to impose a severe punishment to make it absolutely clear to the rest of the community that those who behave in the manner in which you did will properly forfeit their right to be part of our community for a substantial part of their own lives.
>
> (*R v Athuai* [2005] VSC 252, per Kaye J)

Even in cases where the offender had attempted to provide a reason for the carrying of the knife (e.g., personal protection following an earlier attack), it was still positioned as unacceptable, dangerous conduct by the judge in sentencing, as evident in *Perera*:

> I accept that you made the decision to take a knife in the context of having been the victim of an unprovoked assault some days earlier and your fear of meeting your attackers. However, your decision cannot in any way be regarded as justified in the circumstances. It is entirely unacceptable for any member of the community to carry a weapon as you did. . . . [T]he pivotal fact that led to the stabbing of Luke Collins [the victim] was your possession and use of a knife. Time and again the young men of our community arm themselves with knives allegedly for protection and repeatedly their action results in tragedy such as this.
>
> (*R v Perera* [2003] VSC 136, per Warren J)

The judicial remarks here place the responsibility for the consequential lethal violence firmly with the actions of the offender, despite his earlier allegations of victimisation and attempted justification for carrying the knife. This judicial approach is somewhat expected given that the carrying of knives amongst young persons has been a focal concern to governments in Australia and the UK in recent years and has motivated a range of punitive policing measures in both criminal justice systems – for example, the introduction of wide-ranging stop and search policies to 'deter' young persons from carrying knives (Carrell, 2014; Office of Police Integrity, 2012).

The construction of dangerous and irresponsible masculinity at sentencing was also inherently linked to the presence of alcohol in the lead up to, during and following the perpetration of lethal violence. In at least ten of the twenty-three cases, the offender was under the influence of drugs and/or alcohol at the time of the offence. In nearly all of these ten cases, the offender was in the company of other friends/acquaintances who were also under the influence of alcohol at the time of the offence. This association between collective drinking and male violence has been recognised by Tomsen (1997: 94), who, in his study of the culture of drinking violence in Western Sydney, argues:

> There is a complex but powerful link between many incidents of public violence and the social process of collective drinking. This link is built around cultural understandings of the connections between rowdy and violent group drinking, the construction and projection of an empowered masculine identity, and the symbolic rejection of respectable social values.

In this context, Tomsen (1997: 97) argues that any violence winds up as 'one more element of the night's entertainment' and is likely to be in the form of 'unprovoked and unjust assaults' (ibid.: 100). While none of the cases of lethal violence in the current study occurred within the confines of a licensed venue, most likely due to the fact that all perpetrators were under the legal drinking age at the time of the offence, this description of the precipitating incidents that incite violence in the context of collective drinking does resonate with cases in the current study (as explored in more detail in the following section).

Interestingly, in one case within the period studied, the responsibility for the public overconsumption of alcohol among young persons in and around Melbourne was directed at the parents of young persons generally, as opposed to the children themselves:

> It is a reflection on our society and not a positive reflection that so many young people can be out on the streets of Melbourne intoxicated, without their parents having any knowledge of their whereabouts. If there had been more knowledge and more supervision, perhaps these tragic events would not have occurred.
>
> (*R v Simpas and HR* [2008] VSC 222, per King J)

However, while this suggests some leniency among judges in how they assign individual responsibility and view guardians as bearers of secondary responsibility, this deflection of responsibility was not evident in other cases. By and large Victorian judges provided clear condemnations of alcohol-fuelled violence[5] and utilised the child's overconsumption of alcohol and/or drugs as confirmation of his alignment with a dangerous and irresponsible form of masculinity.

Collective male violence

Over the ten-year period, six of the twenty-three cases involved multiple persons either directly or indirectly involved in the lead up to, perpetration of or cover-up of the lethal violence. In five of these six cases, the child offender was joined in the perpetration of lethal violence by at least one other male who was over the age of eighteen years at the time of the offence. In terms of judicial constructions of responsibility in sentencing, the case analysis revealed that while the group perpetration of lethal violence was used to better understand and explain the child's perpetration of homicide, it was not explicitly referenced as a mitigating or aggravating factor in the majority of cases. In these cases, responsibility for the violence became collectivised and understood as the actions of a group, as opposed to the actions of any one individual involved.

The exception to this trend towards collectivised responsibility was noted in cases where the child offender was singled out as having led or incited the actions of the group. In these cases, members of the judiciary condemned the individual child offender for having taken the opportunity to 'step up' and perform the act of violence among his peers. The resulting condemnation and clear identification of individualised responsibility is illustrated in the Honourable Justice King's remarks in *Simpas and HR:*

> You HR were being aggressive and saying, "Do you want to fight" and you were encouraging others, encouraging them to come closer. There was pushing and shoving, punching, and Mr Spinks [one of the victims] came back

into the park and ran towards the group. . . . You are encouraging your friends to come and fight these men, saying, "We are many" or in the words of one witness, "There are heaps of us and just three of them". . . . Every time you are tempted to become involved in alcohol or hanging out in the streets with too many other young people, remember this and remember where it leads; to the totally senseless loss of another young life.

(*R v Simpas and HR* [2008] VSC 222, per King J)

This excerpt aptly captures several important characteristics of dangerous and irresponsible masculinity and the collective contexts within which violence becomes a performance of one's manhood. This notion of the social performance of one's masculinity has been explored extensively by Messerschmidt (1993), who argues that for some men, participating in crime can be a form of 'doing masculinity'.

Discourses of collective violence also emerged in several cases involving child offenders of an ethnic minority. In these cases, constructions of responsibility in representations of collective masculine violence were more difficult to discern, as the child's engagement in lethal violence was understood (and that is not to say excused) by the judge as a consequence of wider feelings of marginalisation in the community. While on the one hand belonging to a group was viewed as offering the young person a sense of identity, the benefit of achieving that sense of belonging is obscured when the youth is drawn into violence as a way of achieving and maintaining that group membership. The difficulty of understanding the dynamics of group membership in such cases is well captured in the sentencing of a seventeen-year-old offender in 2005, where the Honourable Justice Kaye stated:

You gravitated to the company of other Sudanese boys. You did so in order to evade the racism, which had been directed towards you at school. Unfortunately the Sudanese boys with whom you associated were undesirable, and your mother described them as troublemakers.

(*R v Athuai* [2005] VSC 252, per Kaye J at 16)

What this short excerpt encourages is a retelling of the event of collective male violence in cases involving youth from ethnic minorities where the violence is better understood as a last chance attempt at social inclusion and the protection achieved through group membership. This case was not unique in the period studied, a similar retelling of collective violence was evident in the sentencing of AO, who was convicted of manslaughter when he was 16 years old. AO was born in Ethiopia and in the period before he came to Australia at age twelve had lived in a community where there was active fighting between Ethiopian and Somali troops and local rebel groups. While conceding that AO's use of violence was 'vicious and sustained', the Honourable Justice Coghlan at sentencing cited a psychological report that described the offender as having 'learnt to do whatever [he] had to to survive' (*R v AO* [2009] VSC 13). As a result of this 'tendency', the judge provided the following statements at sentencing:

You have a tendency to see things in competitive terms, having lived through a period when only the strong were to survive. In that context, you do not trust others and suspect them of exploitation. . . . You had also developed a sense of powerlessness and alienation. You addressed those feelings in part by your association with other young African men who had had experiences similar to your own. That association did not help and increased your tendency for aggressive behaviour.

(R v AO [2009] VSC 13)

Through this lens, AO's responsibility for being part of an act of collective violence and his own violent actions are presented in a way that displaces responsibility from the individual. Like the earlier analysis of *Athuai*, the child offender's actions are presented by the judge as an inevitable consequence of social isolation and a misguided, albeit justifiable, attempt at achieving one's identity through group membership. This representation builds on work previously undertaken by Treadwell and Garland (2011: 5), who in examining constructions of masculinity among members of the English Defence League recognised the value of examining how 'social marginalisation' and masculinity intersect with violent offending. This point of the analysis also marks a starkly different approach to that explored earlier in relation to traditional notions of collective violence through the lens of dangerous and irresponsible masculinity and merges into the following analysis of judicial discourses of understanding.

Judicial discourses of understanding

In contrast to the heavily explored notions of collective, dangerous and irresponsible masculinity, expressions of fear and vulnerability and experiences of social isolation do not feature as characteristics of Connell's 'idealised' masculinity. For this reason, it is argued that the conceptualisation of a 'vulnerable' masculinity provides a lens through which to understand the perpetration of violence by children for whom those emotions and experiences are woven throughout their childhood backgrounds and the events immediately preceding their perpetration of lethal violence. The analysis revealed that prior experiences of family violence, parental separation, childhood dysfunction, political violence and being a refugee and/or homeless were integral to the judicial retelling of what contributed to that child's perpetration of lethal violence. In this respect, as opposed to focusing on the offence itself, judicial discourses of understanding allowed for a retelling of the event of homicide in a way that shifted the focus onto the background of the offender and the event leading up to the offence, as opposed to the act of lethal violence itself.

To provide a somewhat quantitative overview of the vulnerability that spanned these cases, of the twenty-three cases under examination, five involved a child offender who had spent time in a refugee camp during his childhood, four involved a young offender who had been a victim of family violence during his childhood, eight cases involved children whose parents had separated during their early childhood (of which, in several cases the child was consequently estranged from one parent)[6] and one case involved a child who had witnessed his mother attempt suicide, including observing her shoot herself in the stomach (*R v Tipas* ([2004] VSC 25). Aligning with the underpinnings of a welfare approach to juvenile justice, the influences of childhood dysfunction and trauma in these cases highlight the importance of adequately recognising the contributing factors that lie outside the control of the young offender (Richards, 2011) and add to research which notes the relationship between experiences of trauma in childhood and subsequent displays of violent and aggressive behaviour (see, e.g., Abrahams and Jewkes, 2005). In the context of this analysis, while the lethal violence that each child perpetrated cannot be overlooked in light of their backgrounds, a discourse of vulnerable masculinity and understanding ensures that the child's decision to engage in violence is appropriately contextualised through the sentencing process.

This need to consider the child's responsibility for the perpetration of violence in the context of his childhood experiences was particularly apparent in judicial responses to cases where the offender had been a victim of family violence. In several of these cases, the judge acknowledged that the offender's upbringing had played a central role in his later perpetration of lethal violence. In particular, judicial remarks at sentencing recognised that the presence of a negative environment at home had contributed to the child's perception that violence offered an appropriate, and even in some cases normal, response when challenged. This was particularly apparent in the 2005 case of *R v TY* ([2005] VSC 109). In *TY* the offender was fourteen years old at the time of the offence and was found guilty of the murder of an eighteen-year-old male stranger whom he struck in the head with the steel tip of a golf umbrella. The assault occurred at a public tram stop and was precipitated by verbal taunts that the offender directed at a female friend of the victim's. When the victim questioned the offender about these remarks, the offender thrust the umbrella tip twice at the victim's head. TY had migrated to Australia with his parents and two older brothers from war-torn Lebanon when he was young, following which he was exposed to 'harsh physical discipline' and 'domestic violence' (*DPP v TY (No 3)*[2007] VSC 489, per Bell J). In sentencing TY, the Honourable Justice Teague acknowledged that his dysfunctional family environment had directly contributed to his perception that violence offered an appropriate response when challenged. As stated at sentencing:

> I can accept that, because of the violence and other abuse you were exposed to at home, you came to treat violence as an appropriate response to a situation where you were, or where you perceived that you were, challenged.
>
> (*R v TY* [2005] VSC 109, per Teague J)

Weaving this discourse of understanding throughout the judgment, the judge remarked earlier that TY's offending could be 'linked' to his dysfunctional family upbringing. Through these remarks the normalisation of violence in TY's background was understood by the judge to have limited his capacity to respond to a challenge in a non-violent way. While not ameliorating responsibility, the framing of the child's actions in this way serves to appropriately contextualise the child's tendency towards violence by placing it directly in the context of an abusive childhood. Within this discourse, it is unsaid but implicit that the abusive actions of those who were around TY during his childhood are indirectly held responsible for the child's perception that violence offered an appropriate response when challenged.

Judicial discourses of understanding were evident in cases beyond this one example. In another case involving a history of family violence, the judge noted that the child offender had been given 'the wrong kind of example by disciplining you with violence' (*R v LMA* [2005] VSC 152, per Teague J). Given that this study was undertaken at a time when domestic violence has been declared a 'national emergency' in Australia (Hudson, 2015), this analysis raises broader concerns about the number of Australian children growing up in households where the use of violence is normalised. While the impact of this in terms of safety of women and children victims of violence has been placed under the political and academic microscope, this analysis illustrates why the effects of witnessing routine violence in childhood upon children's own understandings of violence and engagement with violent activity requires further attention.

In addition to family violence and parental separation, and as already touched on in the case of TY, there were five cases during the period examined involving young male offenders who had spent part of their childhood in either a refugee camp or a civil war zone. These included two children who had sought refuge from Syria and Somalia, and two children who had spent part of their childhood in an Egyptian and Malaysian refugee camp. In the sentencing of ZN, who was seventeen years old at the time of the murder and had been born in Sudan during the civil war (*R v ZN* [2012] VSC 616), the judge quoted large excerpts from a psychiatric report tendered to the court to provide context to ZN's use of lethal violence. The length and space that these excerpts are given within the judgment clearly highlight the priority that the judge afforded these explanations in explaining the offender's violence. One excerpt is particularly salient in explaining why ZN's responsibility for the use of violence must be contextualised with reference to his childhood background:

> [T]here are likely to be aspects of [ZN]'s personal history that contribute to him at [the] time making poor judgments and decisions. [ZN]'s early experiences in childhood have resulted in him seeking his own territory, which can be a safe and protected place. He has learned from an early age that aggression and physical superiority can give him this, as well as a sense of freedom.
> (*R v ZN* [2012] VSC 616, as cited by Coghlan J)

These remarks reflect arguments previously made by Messerschmidt (1993: 83) that 'crime by men is a form of social practice invoked as a resource, when other resources are unavailable, for accomplishing masculinity'. In cases such as ZN, the perpetration of violence was framed at sentencing as reflective of the offender's perceived lack of legitimate resources to achieve a sense of belonging in the community rather than an indication of a propensity towards violence. This sense of understanding afforded the circumstances of the child's background is arguably refreshing given the increasingly punitive direction of juvenile justice in Australia.

These cases are important in that they highlight, beyond the usual focus on collective, dangerous and irresponsible masculinity, the vulnerability of those who come before the law as children charged with a homicide offence. While it is recognised that in cases involving the perpetration of heinous offences, such as murder and manslaughter, a punishment-focused response by the justice system is necessary, this analysis of judicial discourses of understanding illustrates why it is equally important to recognise the influence of childhood environments and family characteristics and to pay adequate attention to the contributing factors that were outside the control of the young offender.

Discourses of redemption and rehabilitation

Building on the preceding analysis, judicial remarks at sentencing revealed that for several of the young offenders removal from their disruptive family environment following their perpetration of lethal violence allowed them to flourish. This gave rise to a judicial discourse of redemption and rehabilitation that described a clear passage 'out of crime' for several of the vulnerable young offenders under study. This discourse emerged most clearly in cases where the offender had been on remand for an extended period of time between charge, conviction and sentencing, and where the young offender had been provided with the opportunity to engage in a range of rehabilitation and educative courses prior to the point of sentencing. Consequently, in evaluating the impact of that engagement, judicial discourses of redemption and rehabilitation focused on the importance of these programs in terms of addressing behavioural issues but also of providing the child with legitimate means and strategies to overcome the legacies of problematic home environments and backgrounds. This discourse was characterised by consistent judicial praise for the positive engagement that the offender had shown to date.

This discourse is clearly illustrated through the remarks made on sentence by the Honourable Justice Kellam in *R v BTP* ([2006] VSC 374). BTP committed manslaughter at the age of fifteen years. Throughout his childhood BTP suffered from a severe intellectual disability, experienced parental separation, engaged in high levels of chroming and had been allegedly sexually assaulted by a male family friend (his eventual victim). Upon setting out this background of 'considerable deprivation', the judge cited a Juvenile Justice Centre report to highlight the positive response of BTP to youth imprisonment: 'He [BTP] thrives in a situation with structure and routine and is able to manage relationships with his peers and staff without majority difficulty'. Justice Kellam went on to note that the fifteen months of imprisonment between the date of the offence and sentencing appeared 'to be the most stable period yet experienced by you in your life' (*R v BTP* [2006] VSC 374). While not seeking to minimise the seriousness of the offence perpetrated, the offender's responsibility for this offence is understood against a backdrop of vulnerability and in a judicial discourse that emphasises not the need for punishment or deterrence, but rather the already positive impact of rehabilitation.

Beyond *BTP*, the general value of education for young persons is further captured in remarks made by The Honourable Justice Bongiorno in another child-perpetrated homicide case:

> There is little hope for the prison system as a rehabilitative force for good if prisoners such as you are deprived of the opportunities for self advancement and education such as those you have available at present. There is probably no greater indicator of potential for rehabilitation than a positive attitude towards education.
>
> (*R v Tipas* [2004] VSC 25)

Acknowledging discourses of redemption and rehabilitation in the sentencing of child homicide offenders, albeit briefly canvassed here, is important in that it shines a light on individual stories of the positive impact of rehabilitation programs in the youth justice setting. Given the current political trend towards de-investing in prison services and programmes in Australia (Flynn and Carlton, 2013), it is essential that the value of these rehabilitative programs be critically examined and indeed highlighted wherever possible. In the context of this analysis, these cases emphasise the need to invest specifically in the development and re-education of vulnerable young persons who are brought within the confines of the criminal justice system.

Conclusion

This research is undertaken at a time when the perpetration of violent acts by young males has been central in political campaigns and media debates across Australia. While these debates have not been exclusively focused on offenders under eighteen years old, they have encouraged a national image of childhood and male youth as 'out of control'. In particular, debate surrounding the perpetration of violence by youths, alcohol-fuelled violence and the carrying of knives in the nighttime economy have been focal across Australian state and territorial jurisdictions. While this research in some ways lends support to this focus and to the proliferation of discourses of dangerous, irresponsible and collective-masculinity violence, it is argued that we need to reconsider how we construct the child who commits lethal violence. While the populist view of youths 'at risk' is certainly supported by the analysis in the first half of this chapter, the second half suggests a somewhat more complex picture. Child-perpetrated lethal violence is undoubtedly linked to broader concerns in the Australian community, including what is now being recognised as a national epidemic of family violence as well as the treatment and limited opportunities for support provided to those who migrate or seek refuge in Australia. For this reason, a more nuanced – and less punishment focused – discourse at a criminal justice level but also in the community and political space is arguably required to more accurately illuminate the contributing features of child-perpetrated lethal violence.

The case analysis also highlights the ways in which members of the judiciary can be complicit in encouraging traditional notions of masculinity to proliferate through their retelling of the fatal event in sentencing and in their constructions of responsibility in the cases of child-perpetrated homicide. Interestingly, while all cases in this analysis involved a male offender and (with one exception) a male victim, the language employed by judges at sentencing to allocate responsibility is neither gendered nor sexed. However, while framed in gender-neutral terms, the judicial discourses – particularly in their construction of lethal violence as collective, alcohol fuelled and the irresponsible result of knife carrying – reignite traditional images of male violence and masculinity without the explicit recognition of the act of violence as sexed.

This chapter contends that by viewing the actions of young men convicted of a homicide offence through the lens of vulnerable masculinity and a discourse of judicial understanding, the intricacies of masculine lethal violence and an offender's background can be better understood and contextualised. The case analysis reveals how a child offender can be held individually responsible for an act of lethal male violence at sentencing whilst also being represented by the sentencing judge as among the more vulnerable of young persons in our community. Within the rich tapestry of the Australian cultural community it is perhaps unsurprising that vulnerabilities associated with the legacy of war, migration and refuge would emerge in the stories of children in conflict with the law; however, the analysis extends upon the existing body of research that has examined masculinity and social marginalisation to consider the ways in which children may be drawn into undesirable group membership and the perpetration of lethal violence as a means through which to perform their masculinity. In that context it is arguably not the individual who is responsible for that act but the society that has collectively failed them prior.

Notes

1　For examples of recent Australian media coverage of youth violence, see Drape, 2010; Hasham and Olding, 2014; Weatherburn, 2014.
2　Constructions of masculinity and its relationship to crime remain heavily debated, including a body of work that has critiqued the theories of Connell and Messerschmidt. See, for example, Hood-Williams (2001) and Jefferson (2002).
3　It is acknowledged that where a judgment has been restricted, or was unreported, the case would not have been identified and therefore is not accounted for within this analysis.
4　In terms of case resolution, of the twenty-three cases, ten were resolved by way of a jury verdict, while the remaining thirteen convictions were the result of a guilty plea entered by the offender prior to trial.
5　For example in *DJE,* the Honourable Justice Teague stated that 'while the alcohol may partly explain what you did, it provides no excuse' ([2006] VSC 339).
6　There were five cases within the period studied where the judge noted that the offender had come from a 'supportive' family and there was no history of family abuse, negative childhood environments or parental separation, so it is certainly not purported that this vulnerability was woven throughout all incidences of child-perpetrated homicide.

References

Abrahams, N. and Jewkes, R. (2005) Effect of South African men's having witnesses abuse of their mothers during children on their levels of violence in adulthood. *American Journal of Public Heath*, 95: 1811–1816.

Alder, C. and Polk, K. (1996) Masculinity and child homicide. *British Journal of Criminology*, 38(3): 396–411.

Asquith, S. (1996) When children kill children: The search for justice. *Childhood*, 3(1): 99–116.

Bondy, J., Ogilvie, A. and Astbury, B. (2005) *Living on the Edge: Understanding the Social Context of Knife Carriage among Young People*. Melbourne: RMIT University Press.

Bryant, W. and Cussen, T. (2015) *Homicide in Australia: 2010–11 to 2011–12: National Homicide Monitoring Program Report*. Monitoring Report No. 23. Canberra: Australian Institute of Criminology.

Burman, M. (2010) The ability of criminal law to produce gender equality: Judicial discourses in the Swedish criminal legal system. *Violence Against Women*, 16(2): 173–188.

Carrell, S. (2014) Police stop and search rates in Scotland four times higher than in England. *The Guardian*, 17 January.

Chan, A. and Payne, J. (2013) *Homicide in Australia: 2008–09 to 2009–10: National Homicide Monitoring Program Annual Report*. Monitoring Report No. 21. Canberra: Australian Institute of Criminology.

Children, Youth and Families Act 2005, Act. No. 96/2005 (Vic.)

Collier, R. (2010) *Men, Law and Gender: Essays on the "Man" of Law*. Oxon: Routledge.

Connell, R. W. (1987) *Gender and Power*. Cambridge: Polity Press.

Connell, R. W. (2000) *The Men and the Boys*. New South Wales: Allen and Unwin.

Connell, R. W. (2005) *Masculinities*. (2nd ed.). New South Wales: Allen and Unwin.

Connell, R. W. and Messerschmidt, J. W. (2005) Hegemonic masculinity: Rethinking the concept. *Gender and Society*, 19(6): 829–859.

Cunneen, C. and White, R. (2007) *Juvenile Justice: Youth and Crime in Australia.* (3rd ed.). Melbourne: Oxford University Press.

Drape, J. (2010) Youth violence on the rise: Report. *The Age*, 16 July.

Fitz-Gibbon, K. (2012) The Victorian operation of defensive homicide: Examining the delegitimisation of victims in the criminal justice system. *Griffith Law Review*, 21(2): 555–581.

Fitz-Gibbon, K. (2014) *Homicide Law Reform, Gender and the Provocation Defence: A Comparative Perspective*. Hampshire, UK: Palgrave Macmillan.

Flynn, A. and Carlton, B. (2013) Go directly to jail: Not always the best move. *The Age*, 24 June.

Franklin, B. and Petley, J. (2006) Killing the age of innocence: Newspaper reporting of the death of James Bulger. In Pilcher, J. and Wagg, S. (eds.) *Thatcher's Children? Politics, Children and Society in the 1980s and 1990s*. New York: Psychology Press, pp. 134–154.

Goodey, J. (1997) Boys don't cry: Masculinities, fear of crime and fearlessness. *British Journal of Criminology*, 37(3): 401–418.

Green, D. (2007) Comparing penal cultures: Child-on-child homicide in England and Norway. *Crime and Justice*, 36(1): 591–643.

Green, D. (2012) *When Children Kill Children: Penal Populism and Political Culture*. Oxford: Oxford University Press.

Harland, K. and McCready, S. (2014) Rough justice: Considerations on the role of violence, masculinity and the alienation of young men in communities and peace building processes in Northern Ireland. *Youth Justice*, 14(3): 269–283.

Hasham, N. and Olding, R. (2014) Safer Sydney: Alcohol link to young criminals. *Sydney Morning Herald*, 8 January.

Hood-Williams, J. (2001) Gender, masculinities and crime: From structures to psyches. *Theoretical Criminology*, 5(1): 37–60.

Howe, A. (2008) *Sex, Violence and Crime: Foucault and the 'Man' Question*. London: Routledge.

Hudson, P. (2015) Domestic violence really is a national emergency. *The Australian*, 13 April.

James, A. and Jenks, C. (1996) Public perceptions of childhood criminality. *British Journal of Sociology*, 47(2): 315–331.

Jefferson, T. (2002) Subordinating hegemonic masculinity. *Theoretical Criminology*, 6(1): 63–88.

McCallum, F. (2011) Children and the Scottish criminal justice system. In *Scottish Parliament Information Centre Briefing 11/53*. Edinburgh: Scottish Parliament, pp. 1–19.

Messerschmidt, J. W. (1993) *Masculinities and Crime*. Lanham, MD: Rowman and Littlefield.

Messerschmidt, J. W. (1994) Schooling, masculinities and youth crime by white boys. In Newburn, T. and Stanko, E. A. (eds.) *Just Boys Doing Business?* London: Routledge, pp. 81–99.

Morgan, D.H.J. (1987) Masculinity and violence. In Hanmer, J. and Maynard, M. (eds.) *Women, Violence and Social Control*. London: Macmillan, pp. 180–192.

Naffine, N. (1990) *Law and the Sexes*. London: Allen and Unwin.

Office of Police Integrity. (2012) *Review of Victoria Police Use of 'Stop and Search' Powers*. Melbourne: Victorian Government.

Polk, K. (1994) *When Men Kill: Scenarios of Masculine Violence*. Cambridge: Cambridge University Press.

Richards, K. (2011) *What Makes Juvenile Offenders Different from Adult Offenders?* Trends and Issues in Crime and Criminal Justice No. 409. Canberra: Australian Institute of Criminology.

Sheehy, E. A. (2014) *Defending Battered Women on Trial: Lessons from the Transcripts*. Vancouver, BC: UBC Press.

Tomsen, S. (1997) A top night: Social protest, masculinity and the culture of drinking violence. *British Journal of Criminology*, 37(1): 90–102.

Treadwell, J. and Garland, J. (2011) Masculinity, marginalization and violence: A case study of the English Defence League. *British Journal of Criminology*, 5(4): 621–634.

Virueda, M. and Payne, J. (2010) *Homicide in Australia: 2007–08: National Homicide Monitoring Program Annual Report*. Monitoring Report No. 13. Canberra: Australian Institute of Criminology.

Walker, L. (1998) Chivalrous masculinity among juvenile offenders in Western Sydney: A new perspective on young working class men and crime. *Current Issues in Criminal Justice*, 9(3): 279–293.

Weatherburn, D. (2014) Violence in Sydney: Young men, alcohol and hot summer nights. *The Age*, 2 January.

White, R. and Mason, R. (2006) Youth gangs and youth violence: Charting the key dimensions. *Australian and New Zealand Journal of Criminology*, 39(1): 54–70.

Whitehead, A. (2005) Man to man violence: How masculinity may work as a dynamic risk factor. *The Howard Journal*, 44(4): 411–422.

Part II

Blurring the boundaries between homicide, gender and responsibility

5 Murderousness in war

From My Lai to Marine A

Sandra Walklate and Ross McGarry

It is not new to observe that murderous behaviour, both inter- and intra-combatants and civilians, occurs in times of war. Neither is it particularly startling to observe that the violence and aggression of wartime situations is largely, though not exclusively, associated with men and a version of masculinity that is valorised in these contexts. The legitimising of such gendered behaviour is made forthright within British Army Doctrine (Ministry of Defence, 2012: 2–18, para. 0235e):

> The British soldier should embody a warrior spirit. He should be tough, resilient, innovative, highly-motivated, and compassionate. He should have an offensive spirit and a desire to get to grips with adversaries and challenges. He should not hesitate to engage in combat – to fight – using controlled violence when necessary.

This vision of military manhood, with its emphasis on the 'warrior spirit', has been readily translated into highly successful media representations such as the series of *Rambo* films (the first of which was released in 1982) and the more recently successful film entitled *American Sniper*, released in 2014. Both of these mediated versions of the soldier represent images of soldiering that valorise this warrior spirit, with particular emphasis on its translation into the act of killing and less focus on the use of compassion. They are also images derived from the two conflicts from which the case studies used in this chapter are taken: Vietnam on the one hand and Iraq and Afghanistan on the other. However, the representations of military manhood in the genre of films we mentioned are neither simple nor straightforward. The *Rambo* films feature a Vietnam survivor troubled by survivor's guilt. *American Sniper* is a more factual representation of a hugely successful military sniper who is troubled by how he now fits with his domestic responsibilities. This chapter is not concerned to examine the efficacy or otherwise of these representations either in terms of the warrior spirit of Army Doctrine or how this has been interpreted by the film industry. This chapter is concerned with the underbelly of this spirit, the images of it portrayed in its name, as experienced by those actually expected to deliver it. Specifically it will endeavour to address the consequences of failing to use '*controlled* violence when necessary' (ibid: our emphasis): consequences that – even in the context of war – result in murder. In particular it will consider who is made responsible for murderousness in war and why. In so doing we shall reflect upon the extent to which the concept of gender facilitates the sense-making practices that assign responsibility for the illegitimate uses of violence within violent environments.

In order to do this the chapter falls into four parts. The first section will discuss the legal context in which killing in wartime is viewed as legitimate or illegitimate. The second section will present two case studies. Both of these brought to the fore, in different ways, the question of what counts as the use of 'legitimate' (read 'controlled') violence in conflict situations. The first considers the massacre at My Lai in 1968 during the Vietnam War. The second considers the conviction of 'Marine A' for the murder of an 'unknown member of the Taliban' in September 2011. The third part of this chapter will offer an analysis of what was made visible in the understandings offered about each of these events and will draw on the pleas made in mitigation for them. In the fourth part we shall dig a little deeper into these understandings and reflect upon what has remained invisible within them. It is at this deeper level, we shall argue, that it is possible to discern the powerful influence of gendered understandings of both the responsibility of the individual(s) for the events that took place and the (gendered) role of the state.

The laws of war

Walker (2012: 417) observes that the law of armed combat 'privileges certain forms of lethal violence, in particular that between soldiers'. Whilst such an observation may appear obvious, behind it lies quite a complex puzzle concerned with how and under what conditions that privilege is given primacy. The role of law in war, and the appeal to such jurisdiction in times of war, is a profound feature of the contemporary world. Advocates and concerned parties, both for and against the legality of particular conflicts, look to the law for a resolution of their concerns – so much so that Sarat et al. (2013: 4) assert, 'The waging of war and the doing of law are inextricably bound.' The intermeshing of these two domains stretches back to the work of Hobbes, for whom war was a condition of lawlessness in which the state had no presence, since there were no limits on the kind of violence a person might commit. Yet for Hobbes, the rule of law, as promulgated by the state as a Leviathan, also had a central role in preventing war of all against all. This view put the soldier and the act of killing in a particular place in relation to the state and/or the sovereign. Echoing Weber's (1919) illustration between 'legitimate' violence and state power, Walker (2012: 425) comments: 'He [a soldier] kills without personal desire, on behalf of a sovereign to whom he has pledged his duty. The responsibility therefore lies with authority.' Hence the soldier kills, legitimately, on behalf of the state. However, the laws of war are contemporarily not as simple or straightforward as this summary might suggest; whether the war being fought is 'just' or not adds a further layer of complexity.

Writing a little earlier than Hobbes, Grotius, a Dutch scholar, published *On the Law of War and Peace* in 1625. Here, invoking a more overtly moral stance to war, he offered the seminal intervention that made the distinction between *jus ad bellum* and *jus in bello*. The first refers to the concept of a 'just war' and considers the conditions under which the recourse to war is permissible. The second refers to the practice of war and considers how to conduct war permissibly. This distinction has informed the increasing presence of international law in times of conflict and lies behind, to a greater or lesser degree, the Lieber Code and the Hague and Geneva Conventions. More specifically it is a distinction that frames the Laws of Armed Conflict. The principles of *jus in bello* provide the backdrop against which the kinds of lethal violence engendered in war are made lawful and legally authorised. They are guided by three norms: necessity, distinction and proportionality. Necessity means that the violence perpetrated must be justified in military terms. Distinction means that the aggressors must target only combatants, not civilians. Finally, proportionality implies that the harm caused to combatants should not be excessive but in line with the military benefits being sought. Historically the norms of *jus in bello* have offered some protection for prisoners of war, those *hors de combat* and for civilians. However they also reflect historical and traditional distinctions between war and peace alongside the presumption of a distinction between international and domestic engagement. Nonetheless, despite the observation by Sarat et al. (2013) that they no longer match with what is practically possible in contemporary conflicts, they still inform current legal understandings and military doctrines concerning the conditions under which lethal violence is considered to be legitimate – that which British Army Doctrine (referred to above) cites as 'controlled violence'. In other words, the Laws of Armed Conflict mark the boundary between the legitimate use of violence, as endorsed by the soldier's duty to the state, and illegitimate violence (read murder), for which the soldier will ultimately be held *individually* responsible.

The laws of war, as described above, provide legal and ethical boundaries within which people may take the lives of other warring parties with 'legitimacy'. However, the more domestic issue of murder adds a final layer of complexity to the uses of violence at war. Writing during the same century as Hobbes and Grotius, Sir Edward Coke (1680: 47, cop. VII.b) is attributed with defining murder in the context of English law in the *Institutes of the Laws of England*:

> Murder is when a man of sound memory, and of the age of discretion, unlawfully killeth within any county of the realm any reasonable creature in *rerum natura* under the king's peace, with malice fore-thought, either expressed by the party or implied by law, so as the party wounded or hurt etc. die of the wound, or hurt etc. within a year and a day after the same.

This definition was later implied within the Crime Against the Persons Act (1861) to constitute an understanding of homicide, with its only amendment in the present day pertaining to the revoking of the 'year and a day rule' (D'Cruze et al., 2006). As such, this definition holds some important contextual information regarding the uses of violence at war outside of the laws of war, i.e., illegitimately. To judge the taking of another person's life as murder, the act must be a violation of an existing law (*actus reus*) with intent having been demonstrated to do the same (*mens rea*). However, the circumstances of war are not considered to constitute the 'king's (or queen's) peace' and are therefore governed by the laws of war. The domestic offence of murder occurs within the war setting when the contemporary operational environment no longer holds an immediate threat to serving soldiers, thus restoring the 'king's peace'. There are therefore unlawful ways to kill in war within two sets of circumstances: the illegitimate use of violence under the laws of war during hostilities and the illegal taking of another person's life under the laws of murder, where hostilities appear to have abated, regardless of how ambiguous this may be.

Before unpicking these issues further, we shall consider two case studies. Separated by over forty years, they nevertheless afford some interesting and provocative insights into the question of murder/uncontrolled violence and responsibility in times of war.

The My Lai massacre

For those who lived with the presence of the Vietnam War, the coverage and images associated with what came to be called the My Lai massacre (which took place in March 1968) brought to bear the continuing horrors of war and its violence(s). Indeed, mediated events such as this one did much to damage the American claim, both at home and abroad, to be prosecuting a 'good' war against the evil of communism (Alexander, 2012). The American journalist, Seymour Hersh, who reported on My Lai in November 1969, was awarded the Pulitzer Prize for his work in 1970. Indeed, newspaper reports on the killings committed by US Marines in Haditha, Iraq, in 2005 (see MacArthur, 2006; Pyle, 2006) commented on the similarities between My Lai and this more recent event, suggestive of some ongoing issues in relation to the dispensation of controlled and legitimate violence.

My Lai was a village in an area designated 'Pinkville' by US Forces, known as a Viet Cong stronghold. American Forces had sustained severe casualties from several attempts to secure this area in early 1968. Defined as a 'free fire' area, with civilians having been encouraged to leave by dropping leaflets and by other means, a further offensive was ordered. Lieutenant William Calley was the platoon leader of the Eleventh Brigade of the American Division at this time. This platoon had sustained considerable losses in the earlier offensives. As part of this third offensive, Calley and his platoon were ordered to clear the area that included the village of My Lai. This order was relayed from the battalion commander to the company commander to Calley, the platoon commander. That civilians were killed as part of this clearing process is not in dispute, though estimates on how many is, varying from 109 (the figure acknowledged by the US military) to 700 estimated by local people. Neither is it in dispute that these casualties included women and young children. Photographic evidence and witnesses testified to this. What was in dispute was the nature, extent and motivation for these killings: put simply, whether or not these actions constituted premeditated murder. On this point, military opinion was significantly divided at the time. Clearly those who produced evidence about these killings and subsequently offered testimony to the court at a minimum felt uncomfortable about what had transpired. Indeed, questions about what had happened were raised at the time, although, as indicated below, there was a considerable time lapse before any proceedings were instigated. Equally, there was a body of opinion expressing the view that Calley was just following orders, perhaps rather too literally, to clear the area. Moreover, given the prevailing uncertainty about who was and who was not a member of the Viet Cong, some took the view that the actions that took place were 'understandable'.

Calley was formally charged in September 1969 with the murder of 109 South Vietnamese civilians during this attack, almost a year after the event and just a few days before he was due to be released from active service. Others under his command were also charged with offences, but as platoon commander Calley was considered to be the main culprit. Until this incident, he had received repeated high ratings from his superior officers and was scheduled to receive Bronze and Silver Stars for his efforts. Calley was found guilty as charged and though sentenced to life imprisonment actually served three years under house arrest, his sentence having been commuted by President Nixon.

Marine A

The sentencing remarks by Judge Blackett provide the details of this particular case. In it Blackett (2013) states what Royal Marine Sergeant Alexander Blackman (Marine A) had done:

> On 15 September 2011, while on patrol near CP Omar in Helmand Province, you shot an unknown Afghan insurgent in the chest and killed him. . . . Having removed his AK47, magazines and a grenade, you caused him to be moved to a place where you wanted to be out of sight of your operational Headquarters at Shazad so that, to quote what you said: "PGSS can't see what we're doing to him." . . . When you were sure the Apache Helicopter was out of sight you calmly discharged a 9mm round into his chest from close range.

Sergeant Blackman was stripped of his rank and given a ten-year prison sentence in December 2013 for the murder of this member of the Taliban. Throughout his trial he never denied his actions, nor could he, given the recording available from the helmet camera of one of his colleagues who was present at this incident. Indeed, he is also reported as saying at the time, 'Obviously this doesn't go anywhere, fellas. I've just broken the Geneva Convention.' In 2014 his sentence was reduced from ten to eight years, the court having ruled that the prior hearing should have given greater weight to the combat stress he was under when the offence occurred.

As with the case of Lt. Calley, Sergeant Blackman was well respected, had served five tours of duty abroad and witnessed heavy fighting and military losses in Iraq and Afghanistan. However, the bald statements of the case as summed up by Judge Blackett notwithstanding, commentaries about these events also provoked some differences of opinion on the appropriateness of the criminal charge for murder. On this occasion these differences were not so much about the nature and extent of this crime, but about its intent. The report by filmmaker Chris Terrill (2013) offers a flavour of this:

> Soldiers are not automatons. They are flesh-and-blood human beings with frailties and vulnerabilities like all of us. They are ordinary people doing extraordinary things on our behalf; risking their lives in combat and having to make difficult and morally confusing judgments in the heat of battle. They don't always get it right because, sometimes, the stakes are just too high for any one man to cope with. I believe that if Marine A is a criminal of war, then he is also a casualty of war.

Of course, as intimated above, one of the questions at issue here is what murder might mean in the context of war in general, but it is particularly pertinent in the context of this conflict. The conflict in Iraq and Afghanistan has been subjected to severe critical scrutiny casting some doubt as to whether or not it meets the requirements of *jus ad bellum* (see *inter alia* Kramer and Michalowski, 2005). Thus it might be argued that it is rather anomalous to charge a soldier for an act of killing committed when acting on behalf of the state when the state's engagement in the conflict is legally equivocal. Moreover, the nature of the conflict (as in Vietnam) also cast some doubt on whether or not the requirements of *jus in bello* could be met. Here the view might be expressed that given the melding of combatants with civilians (making distinctions difficult), the questionable necessity of some of the military engagement (particularly in relation to the weapons used) and 'local knowledge' about the dubious proportional response of the enemy, the laws of war as expressed by the principles of *jus in bello* were inappropriate. Such issues aside, it is important to remember that Marines, in the UK and the US, are expected and trained to kill, the validity or otherwise of their actions in particular circumstances notwithstanding. So, with particular reference to Marine A, a pertinent question might be, did his training provide him with intent to kill or was he engaged in an intent to kill without the expectations of such in his role at that particular time? How might it be possible, then, to make sense of the actions that resulted in the massacre at My Lai or the murder of a member of the Taliban by Marine A?

Context, *jus in bello* and 'controlled violence'

Brutal violence and killing are endemic to war and conflict – the evidence of history stands as testimony to this. However, what remains at issue is how to make sense of such behaviour, beyond the persistent recourse to law. As King (2013) documents, literature in all its forms has been an important source of information about the nature and extent of different kinds of conflict violence and sometimes offers graphic detail about the worst excesses and consequences of such behaviour. Memoirs, poetry, photography and embedded journalism all provide rich sources of data about the horrors of war and, more importantly in some respects, the changing nature of combat. However, King (2013: 8) also observes that

> while these artistic representations are impressive and . . . have been taken up in popular imagination as definitive depictions of these conflicts, it may not be necessary to accept them as entirely accurate, still less comprehensive, accounts in sociological terms.

Hence, the popular image of the warrior soldier commented on at the beginning of this chapter has done much to deny the totality of the war experience from the soldier's perspective. A less visible literature has also drawn attention to the less heroic aspects of soldiering. From Wilfred Owen's popular poem 'Dulce et decorum est' to Barker's (1992) *Regeneration Trilogy*, we are presented with a keen sense of the dilemmas associated with being a soldier. Keegan and Holmes (1985: 282) express it this way: '[T]he soldier is both victim and executioner. Not only does he run the risk of being killed and wounded himself, but he also kills and wounds others.' Recognition of the intrinsic contradiction embedded within this role, of course, constitutes a fundamental challenge to the popular imagery of the soldier as 'hero': the warrior spirit. This is a contradiction for which soldiers can pay a price, sometimes illustrated in their personal memoirs (see, e.g., Beattie, 2008). Indeed, in relation to the two case studies above, it is easy to look to the individual soldier for both explanation and blame.

With reference to the My Lai massacre, Collins (2008) makes the point that whilst all the platoons were subjected to a morale-raising speech by their commanding officer the night before the action that took place, it was only Calley's platoon that went on a rampage, with some suggestion that it was only he and a handful of others who participated in the massacre. This has led some commentators – most notably Scheff (2006) – to look to Calley's personal disposition, and the influence he had over his men, as a source of explanation for what took place. On the basis of this evidence, Collins (2008: 101) intimates that Calley was a 'frozen personality' who had experienced failure repeatedly throughout his life and, as a result, turned his repressed anger onto non-combatants. Of course, as Collins (2008) is keen to point out, Calley's platoon was not the only one to have engaged in such behaviour in the Vietnam War, but he does suggest that the disappointment at not finding any Viet Cong in the village was the trigger for the 'emotional contagion' that resulted in the massacre. Scheff (2006) adds to this by suggesting that Calley also epitomised a hyper-masculine personality which afforded some added legitimacy, for Calley himself, for the kinds of actions that took place. Much of this kind of analysis is, of course, a product of its time and arguably suffers from the problem of looking at events in the past through the eyes of the present. However, it remains the case that focusing on the individual and assigning responsibility to him for what took place neatly side-steps the organisational and structural conditions under which the individual was required to operate. It should also be noted that the US Armed Forces in Vietnam was for the most part a conscripted force; a factor that inevitably sets a different tone for practices of engagement than the fully professional military forces engaged in Iraq and Afghanistan (King, 2013).

Marine A was a fully professional soldier, described by Farmer (2012) as 'a brave and modest man who lost his head under the pressures of brutal combat in the Afghanistan'. McGarry (2015) reports that he was a mature family man, of previous good service, again well respected by his colleagues, convicted of the murder of a member of the Taliban (not a civilian) about whom it was deduced that he would never commit such a crime outside of his role as a Marine. However, rather like Calley and his platoon, Marine A, on his fifth tour of duty in Iraq and Afghanistan, had witnessed the loss of colleagues and had been operating from an isolated outpost with two other soldiers for a significant period of time away from direct supervisory contact. At his appeal it was felt that not enough attention had been paid to the possibility that he may have been suffering from combat stress that had been compounded by the recent death of his father. Nonetheless the vulnerability of his victim and the fact that his act brought the British military into disrepute, and likely greater risk of retaliation, weighed heavily against him. Indeed, as documented earlier, the presence of a helmet camera afforded undeniable evidence of what he did and said. Interestingly, reports do not suggest that a case was made in support of his actions as providing protection for the men he was with, in what was undeniably a highly volatile and unpredictable conflict situation. Thus Marine A was presented as someone who had been pushed to the limit rather than someone who had an inherently problematic personality. However, he was nonetheless someone who was responsible and indeed was made to take responsibility for what happened.

Contributory factors: combat stress?

There is (at least) one interesting parallel between these two cases worthy of comment at this juncture. This concerns the prevailing understandings of 'combat stress'. As was noted earlier, recognition of atrocities taking place in Vietnam in the name of democracy shocked the American public and fundamentally called into question the US engagement in that conflict. Alongside this came the question: how could ordinary men (then mostly men) do such awful things? Chamberlin (2012: 362) comments that the *Diagnostic and Statistical Manual of Mental Disorders* (DSM-III) brought the category of PTSD into psychological and popular discourse following the war in Vietnam. Thus:

> The type of traumatic events that were now understood as potentially leading to PTSD included . . . military combat, violent personal assault, being kidnapped or taken hostage, terrorist attack, torture, incarceration as a prisoner of war . . . natural or manmade disasters, severe automobile accidents, or being diagnosed with a life-threatening illness.

The inclusion of military combat in the definition of PTSD, though not published until 1980, was crucial in enabling sense to be made of the relationship between the horrors of war and subsequent problematic behaviour (see *inter alia* Fassin and Rechtman, 2009). It is at this juncture that the unintended consequences of valorising the 'warrior soldier' become visible for the soldiers themselves. Not perhaps of any great value for Lt. Calley at the time of his trial, but such considerations were certainly present in the deliberations at the trial of Marine A. Some of this is captured in Beattie's (2008) autobiographical account of engagement in Afghanistan. Early on in the book Beattie tells us about the aftermath of witnessing a suicide bomber attack: 'The effects of the detonation assaulted all my senses. . . . [H]ere laid out in front of me, all the possible horrors of war had come together in one nightmarish scene' (Beattie, 2008: 4). Later, learning that another attack might be imminent and that only he and one colleague were left to deal with it, he says, 'I was terrified. My stomach churned and my heart raced. . . . This was now a game of chance with the odds stacked against me' (ibid.: 6). Experienced on a routine daily basis in relative isolation, it is perhaps no great surprise that it was suggested that Marine A may have been suffering from paranoia at the time of his crime. Interestingly, however, whilst commented on, little is made of responsibility or of the inability of more senior commanders to assess his mental condition.

Of course, both of these case studies offer potentially different readings of the role of the mental state and/or personal disposition of either Lt. Calley or Marine A as a contributing factor in the commissions of their offences. However taken together with the specific context of the events that took place and the influence of 'local knowledge' pertaining to those events it is not difficult to envisage the importance of individual capacities to cope. Both contexts were marked by prior poor experiences with the combatants, difficulties in identifying who they were and rumours about their likely treatment should they be captured. For example, Anthony Berry QC, in leading Marine A's appeal case, said Marines feared their enemy would subject them to a horrendous death if they were ever caught 'namely skinning them alive, cutting off their testicles and displaying their body parts in trees' (reported by Farmer, 2012). In conflict situations, as Collins (2012) argues, the role of such rumours, whether founded in fact or not, should not be underestimated. In contexts in which conflict is escalating (which arguably would be applicable to both the cases under discussion here), 'it is difficult to distinguish between rumours and realities: in the heightened interaction ritual no-one is interested in the distinction' (ibid: 3). Here Collins (2012: 87) is endeavouring to develop analytically what he has called the 'emotional tunnel of violent attack'. This appreciation of the role of emotions is situated squarely within understanding the reality of the situations being faced rather than as individual psychological problems. In other words the issues faced are also social in nature. The interaction rituals, to use a concept developed by Collins (2004), are not individually produced. They are shared. This affords a differently nuanced insight into the practice of *jus in bello* and 'controlled violence'.

As the discussion above implies, making sense of combat situations does not necessarily lend itself readily to appeals to rationality. Combat situations are highly emotionally charged contexts. These are situations in which the solidarity and comradeship characteristic of disciplined armed forces also comprise strong emotional bonds between (mostly) men. The actual nature of these bonds can be contagious. King (2013) offers a detailed sociological analysis of the combat platoon in which he proffers that '[w]ar is ultimately a product of inter and intra-group dynamics and combat is, therefore, utterly human inhumanity' (ibid.: 12). Sometimes that product is also the result of what Collins (2008: 94) would call 'hot emotion'. It could be argued that this 'hot emotion' is the by-product of both the demands of solidarity and social cohesion intrinsic to a platoon but delivered in particular circumstances. Collins (2008) calls this 'forward panic'. He observes:

> In forward panic, the pathway is a rapid emotional flow during discrete local episodes. . . . It is like an altered state of consciousness from which the perpetrators often emerge at the end as if returning from an alien self.
>
> (ibid.: 100)

This is what he suggests happened at My Lai. In a collective emotional rush, enthralled by repetitive action, everyone is caught up in the action. It is important to note that the concept of 'forward panic' does not explain all circumstances in which atrocities might occur. Some are clearly deliberate and rational. However, in particular circumscribed contexts, as a concept it carries some analytical weight in facilitating an understanding of not only collective action but also individual action. Put simply, combat generates strong emotions, from flight to the back to flight to the front. However, more than this, the recognition that what soldiers actually accomplish in doing their duty is driven as much by the social context in which that duty is given expression as it is by the laws of war and/or a notion of controlled violence. It is, of course, also driven by their training, and it is to an appreciation of the role of that aspect of these two case studies that we shall now turn.

Contributory factors: military masculinity?

The military constitutes a total institution (Goffman, 1961). This means that the military organisation owns the soldier's body and his capacity for work, gives the soldier orders to follow and dictates what risks and dangers he will be exposed to. In return, of course, a soldier, whether a conscript or a volunteer, is paid, fed and provided with training and accommodation. Through training, soldiers learn a whole range of skills, but for the purposes of this discussion they particularly learn when to use and not use violence. However, this experience of the military as a total institution is incomplete without recognising, as Morgan (1987) did some time ago: '[I]t will make a man of you'. This total institution is a masculine one. Consequently McGarry et al. (2014) state that 'soldiers undergo much more than a change physically and psychologically, they experience a change of culture wherein the individual military body adapts to become a collective part of the larger military organism.' They are re-socialised, in Goffman's terms undergoing a 'mortification of the self', ensuring complete submission to the values, norms and practices of the total institution, complete with its punishments, deprivations and humiliations. Recruits are expected to respond to orders without question and perform every task with precision and efficiency and potentially even to their own personal detriment. This process not only converts a civilian into a soldier, it also seeks to ensure a willingness to risk one's own life, to kill the enemy and to protect the larger collegiate body through unquestioning commitment to military doctrine. Brown (2015: 125), speaking of the armed forces in the United States, expresses these processes in this way:

> Military training continuously reinforces military cultural expectations, while simultaneously expunging the recruit's cultural remnants. . . . Cadence also installs the idea that killing is not only acceptable but also encouraged. Killing human beings is not a natural act that one engages in. Most people require programming and training to willingly take the life of another human being.

This is also a process of indoctrination into a highly masculinised culture.

Woodward (2000) suggests that this 'military masculinity' has two key characteristics. It shares with hegemonic masculinity the valorisation of violence and heterosexuality but has the additional feature of the 'warrior hero' commented on at the beginning of this chapter. This image of 'the hard, sacrificial, heterosexual male soldier' and the expectations associated with it lies behind both Collins' (2008) concept of 'forward panic' and King's (2013) efforts to attend to a sociology of combat. It may be invisible and unspoken but it nonetheless takes its toll on men as soldiers (and more recently women too) and is an important ingredient in our capacity to make sense of the kind of murderous behaviour in war with which we are concerned. Of course, military masculinity is a particular version of hegemonic masculinity. Whilst they each hold features in common, it is the particular emphasis on the 'warrior hero' and the particular valorisation of the recourse to violence that demarcates some differences. These differences are enough to render adherence to them problematic when faced with the inherent middle-class masculinity associated with the man of law (Naffine, 1990). The man of law values normative heterosexuality but also valorises reason over emotion: the recourse to violence through discourse over violence through action. Indeed it is at this juncture, when the man of violence meets the man of law, that the capacity of the law to make sense of this violent man falls short. Thus consider the presumptions contained in the following statement made by Judge Blackett in summing up the case of Marine A:

> You were in a tough operational environment where you were legally entitled to use lethal force against the enemy. Whilst carrying out your duty, you came across a very seriously wounded enemy combatant. You were obliged to care for him but instead you executed him. That is a wholly different matter from the cases of murder in the UK normally considered by the civilian Courts, but we are still required by law to apply the same law which those courts are required to apply.

Here there is not only a clash in masculinities but a denial of the realities of war, and returns us to the question of intent: did Marine A kill as a result of his training and all that had gone before, or did he kill outside of these considerations? Whatever the answer to this question, the court convicted him of murder and sentenced him accordingly under the domestic definition of murder invoked by Sir Edward Coke, outlined earlier in this chapter. In this regard he was deemed *individually* responsible and moreover accepted that responsibility, as did Lt. Calley. Between the latter and the former, there have of course been changes both in the management and delivery of military action. O'Malley (2010) reflects some of the changes in his reference to the emergence of neoliberal military subjects. This 'subject aligns not only with the requirements of the new military but equally with many techniques of the self, associated with a liberal mentality of rule that valorizes self-reliance and responsibility in an uncertain world' (ibid.: 505). Here we are offered a glimpse of another layer to our framework of understanding of these two case studies: the interplay among gender, the law, responsibility and the state.

Contributory factors: individualised responsibility?

O'Malley's (2010) analysis of the changing emphasis within military training to the construction of a military (neoliberal) resilient subject serves as a useful reminder that the military and their personnel do not operate in a vacuum. Whilst some of the actions they are engaged in and that are expected of them consist of actions that many civilians, contemporarily, would find difficult to contemplate, the military and its training are implicitly connected with and can be read through the wider social context of which they are a part. Thus Blum (2013: 49) makes some apposite observations concerning what she sees to be the shift from a collective orientation to war and war-making to a cosmopolitan one in which 'wartime regulation is increasingly aspiring to make war look more like a policing operation, in which people are expected to be treated according to their individual actions rather than as representatives of a collective'. This shift, of course, resonates with wider socio-economic and cultural shifts and sits well with O'Malley's (2010) comments concerning the contemporary neoliberal, resilient military subject. For the purposes of this chapter, these concerns neatly reconnect our analysis with the wider framing of the behaviours under discussion within the context of the law.

It has been observed above that one of the tensions evident in bringing lawbreaking military men to court for murder is that which pertains between the rational man of law (also presumed to be a product of liberal theorising and an entrepreneur to boot; see *inter alia* Naffine, 1990, 2003) and the man trained in the use of violence endorsed by the state. Moreover, as some of the analyses discussed in this chapter have also intimated, this man is a collective man subjected to the 'contagion of emotion' (Collins, 2008) in which he has been expected to operate by the state. That clash is one that is evident as the power of 'white man's law' (Hudson, 2006), serving the interests of some and by definition excluding others, including some men. However, there is perhaps a more fundamental issue at stake here. In raising awareness of the wider shifts commented on by O'Malley (2010) and Blum (2013) alongside the gendered, classed and ethnicised nature of law's rationality as intimated in the work of Naffine (1990) and others, we are reminded of the individualised presumption embedded in both, especially in relation to understandings of responsibility. This latter point requires further elucidation.

In a detailed exposition of the concept of responsibility in English and American criminal law, Lacey (2007) reminds us that 'to be deemed responsible is to be judged responsible' (Gray and Shepherd, 2012: 117). This conflation of legal and moral responsibility, as Lacey (2007: 249) argues, belies other interpretations of responsibility that might take account of 'not what we "could" have helped, or whether we "could" have chosen otherwise, but what prevailing social norms judge us to have had a fair opportunity to help or choose.' This kind of understanding affords the opportunity for the law to appreciate the changing landscape of responsibility through time and across space. This vision implies an understanding of responsibility that can be multilayered and multidimensional. It is a vision that transgresses individualist or collectivist orientations (Griffin et al., 2012). Yet law's subjects, whether under national criminal law or international law, stubbornly remain constituted as individuals (though recent moves towards the recognition of corporate responsibilities in cases of manslaughter might be the exception). This is captured succinctly by Simpson (2013: 56–57) in his analysis of the efforts to call both George Bush and Tony Blair to account for war crimes. If individualised justice was the premise on which the international criminal court operated, then surely as officials directing an unjust war they could be indicted before that court. As he states, 'Abstract entities were out, flesh and blood human beings were in' (ibid.: 57). There are two issues embedded in this sleight of hand, the failure to indict Bush and Blair notwithstanding. The first is, despite the claims of international justice to challenge collective behaviour (or indeed the behaviour of 'rogue' states), its capacity to do so, if at all, is highly circumscribed: 'Only individualized justice could ensure the relevance and meaningfulness of international law' (ibid.: 56–57). To recognise collective responsibility, Simpson (2013: 72) suggests, runs the risk 'where everyone is guilty and therefore, no-one is'. Levinson (1973) referred to this as the 'immaculate deception' of the Vietnam War. The second is that international justice is equally circumscribed by liberal views of responsibility (*qua* Lacey, 2007 above). In essence:

> Liberals focus on individuals as free agents capable of making political choices, consuming freely, and, crucially, of doing wrong as individuals abstracted from the social group to which they belong. Criminal concepts like "intent" go to the heart of this liberal view of human agency.
>
> (Simpson, 2013: 73)

So, despite the fact that notions of the collective infuse international criminal law, in reality it is the question of the individual and his/her responsibility that remains a central focus of the law's practice, as per the domestic definition of murder provided above. Therefore, for all practical purposes the consequences of this liberal subject of law implies, whatever the collective, situated and/or social circumstance alluded to in the discussion of the two case studies above, that the assignation of *individual* responsibility for the events that happened and/or that may happen in the future in like circumstances remains paramount.

Concluding thoughts: and what of the state?

In this chapter we have used two case studies to consider the multifaceted nature of how it might be possible to make sense of murderous behaviour in war. Although posited at the start of the chapter in relation to the domestic definition of murder, our analysis has side-stepped the issues of *mens rea* and *actus reus*, since in many ways their presence in both case studies is self-evident. What is less evident in the debates that acts of this kind might generate is the question not so much of whether or not the individuals charged with murder under these particular circumstances are deemed responsible and therefore judged responsible, but what lies behind this assignation of responsibility. In so doing we have considered the role of combat stress, military masculinity and the legal conception of individual responsibility as contributory factors to the process of who was judged responsible and why. In the process of mapping these contributory factors, we have by implication considered the efficacy of the laws of armed conflict as a way of framing the dispensing of legitimate/illegitimate violence in contemporary warfare. This consideration has pointed to a 'cul de sac' for the soldiers who find themselves with the duty of risking their own lives for civilians rather than civilians themselves constituting a factor in how risky a situation might be deemed to be (Blum, 2013) when their local knowledge might be conveying all kinds of information contrary to the principles of *jus in bello*. They are, nonetheless, contemporarily constituted as responsible neoliberal subjects: emblems of a neoliberal but also gendered state.

The question of gender permeates the considerations of this chapter: from the gendered nature of its subject matter, to the gendered presumptions that are deeply embedded in the concepts on which it has drawn to the practical realities of the tension between the 'man of law' and the subjects over which that man sits in judgement. Thus 'masculinist subjectivities intermingle with the dominant imaginations of neoliberal capitalist practices' (Griffin et al., 2012: 5) with consequences at every level of public and private life. However, those consequences are borne more by some than by others. Moreover, some of those consequences are much more visible than others. As far as the subject matter of this chapter is concerned, the state remains invisibly responsible but visibly irresponsible. Sarat et al. (2013: 7) observe: 'In war, the exceptional state, there is no law, in times of peace, there is only law. In each case the sovereign's powers are plenary.' It would seem that neither domestic laws, the laws of armed conflict nor the international criminal court is equipped to challenge the presumption of such powers.

References

Alexander, J. (2012) *Trauma: A Social Theory*. Cambridge: Polity.

Barker, P. (1992) *Regeneration*. London: Penguin Books.

Beattie, D. (2008) *An Ordinary Soldier*. London: Simon and Shuster.

Blackett, J. (2013) Regina v Sergeant Alexander Wayne Blackman ("Marine A"). Available from: www.judiciary.gov.uk/wp-content/uploads/JCO/Documents/Judgments/r-v-blackman-marine-a-sentencing+remarks.pdf

Blum, G. (2013) The individualisation of war: From war to policing in the regulation of conflicts, human rights, and international law. In Sarat, A., Douglas, L. and Umphrey, A. (eds.) *Law and War*. Palo Alto, CA: Stanford Law Books, pp. 48–83.

Brown, W. (2015) Veteran coming home obstacles: Short- and long-term consequences of Iraq and Afghanistan wars. In Walklate, S. and McGarry, R. (eds.) *Criminology and War: Transgressing the Borders*. London: Routledge, pp. 120–136.

Chamberlin, S. E. (2012) Emasculated by trauma: A social history of post-traumatic stress disorder, stigma, and masculinity. *Journal of American Culture*, 35(4): 358–365.

Coke, E. (1680) *The Third Part of the Institutes of the Laws of England: Concerning High Treason, and Other Pleas of the Crown and Clauses*. London: E. and R. Brooke, Bell-Yard, Near Temple Bar.

Collins, R. (2004) *Interaction Ritual Chains*. Princeton, NJ: Princeton University Press.

Collins, R. (2008) *Violence: A Micro-Sociological Theory*. Princeton, NJ: Princeton University Press.

Collins, R. (2012) C-escalation and D-escalation: A theory of the time-dynamics of conflict. *American Sociological Review*, 77(1): 1–20.

D'Cruze, S., Walklate, S., and Pegg, S. (2006) *Murder*. Cullompton, Devon: Willan Publishing.

Farmer, B. (2012) Marine A: 'brave, modest man who lost his head', appeal hears. *Daily Telegraph*, 10 April.

Fassin, D. and Rechtman, R. (2009) *The Empire of Trauma: An Inquiry into the Condition of Victimhood*. Princeton, NJ: Princeton University Press.

Goffman, E. (1961) *Asylums: Essays on the Social Situation of Mental Patients and Other Inmates*. London: Penguin Books.

Gray, R. and Shepherd, L. (2012) "Stop Rape Now?": Masculinity, responsibility, and conflict-related sexual violence. *Men and Masculinities*, 16(1): 115–135.

Griffin, P., Parpart, J. L. and Zalewski, M. (2012) Men, masculinity, and responsibility. *Men and Masculinities*, 16(1): 3–8.

Hudson, B. (2006) Beyond white man's justice: Race, gender and justice in late modernity. *Theoretical Criminology*, 10(1): 29–47.

Keegan, J. and Holmes, R. (1985) *Soldiers: A History of Men in Battle*. London: Guild Publishing.

King, A. (2013) *The Combat Soldier: Infantry Tactics and Cohesion in the Twentieth and Twenty-First Centuries*. Oxford: Oxford University Press Scholarship Online.

Kramer, R. C. and Michalowski, R. J. (2005) War, aggression and state crime: A criminological analysis of the invasion and occupation of Iraq. *British Journal of Criminology*, 45(4): 446–469.

Lacey, N. (2007) Space, time and function: Intersecting principles of responsibility across the terrain of criminal justice. *Criminal Law and Philosophy*, 1: 233–250.

Levinson, S. (1973) Responsibility for crimes of war. *Philosophy and Public Affairs*, 2(3): 244–273.

MacArthur, J. R. (2006) Guest commentary: Semper why? One more illusion down the drain. *Naples Daily News.* Available from: www.naplesnews.com/opinion/perspectives/guest_commentary_semper_why_one_more_illusion_down

McGarry, R. (2015) War, crime and military victimhood. *Critical Criminology: An International Journal,* OnlineFirst.

McGarry, R., Walklate, S. and Mythen, G. (2014) A sociological analysis of military resilience: Opening up the debate. *Armed Forces and Society,* 41(2): 352–378.

Ministry of Defence. (2012) *Army Doctrine Publication: Operations.* Swindon: Development, Concepts and Doctrine Centre.

Morgan, D. (1987) *"It Will Make a Man of You": Notes on Military Service, Masculinity and Autobiography.* Studies in Sexual Politics No. 17. Manchester University: Department of Sociology.

Naffine, N. (1990) *Law and the Sexes.* London: Allen and Unwin.

Naffine, N. (2003) Who are law's persons? From Cheshire Cats to responsible subjects. *Modern Law Review,* 66(3): 346–347.

O'Malley, P. (2010) Resilient subjects: Uncertainty, warfare and liberalism. *Economy and Society,* 39(4): 488–509.

Pyle, R. (2006) Haditha killings recall Vietnam's My Lai. *Washington Post.* Available from: www.washingtonpost.com/wp-dyn/content/article/2006/06/02/AR2006060200936.html

Sarat, A., Douglas, L. and Umphrey, A. (eds.) (2013) *Law and War.* Palo Alto, CA: Stanford Law Books.

Scheff, T. (2006) Male emotions/relationships and violence: A case study. *Human Relations,* 56(6): 727–749.

Simpson, G. (2013) *Law, War and Crime: War Crimes, Trials and the Reinvention of International Law.* Hoboken: Wiley.

Terrill, C. (2013) Marine A: criminal or casualty? *The Daily Telegraph,* 1 December.

Walker, S. G. (2012) Lawful murder: Unnecessary killing in the land of war. *Canadian Journal of Law and Jurisprudence,* XXV(2): 417–446.

Weber, M. (1919) Politics as vocation. In Whyte, D. (ed.) *Crimes of the Powerful: A Reader.* Maidenhead: Open University Press, pp. 13–15.

Woodward, R. (2000) Warrior heroes and little green men: Soldiers, military training, and the construction of rural masculinities. *Rural Sociology,* 65(4): 640–657.

6 'He seems to come out as a personally cruel person'

Perpetrator re-presentations in direct murder cases at the ICTY[1]

Anette Bringedal Houge

> If you were born in a country or at a time not only when nobody comes to kill your wife and your children, but also nobody comes to ask you to kill the wives and children of others, then render thanks to God and go in peace. But always keep this thought in mind: you might be luckier than I, but you're not a better person.
>
> (Littell, 2010: 20)

Jonathan Littell's controversial and award-winning novel, *The Kindly Ones*,[2] tells a story about World War II from the point of view of the former SS officer Max Aue, a fictional character. Over 900 pages in length, the book recounts the experiences of the main protagonist on the Eastern front and his participation in pogroms and mass executions and details for the readers what it was like, for him, to be part of the Nazi regime. In-between and alongside graphic descriptions of mass violence, Aue portrays himself, and comes forth, as an intellectual; he is cultured, holds a PhD in law and treasures classical music. The above quote from the very beginning of the book has stuck with me. Littell's initial and uncomfortable insistence that what Aue did, anyone could do, given the circumstances his protagonist lived and persisted under, directly and eloquently captures the essence of what scholars researching mass violence and war crimes have stated for decades: that perpetrators of mass violence are ordinary men under extraordinary circumstances (Browning, 1998; Drumbl, 2007).

However, as Littell's story progresses, Aue does not quite emerge as an average Joe; he is no ordinary man. Even more than his participation in and rationalization of the tasks he and his peers are put to, his personal life – including an incestuous relationship with and fantasies about his twin sister, a disturbed emotional life, him possibly murdering his parents – makes the book 'a study in the exoticism of evil', to quote one critical reviewer (Lasdun, 2009). This choice, to turn the storyteller into a character of major dispositional "traits", strongly contrasts the ordinary-man paradigm, or the influential banality-of-evil thesis posed by Hannah Arendt (2006) in her analysis of the Eichmann trial. In this respect, *The Kindly Ones* illustrates a paradox of international criminal prosecution, in particular in terms of the international criminal institutions' ambitions to provide accurate historical accounts of what happened, and to counter historical revisionism (see, e.g., Ewald, 2008): On the one hand we have the overall scholarly narrative of historical war crimes and mass violence that emphasizes the meaning of situational pressures and the collective nature of the crimes.[3] The experiments by Stanley Milgram (1974) and Philip Zimbardo (2008), respectively, illustrate these social processes well. On the other hand, the principle of individual criminal responsibility necessitates a focus on individual defendants however it may be that the offences the prosecution responds to are in part the result of extraordinary circumstances and premised by collective action. There is no recourse to collective guilt or responsibility in the legal sphere of individual prosecution. Furthermore, if extraordinary circumstances per se were allowed to alleviate guilt, few could ever be held responsible for crimes committed during wars and conflicts. In addition comes the selectivity that international criminal justice is bound by: Prosecutors cannot prosecute all perpetrators. They have to select whom to accuse and put on trial, whom they will use as symbols to state that there is no longer impunity for war crimes, crimes against humanity and genocide. As a result, international criminal justice primarily targets those "most responsible", which in international criminal justice lingo equals those with superior responsibility.[4] However, common foot soldiers have also been on the stand at the ICTY. In the case against Hazim Delić, the prosecutor rejected

> categorically that this tribunal should only be concerned with deterring superiors. To the contrary. It is crucial that all participants in a war, be they superior or common foot soldiers, understand that the laws of war mean something and that everyone can be held accountable for the crimes. To suggest that the conduct of individual soldiers or guards, all of whom have the power of life and death over others, may not be influenced, or it's not important to influence them is, in our view, fundamentally wrong and fundamentally against one of the reasons why this Tribunal was created.
>
> (15.10.1998, T. 16300)[5]

The laws of war and the international tribunals are there to distinguish between legitimate and illegitimate war violence, to prevent people at *all* levels from engaging in the latter and to hold accountable those who do not respect that distinction. But when "those on the ground" have been prosecuted, the prosecutors do not do so randomly. When prosecuting individuals at the lower levels of the chain of command, the prosecutors tend to select those "most notorious" for their involvement (Guariglia, 2012; Smeulers et al., 2013). Thus, the trials that this selection process result in are expected to not only focus on the worst offences, but also on individuals who distinguish themselves in the degree and form of their participation. This, in turn, lays the ground for prosecutors' dispositional narratives about the defendants. Defendants, too, may opt for dispositional narratives as a defence strategy or for mitigating purposes – arguing that dispositional personality traits limit their responsibility for the crimes they participated in.

Twenty years after the establishment of the ICTY, this paper explores the ways in which defendant perpetrators are constructed, explained and re-presented by primary actors in direct murder cases at the ICTY. What narratives about direct perpetrators of illegitimate killings does the individual-actor perspective of the court provide through its proceedings? It follows that the analysis is not about the individual perpetrators on the stand as such, but about what re-presentations of them court processes produce. The defendants in these cases have been finally convicted for their direct and active involvement in the lethal violence charged. "Primary actors", in turn, refers to prosecutors, defence counsels and judges at the ICTY.

The primary actors' re-presentations reproduce five typical narratives about defendant perpetrators in sexual war violence cases identified in Houge (2015). These narratives constitute two primary categories: one emphasizing dispositional re-presentations of the defendant and his motives for committing murder(s). The other category captures narratives that portray the defendant as an ordinary individual who either didn't commit the crimes charged or did so due to situational pressures or for reasons other than that held by the prosecution. As the analysis proceeds, I look particularly at how narratives about defendant perpetrators in direct murder cases compare with narratives about defendants in sexual war violence cases, and ask if illegitimate killing more easily lends itself to various forms of justification or neutralization narratives.

Background

The conflicts in the former Yugoslavia became infamous for sexual violence. The ICTY started operating in the midst of campaigns building a political and legal momentum for prosecuting sexual violence during conflict. In brevity, organized feminist campaigners, legal scholars and politicians managed to alter the age-old perception of sexual violence as an inevitable part of warfare against which nothing could (or should) be done to a conception of sexual violence that emphasized it as a serious crime that could and should be prosecuted and prevented (see, e.g., Engle, 2005). As a result, thirty individuals have been convicted at the ICTY for their involvement in sexual violence crimes, twelve of whom are direct perpetrators as here defined.[6] Important as these convictions are, widespread impunity remains the rule. According to conservative estimates, 20,000 women were raped during the period covered by the ICTY, in addition to an unknown number of men. These numbers explain the basis of the main slogan of activists and organizations in this field: "End impunity!"

In comparison, Zwierzchowski and Tabeau (2010) estimate that about 90,000 individuals were killed during the same conflict. This, too, is a conservative estimate, and the authors emphasize that the true death toll is probably closer to 105,000. These are directly war-related deaths, meaning both combat deaths and deaths that result from war-related violence committed outside of combat situations, such as mass executions and detainee killings. The authors estimate that 35–40 percent of the victims were civilians, whereas 60–65 percent were military personnel. This distribution, however, does not correspond to a measure of legal versus illegal lethal violence during the war (Zwierzchowski and Tabeau, 2010: 17). Not all civilians killed were unarmed or non-combatants, nor were all soldiers killed during combat or while armed. According to military sociologist David Grossman (2009: 197), 'the problem of distinguishing murder from killing in combat is extremely complex'. Whilst rape/sexual violence is never legal, killing may be.[7] Considering that only fifteen individuals have been finally convicted by the ICTY for their direct participation in murder(s), it is nevertheless safe to say that impunity is widespread also with regard to murder.[8] But aside from the massacre at Srebrenica, murder appears not to be as prevalent in the 'End Impunity' realm as is sexual violence. This may have many explanations, amongst them the commonsensical one that death is an expected and necessary part of warfare. Murder, although distinct from killing in legal terms, also has death as its result: comes war, comes death.[9]

Another explanation might be gendered. I follow Carpenter (2006: 88) in her argument that sexual violence is not the only gender-based offence in war: 'sex-selective violence' that targets men and boys is also gender-based – both in its purpose and in the ways we respond to them, because they rest on 'assumptions about male wartime roles [. . .] that both reflect and reproduce gendered hierarchies'. Much like sexual war violence, wartime killing in the former Yugoslavia was an overwhelmingly sex-selective offence. According to Zwierzchowski and Tabeau (2010: 17) 92 percent of the victims who were killed during the wars in the former Yugoslavia were men. As a category of war violence, neither sexual violence nor murder can be reduced to gendered explanations, nor can either be fully understood without such consideration. Men are targeted in wartime murders because their gender posits them as targetable – as potential combatants and representatives of the enemy. It is on this basis that I ask if illegitimate killing more easily lends itself to various forms of justification or neutralization narratives in courts' re-presentations of perpetrator defendants than do sexual war crimes.

Empirical material

The fifteen cases analyzed for this chapter were identified initially by screening the judgments of all the completed tribunal cases. The court files are publicly available[10] and consist primarily of verbatim transcripts of the proceedings,[11] plea agreements and factual bases, appeal briefs and judgments. It follows from my focus on cases that ended in convictions before the ICTY that the lethal violence forming the material origin in this paper constituted illegal acts, were charged as murders and sustained convictions as such. Not only were they illegitimate; in contrast to Grossman's focus on uncertainty in this regard, these murders were clearly so. None were committed during combat, all victims were unarmed. They were detainees, civilians, men, women, elderly and children. The victims were executed at close range, by firing squads, burned in barricaded houses, beaten to death (including by baseball bats, police truncheons and by pinning a metal badge to the victim's forehead) or stabbed. Accordingly, and importantly, this paper does not concern killing in war as such, or possible grey areas of murders/killings committed during combat – these deaths constituted clear violations of laws of war and conflict.

Table 6.1 Defendants convicted by the ICTY for direct participation in illegitimate lethal violence

Defendant	Case Number	Ethni-city[1]	Age at Time of Offence	Location	Individu-als Killed according to Final Judgment	Guilty Plea	Final Sentence
Bala, H.	IT-03–66	A	40	Lapušnik	9	–	13
Banović, P.	IT-02–65/1	BS	23	Prijedor	5	x	8
Bralo, M.	IT-95–17	C	25	Lašva Valley	5	x	20
Češić, R.	IT-95–10/1	BS	27	Brčko	10	x	18
Delić, H.	IT-96–21	BM	28	Konjic	1	–	18
Landžo, E.	IT-96–21	BM	19	Konjic	1	–	15
Erdemović, D.	IT-96–22	C	23	Srebrenica	70	x	5
Jelisić, G.	IT-95–10	BS	23	Brčko	13	x	40
Lukić, M.	IT-98–32/1	BS	25–6	Višegrad	>132	–	Life
Mrđa, D.	IT-02–59	BS	25	Prijedor	188	x	17
Nikolić, D.	IT-94–2	BS	35	Vlasenica	9	x	20
Sikirica, D.	IT-95–8	BS	28	Prijedor	1	x	15
Tadić, D.	IT-94–1	BS	37–8	Prijedor	2	–	20
Todorović, S.	IT-95–9/1	BS	34	Bosanski Šamac	1	x	10
Zigić, Z.	IT-98–30/1	BS	33	Prijedor	2 (+1)	–	25

Source: Developed by author
[1]Abbreviations: A = Albanian; BS = Bosnian Serb; C = Croat; BM = Bosnian Muslim

All the defendants were men, and the majority were Serbs, but all sides of the conflicts are represented. Nine were convicted following their guilty pleas. Their sentences ranged from five years to life. The youngest defendant was nineteen years old at the time of his offences, the oldest forty years old. Together, these defendants were found guilty of murdering at least 449 individuals – 390 of whom were killed at the hands of three defendants (Erdemović, Lukić and Mrđa). Three of the defendants were convicted for killing women specifically (Bralo, Jelisić and Lukić). Five of the defendants were explicitly also convicted for their direct participation in sexual violence (Bralo, Češić, Delić, Landžo and Todorović), two of whom were convicted for sexual violence against women (Bralo and Delić). The sexual violence was directed against other victims than those who were killed at the hands of the defendants.

I focus the analysis on closing arguments and sentencing discussions in oral proceedings and briefs submitted to the court. These are the parts of the court files and proceedings in which the counsels most explicitly portray the defendants and explain their involvement in murder – particularly when discussing the gravity of the offences and the claimed mitigating and aggravating circumstances. Importantly, the stories about the defendants and their offences that the primary actors present are constructed within a specific framework – the court – and for specific purposes: acquittals or convictions, which greatly influence the direction these stories take and the focus they have. Whatever truth they may entail, these are trial truths, situated within the court setting and in relation to the pressures and influences at work in this context (see Houge, 2015; Natapoff, 2005). The various narratives summarize the counsels' arguments and reflect their respective procedural strategies – drawing on the testimonies and evidence that most benefit their case. Yet, counsels also need to offer a logical narrative and to the best of their abilities present a story that the judges (and wider public) can find credible beyond a reasonable doubt. This type of sense making, although bound by legal parameters, is not constructed in isolation from extralegal social and cultural narratives about the type of crimes and perpetrators in question. It is both influenced by and influences collective memories and narratives about these historical events (Harris, 2001; Osiel, 2000).

Findings

The counsels re-presented the defendants in ways that could be grouped in two primary categories. One category consists of narratives that emphasize dispositional re-presentations of the defendant and his motives for committing murder(s) – either to ascribe guilt or aggravate the sentencing, or to mitigate. The other primary category captures narratives that portray the defendant as an ordinary individual who either didn't commit the crimes charged, or did so due to situational pressures or for reasons other than that held by the prosecution. The narratives reflect the counsels' explanations for the defendants' participation or non-participation in the charged murders and are constructed based on various explanations that were repeated across cases, and by different counsels. They are not mutually exclusive – rather, each counsel (particularly defence counsels) tends to present various narratives or re-presentations of the defendant that separately and together are intended to eliminate or alleviate guilt and mitigate sentences. The narrative re-presentations reproduce the five typical narratives about defendant perpetrators identified in a study of re-presentations of perpetrators in sexual war violence cases (Houge, 2015). This is not surprising as the legal framework provides counsels with a pre-scripted map with a limited set of trails to choose from and according to which they can argue their cases. Still, some differences emerge, and as the analysis proceeds, the content and implications that these differences entail will be elaborated.

Narratives about deviant defendants

The first category of narratives includes two different typical narratives that emphasize psychological traits of the defendants. The first is formulated by prosecution counsels and portrays the defendants as opportunist sadists. The second rests on psychiatric evaluations and expert witnesses who suggest that the defendant perpetrators have some sort of personality traits or disorders that reduce their responsibility and/or is used for mitigation purposes in sentencing.

Deviance as aggravating: narratives of opportunistic, sadistic pleasure

Most prosecutor narratives about the defendants evoke narratives of opportunist sadistic violence and pleasure. At the extreme end, prosecutors present war only as an opportunity and not as a cause in and of itself. Such was the case in the trial of Duško Tadić, the first case brought before the Tribunal. Tadić was the president of the local board of the Serbian Democratic Party and was convicted of killing two Muslim policemen by slitting their throats, as well as of his participation in offences at notorious camps in Prijedor. The prosecutor listed greed, jealousy, hatred and intolerance as reasons for his conduct (02.07.1997, T.9112). However in the sentencing brief, this is what it came down to: 'It was in the Omarska camp [. . .] that *the true nature* of Duško Tadić fully appeared. The crimes he is responsible for in that camp defy logic and demonstrate an evil that is beyond all boundaries of any civilized society' (09.07.1997: 12, my emphasis). War, in this narrative, is a situation that enables a latent characteristic of the defendant, rather than a context that creates this ability to inflict harm. This was also evident in the prosecutor's re-presentation of the defendant in the case against Jelisić, later echoed by the judges in sentencing. During the months of May and June in 1992, Goran Jelisić had a position of authority at the Serb-controlled Luka camp in Brčko, northeastern Bosnia. He introduced himself for detainees as the 'Serb Adolf' and killed detainees by shots to the neck after interrogations that included severe beatings (judgment, 14.12.1999: 32, 9–11). Jelisić was sentenced to forty years in prison by the ICTY following his guilty plea that included confessions to thirteen murders. According to the prosecution, 'Goran Jelisic was not just a willing executioner. He killed in unquestioning and happy obedience, to any instruction to kill, however minimally expressed. He killed as if for pleasure on his own initiative or on a whim' (25.11.1999, T. 3069). The prosecutor did not stop there:

> What is the relevant background of a man guilty of crime in time of war? Principally it is *the man himself.* He is his own background and he can draw little or no comfort from the wider background of war against which it must be remembered some suffer as victims, some behave innocently, some behave nobly.
>
> (25.11.1999, T. 3083–4, my emphasis)

The prosecutor did not object to the defence claim that the defendant had borderline personality disorder; to the contrary, the prosecutor emphasized his 'delusion of grandeur and narcissistic tendency' (25.11.1999: 3088, 3073). The judges also acknowledged the expert diagnosis, but like the prosecutor, they rejected it as a mitigating circumstance, stating that although his 'borderline, narcissistic and anti-social characteristics [. . .] speak in favor of psychiatric follow-up, the Trial Chamber concurs with the Prosecution and does not agree that [this] diminishes [his] criminal responsibility'.

Typical of these narratives, the defendants are re-presented as opportunists who ceased the opportunities provided by the chaos of war to commit crimes with impunity, be they ordered to do so or not. Češić, who confessed to ten murders and to having forced male detainees to perform fellatio on each other, was characterized by his 'extraordinary barbarity' and 'depravity' of mind by the judges. In the case against Delić, who was convicted for beating a man to death and on rape charges, the judges found 'the manner in which [his] crimes were committed [to be] indicative of a sadistic individual who, at times, displayed a total disregard for the sanctity of human life and dignity' (judgment, 16.11.1998: 433, see also Prosecutor, 15.10.1998, T. 16289). According to the prosecutor, he 'revelled in what he could do, and what he could do, he did' (31.08.1998, T. 15535). Similarly, Lukić, who was convicted for barricading people in houses and setting the buildings on fire, killing more than 130 civilians – men, women and children – was portrayed 'not [as] a victim of the "chaos" of war [. . .] but rather an opportunist who took advantage of an environment in which he could commit crimes against Muslims with impunity' (judgment, 20.07.2009: 326). A judge in the case against Nikolić commented in the midst of proceedings that the defendant 'seems to come out as a personally cruel person' (06.11.2003, T. 496), and in the judgment the judges stated that '[o]ne of the most chilling aspects of the Accused's behaviour was the enjoyment he derived from his acts' (18.12.2003: 48). The guilty pleas in some of these cases are presented by the prosecutors as part of bargains, entered for purely self-serving reasons – re-enforcing their portrayal of the defendant as someone with inherent, constant personality traits that explain their participation in war crimes. In these narratives, the defendants' psychological makeup renders any other explanations unnecessary. As Christie would say, 'the monster becomes his own explanation' (2008: 465, my translation).

Not only prosecutors emphasize defendants' personality characteristics. Defence counsels, too, opt for dispositional narratives as a defence strategy or for mitigating purposes – arguing that dispositional personality traits explain their violence and limit their responsibility for the crimes they participated in.

Deviance as mitigating: narratives of personality traits and disorders

Mental capability and personality traits are presented as mitigating arguments in several defence cases. These narratives are based on expert witnesses and evaluations of the defendants by psychologists and/or psychiatrists. The counsels do not claim that the charged crimes were not committed by the defendants, but deny in whole or in part that the defendants were responsible for their participation. Like the prosecutors' narratives, inherent characteristics of the defendant are emphasized. Expert opinions are used to explain how the defendants' dependent personality traits (Landžo, Todorović) made them vulnerable and particularly obedient to the orders and wishes of others. Banović's counsel argued that his less than average intelligence made him susceptible to believe and follow the propaganda and brainwashing that were so ubiquitous during the war. Although these narratives also underscore the war context and pressures, they argue that the extraordinary circumstances of the war had that effect on them, drew them 'into the maelstrom of violence' (Landžo, defence sentencing brief, 05.10.98: 9) and turned them into war criminals and murderers *because* of their inherent personality traits. As 'the opportunistic sadists' in the prosecutions' narratives, it is these traits that explain the gravity of their crimes, including severe beatings resulting in the death of unarmed detainees, pinning a metal badge to the forehead of a prisoner, and also sexual violence committed against detainees. To this, the prosecution counsels sometimes partly concede, as in the case against Landžo, where they responded, 'many persons, if not most persons, who commit horrific crimes, such as those committed by Mr. Landzo, have personality difficulties' (31.08.1998, T. 15536). However, the prosecution held, 'any explanation of why Mr. Landzo or any other criminal did what [he] did, be it dependency or narcissism or transferred aggression, may explain it, but it certainly doesn't excuse it or, in these circumstances, significantly reduce the appropriate punishment. [. . .] He did what he wanted to do' (15.10.1998, T. 16286). Landžo's case is the only one where personality traits were accepted as mitigating judgment. At the same time, however, the 'imaginative cruelty' and 'sadistic tendencies' that followed from these traits were considered aggravating (judgment, 16.11.1998: 434–438).

Both prosecutors' and defence counsels' representations of deviant defendants stand out in contrast to complete and partial denials and out-of-character narratives that in defence counsels' words portray the defendants as ordinary men. These are also the narratives where differences between primary actors' narratives in sexual war violence cases and murder cases emerge.

Ordinary men

The second primary category of narratives entails three different typical narratives that portray the defendant as ordinary men: Narratives of complete denials, narratives of partial denials (in which the act is accepted but the interpretation of and reason for it denied), and narratives of situational pressures, i.e., the ordinary man under extraordinary circumstances, introduced at the very beginning of the chapter.

'Truth is the first casualty in a war': narratives of complete denial

As their main strategy, the defence counsels of five defendants (Bala, Delić, Lukić,[12] Tadić and Zigić[13]) were in complete denial of any form of involvement by their client in the offences charged: the defendant wasn't there, he'd been misidentified at the scene, the offence didn't happen, the defendant didn't do it. 'Truth', as Delić's defence counsel put it, 'is the first casualty in a war' (31.08.1998, T. 15557). Lukić was portrayed as a scapegoat, an innocent man put on the stand for the want of real war criminals (19.05.2009, T.7192). Hence, much of the closing arguments were dedicated to discrediting witnesses and pointing out the inconsistencies in their testimonies. Both Lukić's and Tadić's counsels explicitly stated that their client was 'not a monster', not the monsters the prosecution portrayed them to be (*Lukić,* defence sentencing brief 13.05.2009: 3; *Tadić,* 04.07.1997, T. 9256). The defence counsels in both these cases implicitly asked the judges to consider what a war criminal looks like – just to point at their defendants and state that it certainly could not be like them. Lukić, according to his counsel, was 'a gregarious, smiling, social person' (19.05.2009, T. 7192). His defence continued:

> Before the war, Milan Lukic was a brother, a teenager, a student, a young man, a clown, a bartender; and when the powers turned on chaos, he became a police officer, a soldier, now a fugitive, and an accused war criminal. But he also became a father in that time. And I ask you, if you look in these photographs, do you see someone that could do exactly what they're saying?

Upon showing the court pictures of him when he was a child, his attorney stated, 'you would never, ever think that he would be an internationally accused war criminal' (19.05.2009, T. 7193). The counsel kept pounding this point in slightly different form – talking of how Lukić as a young student took the time to say hi to a witness in the case, a Muslim, asking again: 'Is that someone we would expect to be a future war criminal? Really?' (19.05.2009, T. 7196). This, of course, was not what the counsel's defence boiled down to – but it is noticeable that this was part of the argumentation at all. Perhaps the counsel was doing the best he could on the basis of the evidence against his client, arguing that such an amicable and ordinary man could not be guilty of extraordinary crimes. The judges, however, were not convinced and sentenced Lukić to life in prison. The Appeal chamber later confirmed the sentence. In the trial against Tadić, his counsel pointed out that the prosecution told 'a story of a man who like a fanatic, is involved in all kinds of atrocities, one after the other'. He continued, 'I wonder where that picture originated from. Is it the stereotypical bloodthirsty Serb as pictured so many times in war-crime stories by the other parties in the Bosnian conflict?' (26.11.1996, T. 8577–8578). During the sentencing hearings, his counsel indicated 'in particular his talent for art', before stating that 'artists are surely not prone to the commission of any grave offenses' (07.07.1997, T. 9244). He also drew attention to Tadić's upbringing, his well-regarded family, that he was a well-liked man in his town prior to the war, and that he used to have friends of all ethnic origins. The court, however, seemed to conclude that his entitled background rather supported the dispositional narrative of the prosecution:

> [T]he Defence portrays . . . Dusko Tadic [as] an intelligent, responsible and mature adult raised by his parents in a spirit of ethnic and religious tolerance and capable of compassion and sensitivity for his fellows. However, this, if anything, aggravates more than it mitigates[. F]or such a man to commit these crimes requires an even greater evil will on his part than that of a lesser man.
>
> (Judgment, 14.07.1997: 32)

The complete denials of the defence counsels do not attempt to explain or explain away the violence. They reject it. Still, these references to what a war criminal is expected to look and act like engage the dispositional narratives so often used by the prosecution in support of their case: war criminals, men guilty of such crimes that the prosecution targets, are hardly ordinary – they have identifiable personality and character traits that enable them and make them capable of committing such harm. It is not sufficient to point to the horrors of the crimes – these must also be reflected in the character of the individual defendant, or else he did not do it.

'Purely personal motives': narratives of partial denials

When defence counsels acknowledge the defendants' participation in lethal violence but offer a different interpretation of the act than the charges or the prosecution, I call these 'narratives of partial denials'. The sexual war violence cases analyzed in Houge (2015) offered two different kinds of narratives of partial denials. One emphasized the tactical purpose and necessity of the violence; the strategy – not sex or lust rationalization. The other constructed the sexual violence as personal – not political, as sex – not violence, and certainly not a part of the warfare. Noticeably, the first narrative concerned sexual violence committed against men, and the defence counsels stressed that there was no personal enjoyment involved – it was conducted as part of operating procedures or for tactical purposes. Some defendants claimed that the sexual violence functioned as a disciplining measure, while the harm of the offences was belittled. Češić, who was convicted by the ICTY also for forcing male detainees to perform fellatio on each other, explicitly argued that he did so to 'cause great humiliation and degradation', not 'to satisfy a sexual impulse' (08.10.2003, T. 83–84). Češić's defence counsel was concerned not to have his client convicted of rape. He was perhaps also concerned not to have his client come forth as an opportunistic sadist, which would aggravate his participation. Yet again, emphasizing the tactical motive of his sexual offences emphasized the offence as a deliberate criminal offence, which also aggravates the crime. In contrast, the second narrative concerned sexual violence directed against women, and emphasized precisely sexual urges as the cause of the offences. The sex-not-violence narrative employed in cases concerning sexual violence against women emphasized the personal motives and individualized the crime, which served the opposite purpose: disconnecting the offence from the overall conflict politics. I speculated whether these narratives could be understood in relation to a wider cultural, heteronormative narrative with which defence counsels' narratives could resonate, and according to which '[i]t is better to be re-presented as a simple sex offender than a war criminal when the victims are female, whereas it is the other way around when the victims are male' (Houge, 2015: 13).

When comparing re-presentations of defendant perpetrators killing unarmed detainees and defendants convicted for committing sexual violence, it seems as if there are available a wider repertoire from which to rationalize sexual offences. The first form of partial denial that emphasizes the violence as tactical on the part of the defendant was not found in the murder cases examined at all. The lethal violence was never argued to have been necessary to enforce control over unruly detainees or to state an example in terms of security. There were, however, some attempts at, if not belittling, at least suggesting that the crimes could have been worse. Češić's counsel argued as a mitigating circumstance that 'in almost all murder cases for which the accused [. . .] was [found] guilty, the victims did not suffer any additional suffering, pain, degradation or humiliation, since they were shot from firearms and thus instantly killed' (defence sentencing brief, 12.11.2003: 11). The court did not consider this a factor in mitigation. Mrđa was convicted upon his guilty plea for war crimes and crimes against humanity pertaining to his participation in a mass execution in which 200 men were killed. He was twenty-five years old at the time of his offence and was sentenced to seventeen years in prison. According to the plea agreement and judgment, he personally participated in the guarding, escorting and shooting of these men. All victims were first taken by bus to the execution spot, after which they were taken away in groups, ordered to kneel, and then shot and killed. In its sentencing brief, Mrđa's defence asked the court to consider 'whether [the crime was] the worst example of the offence likely to be encountered in practice' (13.10.2003: 6), at least implying that it could have been worse. The Trial Chamber responded in its judgment that the offence caused 'extraordinary suffering' that 'went beyond what is usually suffered by victims of murder and inhumane acts' (31.03.2004: 14).

The second partial denial – the personal, not political, narrative – was employed by the Lukić defence in its sentencing brief. They argued that the prosecution had failed to show that Lukić's alleged crimes 'were committed other than for purely personal motives, unrelated to the conflict' (13.05.2009: 19). Perhaps this most of all reflects a difficulty of providing sentencing arguments before the court has announced its finding of guilt or acquittal, because it contradicts the counsel's earlier insisting on Lukić being an amicable, ordinary man. Yet, it also suggests that the defence counsel considers it better to be sentenced on the basis of a dispositional narrative according to which the defendant acted opportunistically, than on a strategic narrative, according to which his crimes would be seen as part of a greater plan targeting victims for political purposes.

As stated, the defence counsels re-present their defendant in numerous ways. The different narrative turns overlap and interact. Order and duress narratives could have been categorized as partial denials, in the sense that they acknowledge the killing but partly or fully attempt to allocate guilt elsewhere than to the defendant. But as these re-presentations refer to different degrees of social pressures. I have grouped them together with so-called out-of-character re-presentations, as narratives of situational pressures. These re-presentations epitomize the notion of the ordinary man under extraordinary circumstances.

'Ordinary people put in extraordinary situations': narratives of situational pressures

Narratives of situational pressures are stories that re-present the defendant perpetrator as an ordinary man who committed lethal violence because of the extraordinary circumstances the war context constitutes. Contrary to defence counsels' narratives of personality traits and disorders that claim the war had such an effect on the defendant because of his psychological makeup, these narratives re-present the defendant as average Joes, and the war-specific circumstances as a sufficient explanation in and by itself.

Dragan Nikolić was the first to be indicted by the ICTY, in November 1994. He later pleaded guilty to, *inter alia*, beating nine detainees to death while he was the commander of a detention camp in eastern Bosnia and Herzegovina. His defence commented about his acts that 'you cannot mitigate easily dreadful things' (06.11.2003, T. 483) and conceded that '[h]e was for a relatively short period of time, 11 years ago, extraordinarily cruel' (06.11.2003, T. 497). This portrayal of the crimes of the defendant by his counsel is rare, also in guilty plea cases, as defence counsels tend to avoid descriptions of the offences and focus on the good deeds and character of the defendant.[14] According to the defence, Nikolić 'can now not understand what it was that caused him to commit those horrid acts. Nobody can' (06.11.2003, T. 485). The defence still attempts an explanation:

> The best that one can say is this, that there are examples throughout history where ordinary people are put in extraordinary situations. If they're not trained for it and they're not mature enough to cope with it and they have a dark side to their character, that's when the dark side of their character is going to come out, and it came out in Dragan Nikolic.
>
> (06.11.2003, T. 485)

The reference to Nikolić's dark side is perhaps indicating dispositional traits, but this is not a comment made for the purpose of mitigating or alleviating guilt – rather, it is based on a lack of better explanations. However, most of the narratives of situational pressures also include specific social pressures and orders in their explanations. The defence counsels in *Landžo, Jelisić, Mrđa* and *Češić* all argued as mitigating that their defendants were only following orders. As put forth by Češić's defence: '[T]he accused was pulling the trigger [but] others were taking aim' (defence sentencing brief, 12.11.2003: 11). In the proceedings against Miroslav Bralo, who according to his defence acted 'wholly uncharacteristically', situational pressures were central in sentencing arguments (sentencing brief, 25.11.2005: 4). Bralo voluntarily surrendered and pleaded guilty to five murders that he personally committed, including killing a woman with a knife, in addition to fourteen murders that he assisted. He also pleaded guilty to numerous rapes of a female detainee. His defence did not take issue with any of the aggravating factors but asked the court to take into consideration that he was following orders and that 'some value system collapsed' in him during the war (20.10.2005, T. 127), as well as the deteriorating political and military situation and the 'enormous pressures placed on many people of good character' (20.10.2005, T. 120). The prosecutor, and the court, accepted that Bralo acted as a useful tool to others but also found that 'there can [. . .] be little doubt that Bralo was a willing participant' and that he displayed a 'shocking disregard for the value of human life and dignity' (judgment 07.12.2005: 10, 19). The court emphasized how most citizens are subjected to severe pressures in times of war but that few respond in the way that this defendant did, echoing the prosecutor in *Jelisić* quoted above (see also *Češić* judgment 11.03.2004: 26–27). Unlike *Jelisić*, however, the prosecutor and the court in *Bralo* found the defendant to be genuinely remorseful and that he had 'embarked on a personal voyage of reconciliation and atonement' (prosecutor, 20.10.2005, T. 109) – suggesting that they did not see his crimes and cruelty as a reflection of constant, inherent personality traits.

At the extreme end of the various situational-pressure narratives comes the case of Dražen Erdemović. Erdemović voluntarily surrendered and revealed a mass execution site that the ICTY had no knowledge about. He estimated that he had personally shot and killed about 70 people during the massacre in which 1,200 men were killed. 'In this crime', argued his defence, 'the accused Erdemović is neither the creator, the ideologist, the one giving the orders, a religious-nationalistic fanatic nor a sadistic soldier, but above all a victim sowing victims, a mere "tool for killing" which has to kill in order not to be killed' (appellants brief, 14.04.1997: 18). He was simultaneously 'a victim of the whirlwind of war and the victim of his deed' (20.01.1996, T. 320). His counsel asked the court to consider if there were 'a worse way of using and abusing a man? Is there a graver punishment?' (20.01.1996, T. 336). In its appellant brief, his defence stated that 'his willingness to appear before this tribunal, to incriminate himself and to testify [is] the finest proof of his attempt to regain, as much as possible, *the human dignity he was forced to sacrifice in the act*' (14.04.1997: 17, my emphasis). In most sexual violence cases, prosecutors and judges portray dignity as something the defendant has deprived his victims of. For instance, the presiding judge in *Kunarac et al.* commented how rape victims, 'Muslims, women and girls, mothers and daughters together, [were] robbed of their last vestiges of human dignity' through the sexual violence (22.02.2001: 6559–6560). Erdemović's counsel, on the other hand, portrayed dignity as something Erdemović, the perpetrator, had lost through his actions. This comment opens up for a different conception of what dignity is, and whose it is to own, construct, give or take away, and maybe also tells us something about the ways we see victims of murder and victims of sexual violence differently. The prosecutor accepted that Erdemović was ordered to kill. Both the court and the prosecutor understood that the defendant followed these orders under threats. Interestingly, it was the prosecutor, not the defence, who raised that duress should be considered in mitigation (sentencing brief, 11.11.1996: 4). The judgment emphasized that 'he took no perverse pleasure from what he did' (29.11.1996: 21). Erdemović's is the only case in which the prosecution did not portray the defendant as someone who enjoyed killing or enthusiastically followed orders. Erdemović was eventually sentenced to five years in prison.

Discussion and conclusion

The archives of the ICTY constitute a seemingly endless source of empirical material pertaining to the international investigation, fact-finding, prosecution and judgment of war crimes committed during the wars in the former Yugoslavia.

This chapter has focused on a particular subset of cases at the trial end of these archives. I have explored how primary actors at the ICTY construct explanations for illegitimate lethal war violence from the individual actor perspective the court necessitates. At the outset, and in the defense counsels' narratives, perpetrators may be perceived as ordinary people put under extraordinary pressures, which aligns well with the dominant scholarly narrative about perpetrators of mass violence. But once prosecutors scratch the surface, another, and dispositional, narrative emerges: the crimes of the defendant are seen as evidence of a depraved mind, of the defendant being an opportunistic sadist, a development much like that of the protagonist in *The Kindly Ones* quoted in the beginning. And this, prosecutors argue, is important to acknowledge. As they state in the case against Delić and Landžo: 'It's a sad truth that people like Mr. Delic and Mr. Landzo exist everywhere' (31.08.1998, T. 15537). The prosecutors' dispositional narratives may serve as a necessary nuance to the narrative of the ordinary man under extraordinary circumstances. That is not to say that it challenges its general applicability. As stated early on, the defendant perpetrators in these court cases are not randomly selected from the universe of perpetrators out there. These re-presentations are intimately connected to the court context in which they were produced.

Early on I asked whether illegitimate killing more easily lends itself to various forms of justification or neutralization narratives than do sexual war violence, as war is a context in which particularly male death is expected, accepted and abounds and where killing is also legal under certain conditions. At the same time, sexual violence is a rather common violent offence in times of peace, hence it could just as well be argued that this constitutes the lesser breach of norms, also during war. Given the limited material, this part of the analysis is somewhat speculative in form. As a first note: most of the victims in these murder cases were men – and most defendants were convicted of killing men only. This was not considered an aggravating factor in light of the general targeting of men for murder in the conflict. In rape and sexual violence cases, women were portrayed as particularly vulnerable and particularly targeted with sexual violence. In one case, the court specifically stated that the sexual violence was committed 'solely against women' and that 'raping a person on the basis of sex or gender is a prohibited purpose for the offence of torture', which in turn aggravated the crime (judgment in *Radić,* 02.11.2005: 560). It is tempting to comment how victims' gender comprises an aggravating circumstance only when victims are female. Vulnerability, too, is a gendered construct.

Pertaining to defendant perpetrator re-presentations, I found that the defence counsels in sexual violence cases drew on a larger repertoire of neutralizing narratives. More specifically, they argue that sexual violence against men was not sexual but political or tactical, whereas sexual violence against women was presented as the acting out of urges, hence not related to politics; it was sex, not violence – seemingly drawing on resonating neutralizing narratives from peacetime discourses on sexual violence. It is noticeable in this regard, though, that none of the murder cases examined concerned battle-related deaths. Provided the killings had taken place in relation to battles or more ambiguous conditions, other neutralization narratives would probably emerge, e.g., pertaining to claims of self-defence. In sum, however, the defendant perpetrators are more or or less similarly re-presented – the rough typology of defendant perpetrators that was constructed in the counsels' respective narratives did not depend on the violence being lethal or sexual/ized. Although the argument of 'only following orders' figured more often in the murder cases, it was also present in sexual violence defence cases. Prosecution counsels relied heavily on re-presenting the defendant as an opportunistic sadist across cases – both where they argued the offences had a political motive and where they emphasized this particular aspect to a lesser degree. The ways we understand and construct wartime murder and sexual war violence within courts share common ground and may also feed and reflect the ways these offenses are understood and constructed outside of the courtroom. That is a relationship that needs to be explored. This chapter can be seen as the beginning of such an exploration.

Notes

1 I would like to thank Kjersti Lohne for constructive comments on a draft version of this chapter.
2 Originally written in French and published as *Les Bienveillantes* (in 2006).
3 As Drumbl (2007: 9) states, '[P]articipation in atrocity becomes a product of conformity and collective action, not delinquency and individual pathology.'
4 As opposed to US courts-martial, where criminal responsibility weighs heaviest on the direct perpetrators of a crime.
5 In the following, transcript pages from oral proceedings are indicated by a capitalized T. Written submission such as sentencing or closing briefs and judgments are specified as such.
6 See ICTY's webpage at www.icty.org/sid/10586 for an overview [last accessed 28.08.2015].
7 What constitutes the act of legitimate killing versus the act of illegitimate murder is regulated by three guiding principles: necessity, distinction and proportionality (see Walklate and McGross' contribution to this book).
8 The total number of final convictions at the Tribunal pertains to 80 individual defendants.
9 It is worth noting that just a few decades ago sexual violence was commonly perceived the same way.
10 ICTY redacted case records are available at http://icr.icty.org/default.aspx.
11 Confidential parts of proceedings and briefs were not available for analysis.
12 The closing briefs of both the defence and the prosecutor are largely confidential in Tadić's case.
13 Closing and sentencing briefs and arguments pertaining to Zigić's case are confidential.
14 Noticeably, Nikolić's lead counsel, Howard Morrisson, was later appointed as a judge at the Tribunal.

References

Arendt, H. (2006) *Eichmann in Jerusalem: A Report on the Banality of Evil.* New York: Penguin.
Browning, C. R. (1998) *Ordinary Men. Reserve Police Battalion 101 and the Final Solution in Poland.* New York: Harper Perennial.

Carpenter, R. C. (2006) Recognizing gender-based violence against civilian men and boys in conflict situations. *Security Dialogue,* 37: 83–103.

Christie, N. (2008) Serberleirene i Nord-Norge. Gjensyn med en studie av fangevokterne [Serb Camps in Northern Norway. Another look at a study of prison guards]. In Hagtvet, B. (ed.) *Folkemordenes svarte bok: Politisk massevold og systematiske menneskerettighets-brudd i det 20. århundre.* [The Black Book of Genocide: Political Mass Violence and Systematic Breaches of Human Rights in the 20th Century]. Oslo: Universitetsforlaget, pp. 461–468.

Drumbl, M. A. (2007) *Atrocity, Punishment, and International Law.* Cambridge: Cambridge University Press.

Engle, K. (2005) Feminism and its (dis)contents: Criminalizing wartime rape in Bosnia and Herzegovina. *American Journal of International Law*, 99: 778.

Ewald, U. (2008) "Reason" and "truth" in international criminal justice – a criminological perspective on the construction of evidence in international trials. In Smeulers, A. and Haveman, R. (eds.) *Supranational Criminology: Towards a Criminology of International Crimes.* Antwerp: Intersentia, pp. 399–432.

Grossman, D. (2009) *On Killing: The Psychological Cost of Learning to Kill in War and Society.* New York: Back Bay Books/Little, Brown and Co.

Guariglia, F. (2012) 'Those most responsible' versus international sex crimes: Competing prosecution themes?' In Bergsmo, M. (ed.) *Thematic Prosecution of International Sex Crimes.* Beijing: Torkel Opsahl Academic EPublisher, pp. 45–58.

Harris, S. (2001) Fragmented narratives and multiple tellers: Witness and defendant accounts in trials. *Discourse Studies,* 3: 53–74.

Houge, A. B. (2015) Re-presentations of defendant perpetrators in sexual war violence cases before international and military criminal courts. *British Journal of Criminology.* Online first. doi: 10.1093/bjc/azv065

Lasdun, J. (2009) The exoticism of evil: Review. *The Guardian,* 28 February. Available at www.theguardian.com/books/2009/feb/28/kindly-ones-review

Littell, J. (2010) *The Kindly Ones.* London: Harper Perennial.

Milgram, S. (1974) *Obedience to Authority: An Experimental View.* New York: Harper & Row.

Natapoff, A. (2005) Speechless: The silencing of criminal defendants. *New York University Law Review,* 80: 1449–1504.

Osiel, M. (2000) *Mass Atrocity, Collective Memory, and the Law.* New Brunswick, NJ: Transaction Publishers.

Smeulers, A., Hola, B. and van der Berg, T. (2013) Sixty-five years of international criminal justice: The facts and figures. *International Criminal Law Review,* 13: 7–41.

Zimbardo, P. G. (2008) *The Lucifer Effect: How Good People Turn Evil.* London: Rider.

Zwierzchowski, J. and Tabeau, E. (2010) *The 1992–95 War in Bosnia and Herzegovina: Census-Based Multiple System Estimation of Casualties' Undercount.* Hague: ICTY.

7 Lethal violence and legal ambiguities

Deaths in custody in Australia's offshore detention centres

Alison Gerard and Tracey A. Kerr

> Geopolitical squabbles between states over regional migration management have embodied effects.
>
> (Lloyd and Mountz, 2014: 33)

In this chapter, we critically examine a death in custody that illustrates the 'embodied effects' (Lloyd and Mountz, 2014: 33) of migration management in the Asia-Pacific region. On 17 February 2014, a twenty-three-year-old Iranian asylum seeker, Reza Barati, was murdered in an Australian-funded detention centre housing male asylum seekers on Manus Island, PNG. His death occurred during violent clashes that took place over three days between 16 and 18 February 2014. Witnesses to Reza Barati's death allege that he was beaten by up to ten people, including employees contracted to provide welfare and security services to the detention centre. The medical officer who attended to Reza Barati said his fatal injuries were consistent with a general beating that ultimately shattered the left side of his skull (Cornall Review, 2014: 64–65). Reza Barati had been sent to Manus Island as part of Australia's RRA, a migration management tool utilised by successive Australian governments to deter asylum seekers from arriving in Australia and seeking refugee protection. His death, allegedly at the hands of service providers funded and managed by the Australian government, gives rise to urgent questions about legal responsibility for lethal violence in offshore detention centres. In this chapter, we analyse how legal responsibility is constructed in official Australian government narratives regarding the death of Reza Barati. We note that even referring to Reza Barati's death as a 'death in custody' challenges official accounts of his death (Powell et al., 2013).

This chapter begins by examining the securitisation of migration – policies that have come to dominate not only Australia's approach to asylum seekers, but refugee policy internationally (Gerard, 2014; Huysmans, 2006; Pickering, 2011). Asylum seekers have become a vehicle for performances of sovereignty and, in particular, the sovereign power to exclude, contain and punish (Weber, 2007). Such policies have made travel more dangerous for asylum seekers and have enhanced the geo-strategic importance of offshore locations, particularly islands, in containing persons deemed to be security risks. Language has become a powerful tool in the securitisation of migration (Huysmans, 2006; Pickering, 2011). The Australian government's latest policy approach to asylum seekers, Operation Sovereign Borders (Hodge, 2015), has entrenched the criminalisation of asylum seekers, referring to those who arrive in Australia by boat as 'illegal maritime arrivals' and 'detainees'. To avoid such 'political loading' (Pickering, 2011: 4), throughout this chapter we will refer to those detained in Manus Island detention centre as 'asylum seekers', as the majority do apply for refugee protection. The detention centre on Manus Island is officially termed the 'Manus Island Regional Processing Centre' by the Australian government (Senate Report, 2014). We use the terminology 'Manus Island detention centre', as this is its primary function.

Legal ambiguities are intrinsic to offshore detention centre arrangements. These legal ambiguities produce major tensions for access to justice, clustered around refugee status determination, competition over the income generated from migration management and, as we analyse here, legal responsibility when lethal violence occurs. This chapter focuses on how the securitisation of migration, constructions of sovereignty, and gendered and racialised punishment operate to obscure legal responsibility for lethal violence in Australia's offshore detention centres and create zones of legal ambiguity. We draw from three sources of official Australian government representations of the death in custody of Reza Barati to investigate constructions of legal responsibility – first, media statements of then Minister of Immigration and Border Protection Scott Morrison in the immediate aftermath of the death in custody in Manus Island detention centre; second, the 'Review into the Events of 16–18 February 2014 at the Manus Regional Processing Centre' (Cornall Review, 2014) (hereinafter referred to as the Cornall Review), the inquiry commissioned by the Australian government in the wake of Barati's death; third, the Australian Senate report produced by the Legal and Constitutional Affairs Committee of the Australian Senate (Australian Senate, 2014) (hereinafter referred to as the Senate Report), which conducted an inquiry into the incidents at Manus Island detention centre between 16 and 18 February 2014. We identify representations of lethal violence within these documents that seek to responsibilise asylum seekers, further their criminalisation and contain state responsibility. We argue that constructions of sovereignty create an ambiguous legal zone driven by political arrangements that enable responsibility to be dispersed and, thereby, remain elusive.

The securitisation of migration, sovereignty and offshore detention

The challenge to sovereignty posed by globalisation has led governments to reassert power through the securitisation of migration (Sassen, 1996). Policies of the securitisation of migration have driven a resurgence in internal and external border controls that target certain populations, including asylum seekers (Gerard, 2014; Huysmans, 2006; Pickering, 2011; Sassen, 1996; Vecchio, 2015; Weber, 2013). These policies have, at their core, an assumption of cultural homogeneity amongst the existing population and a fear of the arrival of a 'racialised' other (Huysmans, 2006). These portrayals are often gendered. Women are depicted as a welfare burden and 'breeders of dependents' (Chang, 2000: 4), whilst Muslim men, in particular, are cast as having a 'primitive masculinity' (Khosravi, 2012).

Policies of the securitisation of migration have also cultivated the criminalisation of asylum seekers (Melossi, 2003). International legal frameworks of refugee protection, and the asylum seekers who rely upon them, are caught in conflict with the policies of the securitisation of migration. Asylum seekers and their methods of crossing international borders have been represented as illegal, notwithstanding refugee protections enshrined in international and domestic law, which stipulate that asylum seekers should not be punished for their method of arrival (Gerard, 2014). In what has been termed 'crimmigration' (Stumpf, 2006), many of the policies, practices and discourses of the securitisation of migration are based on criminal justice practices and represent the merging of immigration and criminal law (Gerard, 2014; Gerard and Pickering, 2013; Welch, 2011). The construction of asylum seekers as 'criminals' makes the application of criminal justice responses to irregular migration appear reasonable (Mountz, 2010). It also functions to distort and obscure the structural causes of mobility, such as violent conflict, transformations in gendered roles and responsibilities and the unequal distribution of wealth in the global economy (Grewcock, 2013; Wonders, 2007). Increased reliance on criminal justice practices has seen prison expansionism across the globe as places to manage 'at risk' groups, most directly in the proliferation of detention centres (Scraton and McCulloch, 2006). Detention centres have mushroomed as a key 'infrastructure of normalized crises' (Lloyd and Mountz, 2014: 32) and have become central to regional migration management agreements that administer refugee status determination offshore.

Australia's deterrence-based border control policies stand out as being particularly punitive (Grewcock, 2013; Weber and Pickering, 2011). Such policies include mandatory detention (in many cases including children), the excision of territory for the purposes of migration control, 'turn-backs' of boats and novel offshore detention arrangements in independent sovereign nations in the Pacific (Foster and Pobjoy, 2011; Weber, 2007). Australia's policies of colonisation are closely linked to the current treatment of asylum seekers as racialised 'others' (Perera, 2002). Indigenous Australians fought frontier violence and state intervention after the establishment of Australia as a British penal colony and are dramatically overrepresented amongst the prison population, particularly women (ABS, 2013; Scraton and McCulloch, 2006). Notions of the racial superiority of Europeans have been embedded within Australia's immigration policy since its independence from Britain. The 'White Australia' policy was introduced in 1901 to promote an ethnically homogenous 'white' Australia (Jupp, 1995). This legacy is reflected in current immigration policies.

The Australian government's asylum seeker policy has created new forms of neo-colonialism in the Asia-Pacific. Internationally, many countries are turning to forms of extraterritorial processing designed to deter and prevent asylum seekers from reaching their shores (Mountz, 2011a; Weber, 2007). Yet, Australia's fierce pursuit of offshore detention arrangements remains relatively unique. Australia has used its geopolitical influence to create an 'enforcement archipelago' in the region, enlisting countries that are enticed by the income from the securitisation of migration (Mountz, 2011a: 120). Australia has played an active role in establishing detention centres in Indonesia (Nethery et al., 2013). Australia has secured a resettlement arrangement with Cambodia after unsuccessful attempts with Timor-Leste and Malaysia (Grewcock, 2014; Hawley, 2015). The Australian government's flagship policy, the 'Pacific Solution', was established in 2001 by former prime minister John Howard to respond to an increase in boat arrivals, who were being portrayed within Australia as diseased, racialised and deviant (Pickering, 2001). The Pacific Solution involved creating an offshore detention centre on Manus Island and one in the Republic of Nauru. At the time, both countries had little experience with processing refugee protection claims and both systems attracted criticism for a lack of safeguards and poor access to legal representation (Foster and Pobjoy, 2011). These offshore detention centres were closed in 2008 by the incoming Rudd (Labor) government as part of an election promise (Evans, 2008). The reopening of offshore detention in 2012, 'Pacific Solution II' (Grewcock, 2014), came about after the Labor government, under new prime minister Julia Gillard, commissioned an expert panel to review solutions to the increase of asylum seekers' deaths at sea en route to Australia. The return to offshore processing was prioritised over increasing humanitarian settlement and other measures within the expert panel report (Pickering and Weber, 2014). The RRA, signed by the Australian and PNG governments in July 2013, dramatically changed asylum policy by refusing resettlement in Australia for asylum seekers who arrived by boat (Senate Report, 2014). Thus, the reliance on offshore detention centres rapidly increased.

Violence at the border

The securitisation of migration has narrowed safe pathways to cross international boundaries to seek refugee protection (Weber and Pickering, 2011). Close to 2,000 people have lost their lives at the Australian border since the start of this century, the majority from drowning (Australian Border Deaths Database, 2015). Thirty-five people have died in custody in Australia's onshore and offshore detention centres (Australian Border Deaths Database, 2015). Travel by sea is particularly dangerous for women, for whom exposure and dehydration are the major causes of fatalities at the border (Pickering and Cochrane, 2012). Violence short of fatality has been documented to include physical and emotional distress, particularly the strain of protracted periods in immigration detention (Steel and Silove, 2001). A recent report about conditions in the Australian-funded detention centre on Nauru found allegations of sexual and physical assault against asylum seekers, many of which went unreported (Moss, 2015).

Governments rarely prioritise accounting for fatalities that occur in the context of crossing borders. Internationally, several non-government organisations have responded to fill this void and make accounting for deaths at the border their mandate. Collecting data regarding deaths at a border presupposes a willingness to acknowledge the phenomena. It would be an acknowledgement that the subject of the inquiry is worthy of counting (Aas and Gundhus, 2015: 12; Weber and Pickering, 2011). In Australia, deaths that occur in immigration custody are not classified as deaths in custody for the purposes of official databases that record incidents of deaths in police and prison custody (Lyneham et al., 2010). These factors led Monash (2015) to establish the 'Australian Border Deaths Database'. Powell et al. (2013: 392) contend that isolating these fatalities from deaths in prison and police custody 'effectively "bureaucratises away" opportunities to consider the deaths of these non-citizens either as homicides or as deaths arising from the specific risks associated with illegalised travel or the ongoing condition of deportability'. They also disable the requirements of official oversight that are triggered when a death in prison or police custody occurs.

Reza Barati sought refugee protection in Australia, arriving by boat shortly after the RRA was signed on 24 July 2013. He was transferred to the Manus Island detention centre shortly thereafter (Laughland, 2014). Barati was part of a global movement of those displaced by conflict: recent figures from the UNHCR suggest that forced displacement is at its highest now since the post–World War II period (UNHCR, 2014). The extent to which this death was 'counted' or met with transparency and accountability mechanisms is visible through an analysis of how constructions of responsibility were narrated in the aftermath of Reza Barati's death in the detention centre on Manus Island.

Manus Island detention centre, Papua New Guinea

The Regional Resettlement Agreement returned Manus Island to the centre of Australia's border protection policies and provided a vital source of economic development for PNG. Papua New Guinea became independent from Australia in 1975 and is ranked 157 out of 187 countries on the United Nations Development Programme's Human Development Index (UNDP, 2013). Manus Island, located some 350 kilometres from the PNG mainland, is a former WWII air and naval staging point (Kneebone, 2006). The detention centre is said to provide valuable employment opportunities for local Papua New Guineans (Senate Report, 2014: 27). As part of the RRA, hundreds of millions of dollars of additional aid was committed for infrastructure improvements to hospitals, roads, policing and administration in order that PNG's immigration department could service Australia's offshore processing policy (Senate Report, 2014: 163).

There was considerable tension on Manus Island between locals and asylum seekers leading up to the death in custody of Reza Barati. Some asylum seekers had directed resentment at being sent to the island towards local PNG staff of the detention centre and engaged in racial abuse (Cornall Review, 2014: 28). Notwithstanding the promises of economic benefit, the establishment of the detention centre attracted criticism from locals on Manus Island (Cornall Review, 2014; Senate Report, 2014: 13). The rapid reopening of the detention centre meant a lack of consultation with the local population, and protests by locals ensued (Senate

Report, 2014: 13–14). Animosity towards the detention centre and its occupants centred around the comparatively better access to food and medical care, the plan to permanently resettle asylum seekers on the island and some environmental concerns (Cornall Review, 2014: 30; Senate Report, 2014: 53). After some initial protests from landowners, the PNG government placed a paramilitary police unit, known as the Mobile Squad, outside the detention centre to guard it from external threats. The Mobile Squad, funded by the Australian government, was heavily armed and inadequately trained (Senate Report, 2014: 20). In correspondence with the Australian DIBP prior to Reza Barati's death in custody, G4S, the global security company contracted by the detention centre, raised concerns about the Mobile Squad and in particular 'its propensity to use disproportionate force to maintain order' (Senate Report, 2014: 20). Some members of the Mobile Squad have been accused of involvement in the murder of Reza Barati.

Conditions for asylum seekers within the Manus Island detention centre have been characterised as hard and inhumane (Amnesty International, 2014a; UNHCR, 2013). Asylum seekers experienced difficulties contacting legal representatives and advocates. Australian lawyers, critical of offshore detention, have been expelled from Manus Island or refused entry, even when in the possession of court orders to enable them to see their clients (Amnesty International, 2014a: 11). A significant factor contributing to tensions amongst asylum seekers was the protracted legal uncertainties over refugee status determination. A clear process for refugee status determination was not in place, and claimants were left confused about their futures and how long they would remain within the detention centre (Cornall Review, 2014; Senate Report, 2014). A lack of activities, mental stimulation and learning opportunities exacerbated mental health issues amongst asylum seekers (Amnesty International, 2014a). Concerns have been raised over the lack of proper protection from the elements, including proper shade and ventilation. There is overcrowding and a lack of privacy and dignity (Amnesty International, 2014a). There has been insufficient access to clean water and hygienic food and issues of unhygienic conditions, including dirt, mould and unhygienic toilets (Amnesty International, 2014a). These issues have been blamed, together with the lack of prompt medical response, for the septicaemia that killed another Manus Island detention centre asylum seeker, Hamid Kehazaei, in September 2014 (Amnesty International, 2014b). Hamid Kehazaei died in Brisbane's Mater Hospital after being medically evacuated from the Manus Island detention centre. He had been one of the first asylum seekers transferred to the Manus Island detention centre from Australia and had been resident there for almost a year. As his death in custody took place on the Australian mainland, it will be the subject of a coronial inquiry (Bourke, 2014). At the time of writing the coronial inquiry had not yet occurred.

The punitive and gendered use of offshore detention is revealed in the reorganisation of the Manus Island detention centre as an all-male facility. When the Manus Island detention centre was reopened, the harsh conditions prompted questions about its suitability for children and families. Manus Island became a single adult male only detention centre from 15 June 2013, and all families and children were sent to Christmas Island or Nauru (Cornall Review, 2014: 22; Senate Report, 2014: 6). 'Vulnerable men' were also removed from the Manus Island detention centre at the same time. Those who remained were presumed to be physically and emotionally able to tolerate the difficult conditions. This gendered use of Manus Island is contrary to statements by the Australian Minister for Immigration and Border Protection (at the time of Barati's death) of the universal application of offshore detention policy:

> It doesn't matter how much education you've had, it doesn't matter whether you've come from Syria, Iran, Iraq, Afghanistan, anywhere else, it doesn't matter whether you're a child, it doesn't matter whether you're pregnant, it doesn't matter whether you're a woman, it doesn't matter whether you're an unaccompanied minor, it doesn't matter if you have a health condition, if you're fit enough to get on a boat then you can expect you're fit enough to end up in offshore processing.
>
> (Jabour, 2013)

In practice, only men were 'fit enough' to be sent to the Manus Island detention centre. The inherent assumption was that men were better placed to withstand the difficult conditions. G4S, the security provider at the time of the incidents, said that having families and children at the Manus Island detention centre was 'a moderating influence on the behaviour' of male asylum seekers, adding that the change to a single adult male only facility 'increased likelihood of tensions leading to violence' and presented additional security risks (Senate Report, 2014: 39). The facility on Manus Island was initially intended to detain 500 people, but when it changed to a single adult male facility and when the RRA was announced, it grew quickly and exponentially (Senate Report, 2014: 12). At the time of Reza Barati's death, there were 1,300 men detained at the Manus Island detention centre (Cornall Review, 2014: 3). Refugee status determination was uncertain, and so asylum seekers were left unsure of when they would leave the detention centre.

Reza Barati's death in custody

On 5 February 2014 asylum seekers asked for responses to a number of questions about their legal claims and status on the island. The answers provided, in a later meeting between Australian and PNG officials and asylum seekers on 16 February 2014, ruled out resettlement in Australia, detailed that there were no plans for resettlement in PNG in place and that refugee status determination would involve a long wait (Cornall Review, 2014; Senate Report, 2014). Asylum seekers were told repeatedly that they had the option of going home (Cornall Review, 2014: 36–39). No answers were provided about the status of their claims or when they might be resolved (Senate Report, 2014). Protests followed the meeting, during which time thirty asylum seekers briefly escaped (Cornall Review, 2014; Senate Report, 2014). In response, guards at the detention centre and locals physically attacked asylum seekers, causing physical injuries, including a man who had his throat slashed by a PNG local who was employed as a G4S guard (Cornall Review, 2014; Senate Report, 2014). After this incident, asylum seekers feared that they were going to be attacked by locals (Cornall Review, 2014; Senate Report, 2014).

Protests continued on the next day. On 17 February 2014, the Mobile Squad pushed down external gates and entered the detention centre (Cornall Review, 2014; Senate Report, 2014). When the Mobile Squad entered the detention centre, PNG nationals and expatriates, including some G4S employees, followed them in. Asylum seekers were attacked and beaten (Cornall Review, 2014; Senate Report, 2014). Multiple shots were fired by the heavily armed Mobile Squad; bullet holes from the shots were found at about chest height, contrary to the initial characterisation that they were merely 'warning shots' (Senate Report, 2014). Reza Barati had been in the detention centre's computer room when the gates were breached. When shots were fired, he headed towards his room, where multiple people, including locals, guards and expats, attacked him. A local Salvation Army employee allegedly hit Reza Barati on the head with a large stone (Cornall Review, 2014: 8; Senate Report, 2014). As a result, 'Mr Barati suffered a severe brain injury caused by a brutal beating by several assailants and died a few hours later' (Cornall Review, 2014: 7).

A criminal investigation into the death of Reza Barati was launched in PNG and is still ongoing. In August 2014, PNG police announced that they had arrested two suspects, both PNG nationals: a former Salvation Army worker and a former employee of the security firm G4S (Cochrane, 2014). Three additional men are still being sought in the investigation: one PNG national and two expatriates (Cochrane, 2014). There have been no arrests for any of the other assaults that occurred during the 16 to 18 February 2014 incidents (Senate Report, 2014). A PNG judge, Justice David Cannings, initiated an inquiry into the Manus Island detention centre after the incidents (Senate Report, 2014). After an initial visit to the Manus Island detention centre, accompanied by journalists, the inquiry was halted by PNG, reportedly with Australian involvement (Gordon, 2014). Concerns remain that some of the people who committed violence against asylum seekers are still working in the Manus Island detention centre (Amnesty International, 2014a; Cornall Review, 2014). In PNG, individual criminal responsibility for these deaths in custody has been pursued, with no convictions at the time of writing.

Zones of ambiguity and lethal violence: investigating deaths at the border in offshore detention

The importance of interrogating official accounts of deaths in custody and at the border is well established (Carlton, 2007; Scraton, 2002; Weber and Pickering, 2011). Official legal discourse produces 'formally sanctioned knowledge' (Scraton, 1999: 275) and systematises legal and administrative processes that confer legitimacy on the state (Carlen and Burton, 1979: 48). Scraton (1999: 275) highlights that 'not only does the state claim legitimacy for the operation and function of power, it proclaims and confers legitimacy on truth'. Weber and Pickering

(2011) have revealed the complex ways in which deaths at the border are discounted and neutralised. The textual analysis that we undertook here enables insight into how narratives about responsibility for lethal violence are constructed (Fairclough, 2013).

Across Australia, when a person dies in custody, coronial inquiries are the main avenue for public transparency and accountability (Freckleton and Ranson, 2006). As this death in custody occurred in PNG, Australian coroners had no jurisdiction. Therefore, we rely on three sources of official Australian accounts for our analysis of how narratives about legal responsibility for lethal violence are constructed: the media statements of the Minister of Immigration and Border Protection in the immediate aftermath of the incident; the Cornall Review (2014); and the Senate Report produced by the Legal and Constitutional Affairs Committee of the Australian Senate that conducted an inquiry into the incidents on the Manus Island detention centre on 16 to 18 February 2014 (Australian Senate, 2014). These texts illustrate how legal responsibility can be outsourced, constructed to criminalise asylum seekers and potentially be reclaimed.

Neoliberal personal responsibility and the criminalisation of asylum seekers

In the immediate aftermath of the death in custody of Reza Barati, the leading official Australian government narrative was to responsibilise asylum seekers for the violence that led to his death. In imputing blame and casting asylum seekers as responsible, this construction bears the hallmarks of neoliberalism. The narrative advanced in public statements by the former Minister for Immigration and Border Protection Scott Morrison at the time of the incident depicted asylum seekers as criminals engaging in risky behaviour for which they ought to be held personally responsible. He reported factually incorrect information to advance this claim. In his first media appearance following the death of Reza Barati, Minister Morrison offers the following explanation of the events that occurred in the Manus Island detention centre:

> [T]his was a very dangerous situation where people decided to protest in a very violent way and to take themselves outside the centre and place themselves at great risk. In those situations our security people need to undertake the tasks that they need to undertake to restore the facility to a place of safety, and equally those who are maintaining the safety of the security environment outside the centre need to use their powers and various accoutrements that they have available to them in order to restore in the way that is provided for under PNG law.
>
> (Hall, 2014)

This narrative recasts responsibility for the death of Reza Barati in powerful ways. Notions of neoliberal, personal responsibility are invoked to construct asylum seekers as being responsible for the violence that they experienced. This construction fits neatly with extant policies that criminalise asylum seekers (Innes, 2013). Asylum seekers are depicted as having protested violently, jeopardising their own safety by escaping the confines of the detention centre; a point later proved to be incorrect. In contrast, the behaviour of those charged with managing the centre is seen as measured and appropriate. The context that may have given rise to the protests is silenced. In responding to a question from the media about guaranteeing the future safety of asylum seekers at the detention centre, the minister continued to depict asylum seekers as violent and disorderly:

> I can guarantee [detainees'] safety when they remain in the centre and act co-operatively with those who are trying to provide them with support and accommodation. When people engage in violent acts and in disorderly behaviour and breach fences and get involved in that sort of behaviour and go to the other side of the fence, well they will be subject to law enforcement as applies in Papua New Guinea. But when people co-operate and conduct themselves appropriately within the centre then yes I can.
>
> (Senate Report, 2014: 109)

Here, very specific narratives about personal responsibility are voiced: asylum seekers who choose to leave the centre are behaving irrationally, in contrast to the rational behaviour of service providers. A great emphasis is placed on the assurance of safety for asylum seekers when they are within the confines of the detention centre. The act of absconding is reasonably equated with forgoing safety and sees the minister absolved of responsibility. Moreover, personal safety is distinguished from Papua New Guinean law enforcement. This statement by the minister is imbued with Orientalist assumptions about tolerated and even expected levels of violence (Said, 1978). Finally, the protests are seen as demonstrating a lack of gratitude on the part of asylum seekers towards their hosts. This characterisation constructs detention as a safe place where people protect and support asylum seekers. The implied message is that law enforcement cannot be held responsible for their treatment of people committing criminal acts, people seen as ungrateful and willingly forgoing their fundamental human rights.

Amongst other characterisations of state denial of human rights abuses, Cohen (2002: 4) talks of 'propaganda, disinformation, whitewash, manipulation and spin'. The official narrative that asylum seekers protested violently, leading to Reza Barati's death outside the detention centre, was allowed to permeate for over three days before the minister acknowledged that it could be untruthful. This delay enabled asylum seekers to be portrayed as criminal and chiefly responsible for the violence that they experienced. It also closed off the narrative that the detention centre itself was the site of extreme brutality; a narrative that eventually transpired as truthful. The minister issued a public statement late on the following Saturday evening, outside of the peak news cycle, correcting the record about the violence taking place within the detention centre (Morrison, 2014). The minister's choice of timing meant that the correction would have reached a smaller audience than his initial claims.

The Senate Report was critical of the minister's choice of narrative in his public statements and accused him of apportioning blame to asylum seekers. The Senate inquiry's terms of reference were broad and aimed to evaluate systemic issues (Senate Report, 2014: 1–3). The inquiry focused on what happened during the incident, including 'the sequence of events that led to, and the cause of, Reza Berati's death' (Senate Report, 2014: 1); the involvement and response of the DIBP, the PNG government and contractors; the conduct of the Minister for Immigration and Border Protection before and after the incident; refugee status determination processing and arrangements; and the Australian government's duty of care obligations (Senate Report, 2014: 1). Evidence was received by way of public submissions and public hearings. The Senate Committee members had the information from the Cornall Review and put questions directly to the DIBP and G4S during the public hearings (Senate Report, 2014: 179–188). The Senate Report found that

> [b]y giving the impression that events primarily occurred outside the centre, and that PNG police were not involved in the violence that occurred in the centre, the minister sought to unfairly apportion blame to the asylum seekers themselves for the violence that was done to them on the night of 17 February 2014.
>
> (Senate Report, 2014: 150)

The Senate Committee members heard evidence that the DIBP, headed by the minister, had knowledge that there were conflicting reports as to the parameters of the centre being breached on 18 February 2014, the morning after Reza Barati's death (Senate Report, 2014). Correct information that the violence, injuries and Mr Barati's death took place inside the detention centre had been confirmed early on the afternoon of 18 February 2014 (Senate Report, 2014). The minister's handling of public statements in the immediate aftermath of the death in custody of Reza Barati accords with 'spin' and 'misinformation' (Cohen, 2002). Despite the Senate Report later issuing a contrasting narrative of the events, the significant delay in correcting the official record further perpetuated the narrative that asylum seekers ought to be responsibilised for this death in custody and served to further their representation as ungrateful troublemakers and criminals.

Containing responsibility: individual criminal responsibility

The privileging of legal responses to incidents, such as criminal trials, often leads to a focus on individual accountability and retributive justice, rather than a structural appraisal of underlying causes and conditions that precede the incident (Bell et al., 2004). The Cornall Review gathered evidence by interviewing asylum seekers detained on Manus, including witnesses to Reza Barati's murder, and conducting group interviews. Feedback forms from individual asylum seekers were distributed and analysed (Cornall Review, 2014). Additionally, the Cornall Review (2014: 10) interviewed departmental and service provider staff and considered internal reports. The Cornall Review, whilst acknowledging that the wider context was key to preventing further issues in the Manus Island detention centre, privileged individual, criminal responsibility. This conclusion limited Australia's contribution to and responsibility for the lethal violence that took place. It wholly defers the matter to the PNG authorities to resolve.

The Cornall Review clearly identified that the protest events were caused, in part, by detainee uncertainty about their futures and Australian government policies (Cornall Review, 2014: 8–9) but stopped short of responsibilising the Australian government policies that led to this uncertainty:

> The responsibility for offences which caused death, injury, loss of personal property or property damage or any other breaches of PNG law lies with the offenders, including expats and transferees. Those matters should be investigated by the police, where appropriate, and prosecuted when the available evidence supports that course of action.
>
> (Cornall Review, 2014: 92)

Moreover, the recommendations are narrow and pertain primarily to how the PNG government can improve its processes and the new contractor managing the facility, Transfield, which also operates the detention centre on Nauru. Recommendations pertaining to the Australian government invite it to review risk management procedures, support Transfield to restore trust and cooperation with asylum seekers and improve communication with asylum seekers and the local population (Cornall Review, 2014: 9). Australia's policy of offshore detention is accepted as rational government policy and escapes further criticism. The Cornall Review does recommend that refugee status determination procedures in PNG be improved, but legal responsibility is primarily outsourced to the Papua New Guinean government to investigate.

Outsourcing responsibility: sovereign power and lethal violence

In contesting responsibility, narratives about sovereignty were heavily relied upon to abdicate the Australian government's responsibility for this death in custody. In establishing these offshore arrangements, the Australian government has effectively secured the 'cooperation of chains of actors who "translate" power from one locale to another' (Garland, 1997: 182). Asylum seekers' experiences of offshore detention shed light on how sovereign power operates to include and exclude (Mountz, 2011b: 386). In this case, the Australian government was able to use its sovereign power to exclude asylum seekers from accessing resettlement in Australia and to limit access to transparency and accountability for asylum seekers detained in offshore detention centres. The Cornall Review cultivates this narrative by deferring legal responsibility to PNG in the investigation of Reza Barati's death in an Australian-funded and -run detention centre, as well as to the Australian government's contention that the PNG government was in charge of and responsible for the Manus Island detention centre (Cornall Review, 2014: 9).

This perpetuates the idea that Australia is not in effective control of the detention centre. The notion of 'effective control' is significant in international law. If Australia is understood to be in 'effective control' of the detention centre on Manus Island, then it is responsible under Australian and international law for the human rights of asylum seekers in the centre. The Cornall Review recommends that Australia 'further and support' (Cornall Review, 2014: 12) Papua New Guinea's investigations into the events, so Cornall turned over copies of the transcripts of his interviews with asylum seekers and medical staff, and the feedback forms to PNG law enforcement authorities. During the Senate inquiry, the Department of Immigration and Border Protection expressed the view that Australia was not in effective control of the Manus Island detention centre, arguing that it was the PNG authorities that administer the detention centre. The Senate inquiry also heard alternative views from legal experts and academics (Taylor, 2010), who argued that several factors pointed to Australia being in effective control or, at least, jointly liable with PNG (Senate Report, 2014: 135–137). These factors included: the Australian government's management of the contracts for service providers at the centre; the funding provided by Australia for the centre's operations; and the fact that asylum seekers had arrived in Australia before being sent to Manus Island and were the only residents in the centre (Senate Report, 2014: 132–135).

The Senate inquiry was emphatic, in its recommendations, that Australia take responsibility for the events that took place on Manus Island and the conditions that led to the death in custody of Reza Barati. It recommended that the Australian government 'acknowledge and take responsibility for violations of human rights in relation to the incident at the Manus Island Regional Processing Centre from 16 to 18 February 2014' (Senate Report, 2014: 153). Part of its reasoning was that the violence was foreseeable and preventable if refugee status determination procedures were transparent (Senate Report, 2014: 145). The Senate Report recommended that the Australian government not only assist the PNG government in its criminal investigation, but 'ensure an adequate and effective investigation into the criminal assaults perpetrated' (Senate Report, 2014: 149), a more strongly worded recommendation than the Cornall Review. Its second recommendation was that 'the Australian Government acknowledge its responsibility to respect, protect and fulfil the human rights of individuals detained at the Manus Island Regional Processing Centre' (Senate Report, 2014: 151). In order to do so, it recommended providing 'compensation to those who have suffered human rights violations, including Reza Barati's family and asylum seekers who were injured during the incident' (Senate Report, 2014: 153). To further enhance accountability, it recommended that Australia and PNG allow appropriate access to the Manus Island detention centre for United Nations representatives, lawyers, the Australian Human Rights Commission and journalists (Senate Report, 2014: 154). It is not clear what lies beyond these recommendations in terms of how they will be achieved. It is clear that the political will to implement these recommendations is absent. The Australian government had several members on the committee who offered a dissenting view. They agreed to most of the recommendations in the report but disagreed that access to the centre was an issue for the Australian government and contested that any human rights violations had taken place (Senate Report, 2014: 162). In agreeing with the majority of the recommendations, the dissenting members were adamant to point out that many improvements had taken place and that the PNG government was responsible for improvements. The blurred and ambiguous legal matrix governing offshore detention ensures that tracing responsibility and developing legal remedies for the systemic violence that led to this death in custody remain elusive.

Dispersing responsibility: the ambiguous legal and political arrangements of offshore detention

Whilst the violence that took place on Manus Island that led to the death in custody of Reza Barati was arguably both foreseeable and, indeed, preventable, the legal and political arrangements of offshore detention have, so far, been insurmountable in achieving transparency and accountability. A lack of progress on resettlement has meant that more people have died on Manus Island than been resettled (HRW, 2015). This chapter has captured narratives from official accounts that serve to narrow the state's culpability for lethal violence. Neoliberal forms of personal responsibility are fostered, as are individual criminal responsibility and the outsourcing of legal responsibility to PNG. The Senate Report seeks to make Australia's immigration policies accountable and conducted a systematic inquiry of the type recommended in the aftermath of a death in immigration custody (Powell et al., 2013), but there is currently little political will to address these recommendations. The portrayal of asylum seekers as being criminals provides the imagery and ideology supporting the 'ready justification for the marginalization' of asylum seekers (Scraton and Chadwick, 1986: 220). The Australian government knew of the tinderbox created on Manus Island and the escalating, racialised tensions between asylum seekers and the local population. Australian policy towards asylum seekers creates not only an 'archipelago of exclusion' (Mountz, 2011a: 120), but also a zone of legal ambiguity with regard to responsibility for violence, even lethal violence. Asylum seekers are constructed as ultimately responsible for arriving in Australia outside of accepted legal pathways.

Zones of legal ambiguity are not confined to offshore detention centres. Internationally, attributing legal responsibility for deaths in custody, particularly those involving racialised victims, is a challenge often met with silence, delays or inaction (Athwal, 2015). This analysis aptly illustrates Weber and Pickering's (2011: 84) contention that accountability for systemic harms is plagued by the problem of 'the diffusion of responsibility'. In offshore detention, obligations are less clear than if asylum seekers were processed in Australia, but diffusion is increased by the lack of safeguards built into offshore and onshore detention arrangements when a death in custody occurs. The United Kingdom and the United States of America have more advanced accountability systems in this regard (Powell et al., 2013). In Canada and the United Kingdom, the same organisations are responsible for investigating deaths in detention and correctional settings. The Australian government has since sought to expand civil immunity to itself and its contractors for force used against asylum seekers detained in its detention centres (Farrell, 2015). This does not augur well for enhancing accountability mechanisms.

The legal ambiguities in offshore detention arrangements have ensured that the state, as well as individuals, have thus far avoided responsibility for the events that occurred between 16 and 18 February 2014 within and outside the Manus Island detention centre. Transfield is now the main service provider running the Nauru and Manus Island detention centres (Senate Report, 2014). The lack of significant change in the aftermath of this death in custody in offshore detention is arguably not unlike that which occurs in domestic deaths in custody across Australia. It is also not unlike the many deaths that occur in immigration custody across the globe. People die in similar circumstances all too often, with little access to justice. In deaths in custody both offshore and onshore, official inquiries present themselves as offering resolutions that fail to provide lasting change.

Reza Barati fled violence in his home country of Iran, only to experience brutal violence in an Australian-funded detention centre. This chapter aims to foster his memory and to urge governments to make the journey to seek refugee protection safer for men, women and children.

References

Aas, K. F. and Gundhus, H. (2015) Policing humanitarian borderlands: Frontex, human rights and the precariousness of life. *British Journal of Criminology*, 55: 1–18.
Amnesty International. (2014a) Australia: This is still breaking people: Update on human rights violations at Australia's asylum seeker processing centre on Manus Island. Papua New Guinea. Available from: www.amnesty.org/en/library/info/ASA12/002/2014/en
Amnesty International. (2014b) Urgent independent review needed into another asylum seeker tragedy. Available from: www.amnesty.org.au/news/comments/35476
Athwal, H. (2015) 'I don't have a life to live': Deaths and UK detention. *Race and Class*, 56(3): 50–68.
Australian Bureau of Statistics. (2013) Women prisoners increasing at a faster rate than men. Available from: www.abs.gov.au/AUSSTATS/abs@.nsf/mediareleasesbyRelease Date/1F2BD14CF87EE4AFCA25751B001AC5FA?OpenDocument
Australian Senate (Legal and Constitutional Affairs References Committee). (2014) Incident at the Manus Island detention centre from 16 February to 18 February 2014. Available from: www.aph.gov.au/Parliamentary_Business/Committees/Senate/Legal_ and_Constitutional_Affairs/Manus_Island/~/media/Committees/Senate/committee/ legcon_ctte/Manus_Island/Report/report.pdf
Bell, C., Campbell, C. and Aolain, F. (2004) Justice discourses in transition. *Social and Legal Studies*, 13: 305–328.
Bourke, L. (2014) Hamid Kehazaei treated as death in custody. *Sydney Morning Herald*, 8 September. Available from: www.smh.com.au/federal-politics/political-news/hamid-kehazaei-treated-as-death-in-custody-20140908-10dse7.html
Carlen, P. and Burton, F. (1979) *Official Discourse: On Discourse Analysis, Government Publications and Ideology*, Abingdon: Routledge.
Carlton, B. (2007) *Imprisoning Resistance: Life and Death in an Australian Supermax.* Sydney: Sydney Institute of Criminology.
Chang, G. (2000) *Disposable Domestics: Immigrant Women Workers in the Global Economy.* New York: South End Press.

Cochrane, L. (2014) 'Manus Island riot: Papua New Guinea police charge two men over Reza Barati's death, search for wanted expats'. *ABC News*. Available from: www.abc.net.au/news/2014-08-19/two-men-charged-over-reza-barati%27s-death-on-manus-is/5681882 (accessed 5 April 2015).

Cohen, S. (2002) *States of Denial: Knowing about Atrocities and Suffering*. Cambridge: Polity Press.

Cornall Review. (2014) *Report to the Secretary, Department of Immigration and Border Protection: Review into the Events of 16-18 February 2014 at the Manus Regional Processing Centre*, Canberra. Available from: www.immi.gov.au/about/dept-info/_files/review-robert-cornall.pdf

Evans, C. (2008) *Refugee Policy under the Rudd Government – the First Year*. Sydney: Refugee Council of Australia.

Fairclough, N. (2013) *Critical Discourse Analysis: The Critical Study of Language*. Abingdon: Routledge.

Farrell, P. (2015) Government seeks immunity over use of force in immigration detention. *The Guardian*, 8 April. Available from: www.theguardian.com/australia-news/2015/apr/08/government-seeks-immunity-over-use-of-force-in-immigration-detention?CMP=soc_567

Foster, M. and Pobjoy, J. (2011) A failed case of legal exceptionalism? Refugee status determination in Australia's 'excised' territory. *International Journal of Refugee Law*, 23: 583–631.

Freckelton, I. and Ranson, D. (2006) *Death Investigation and the Coroner's Inquest*. Melbourne: Oxford University Press.

Garland, D. (1997) 'Governmentality' and the problem of crime: Foucault, criminology, sociology. *Theoretical Criminology*, 1: 173–214.

Gerard, A. (2014) *The Securitisation of Migration and Refugee Women*. Abingdon: Routledge.

Gerard, A. and Pickering, S. (2013) Crimmigration: Criminal justice, refugee protection and the securitisation of migration. In Bersot, H. and Arrigo, B. (eds.) *The Routledge Handbook of International Crime and Justice Studies*. Abingdon: Routledge, pp. 587–611.

Gordon, M. (2014) Abbott and O'Neill agree : No human rights inquiry for Manus Island. *Sydney Morning Herald*, 23 March. Available from: www.smh.com.au/federal-politics/political-news/abbott-and-oneill-agree-no-human-rights-inquiry-for-manus-island-20140322-35a6e.html

Grewcock, M. (2013) Australia's ongoing border wars. *Race & Class*, 54: 10–32.

Grewcock, M. (2014) Australian border policing: Regional 'solutions' and neocolonialism. *Race & Class*, 55: 71–78.

Hall, B. (2014) Scott Morrison admits information he gave on Manus riot was wrong. *Sydney Morning Herald*, 22 February. Available from: www.smh.com.au/federal-politics/political-news/scott-morrison-admits-information-he-gave-on-manus-riot-was-wrong-20140222-339hs.html

Hawley, S. (2015) Cambodia refugee resettlement: Asylum seeker deal a step closer as international organisation for migration agrees to oversee transfer from Nauru. Available from: www.abc.net.au/news/2015-01-20/deal-to-transfer-asylum-seekers-from-nauru-to-cambodia-closer/6026604

Hodge, P. (2015) A grievable life? The criminalisation and securing of asylum seeker bodies in the 'violent frames' of Australia's Operation Sovereign Borders. *Geoforum*, 58: 122–131.

HRW. (2015) Australia/Papua New Guinea: The Pacific non-solution. *News, Human Rights Watch*, 15 July. Available from: www.hrw.org/news/2015/07/15/australia/papua-new-guinea-pacific-non-solution

Huysmans, J. (2006) *The Politics of Insecurity – Fear, Migration and Asylum in the EU.* London: Routledge.

Innes, A. J. (2013) International migration as criminal behaviour: Shifting responsibility to the migrant in Mexico–US border crossings. *Global Society*, 27: 237–260.

Jabour, B. (2013) Asylum seekers: Scott Morrison orders review of mother-baby separation. *The Guardian*, 15 November. Available from: www.theguardian.com/world/2013/nov/15/morrison-orders-review-of-mother-baby-separation

Jupp, J. (1995) From 'White Australia' to 'Part of Asia': Recent shifts in Australian immigration policy towards the region. *International Migration Review*, 29: 207–228.

Khosravi, S. (2012) White masks/Muslim names: Immigrants and name-changing in Sweden. *Race & Class*, 53: 65–80.

Kneebone, S. (2006) The Pacific plan: The provision of 'effective protection'? *International Journal of Refugee Law,* 18: 696–721.

Laughland, O. (2014) Manus violence: Dead asylum seeker named as Iranian Reza Barati, 23. *The Guardian*, 21 February. Available from: www.theguardian.com/world/2014/feb/21/manus-dead-asylum-seeker-iranian-reza-berati

Lloyd, J. and Mountz, A. (2014) Managing migration, scaling sovereignty on islands. *Island Studies Journal*, 9: 23–42.

Lyneham, M., Larsen, J. and Beacroft, L. (2010) *Deaths in Custody in Australia: National Deaths in Custody Program 2008.* Canberra: Australian Institute of Criminology.

Melossi, D. (2003) 'In a peaceful life': Migration and the crime of modernity in Europe/Italy. *Punishment and Society*, 5: 371–397.

Monash University. (2015) Australian border deaths database. Available from: http://artsonline.monash.edu.au/thebordercrossingobservatory/publications/australian-border-deaths-database/

Morrison (2014) The Hon Scott Morrison MP, Minister for Immigration and Border Protection, 'Manus Island Update', Media release, 22 February, available from: www.minister.immi.gov.au/media/sm/2014/sm212031.htm (accessed 4 April 2015).

Moss, P. (2015) *Review into recent allegations relating to conditions and circumstances at the Regional Processing Centre in Nauru,* Canberra. Available from: www.immi.gov.au/about/dept-info/_files/review-conditions-circumstances-nauru.pdf (accessed 6 February).

Mountz, A. (2010) *Seeking Asylum: Human Smuggling and Bureaucracy at the Border.* Minneapolis: University of Minnesota Press.

Mountz, A. (2011a) The enforcement archipelago: Detention, haunting, and asylum on islands. *Political Geography*, 30: 118–128.

Mountz, A. (2011b) Where asylum-seekers wait: Feminist counter-topographies of sites between states. *Gender, Place & Culture*, 18: 381–399.

Nethery, A., Rafferty-Brown, B. and Taylor, S. (2013) Exporting detention: Australia-funded immigration detention in Indonesia. *Journal of Refugee Studies*, 26: 88–109.

Perera, S. (2002) What is a camp . . . ? *Borderlands E-Journal*, 1: 1.

Pickering S. (2001) Common sense and original deviancy: News discourse and asylum seekers in Australia. *Journal of Refugee Studies*, 14: 169–186.

Pickering, S. (2011) *Women, Violence and Borders.* London: Springer.

Pickering, S. and Cochrane, B. (2012) Irregular border-crossing deaths and gender: Where, how and why women die crossing borders. *Theoretical Criminology*, 17(1): 27–28.

Pickering, S. and Weber, L. (2014) New deterrence scripts in Australia's rejuvenated offshore detention regime for asylum seekers. *Law & Social Inquiry*, 39(4): 1006–1026.

Powell, R., Weber, L. and Pickering, S. (2013) Counting and accounting for deaths in Australian immigration custody. *Homicide Studies*, 17: 391–417.

Said, E. (1978) *Orientalism*. New York: Vintage Books.

Sassen, S. (1996) *Soverignty in an Age of Globalisation*. New York: Columbia University Press.

Scraton, P. (1999) Policing with contempt: The degrading of truth and denial of justice in the aftermath of the Hillsborough disaster. *Journal of Law and Society*, 26: 273–297.

Scraton, P. (2002) Lost lives, hidden voices: 'Truth' and controversial deaths. *Race & Class*, 44: 107–118.

Scraton, P. and Chadwick, K. (1986) Speaking ill of the dead: Institutionalised responses to deaths in custody. *Journal of Law and Society*, 13: 93–115.

Scraton, P. and McCulloch, J. (2006) Introduction: Deaths in custody and detention. *Social Justice*, 33: 1–14.

Senate Report. (2014) *The Australian Senate Legal and Constitutional Affairs References Committee, 2014. Incident at the Manus Island Detention Centre from 16 February to 18 February 2014*, Canberra. Available from: www.aph.gov.au/~/media/Committees/Senate/committee/legcon_ctte/Manus_Island/Report/report.pdf

Steel, Z. and Silove, D. (2001) The mental health implications of detaining asylum seekers. *Medical Journal of Australia*, 175: 596.

Stumpf, J. P. (2006) The crimmigration crisis: Immigrants, crime and sovereign power. *Bepress Legal Repository*. Available from: http://law.bepress.com/expresso/eps/1635

Taylor, S. (2010) Australian funded care and maintenance of asylum seekers in Indonesia and PNG: All care but no responsibility? *University of New South Wales Law Journal*, 33: 337.

UNDP. (2013) UNDP human development reports. Available from: http://hdr.undp.org/en/content/table-1-human-development-index-and-its-components

UNHCR. (2013) *UNHCR Monitoring Visit to Manus Island, Papua New Guinea 23 to 25 October 2013*. Canberra: United Nations High Commissioner for Refugees.

UNHCR. (2014) World refugee day: Global forced displacement tops 50 million for the first time in post–World War II era. Available from: www.unhcr.org/53a155bc6.html

Vecchio, F. (2015) *Asylum Seeking and the Global City*. Abingdon: Routledge.

Weber, L. (2007) Policing the virtual border: Punitive preemption in Australian offshore migration control. *Social Justice*, 34: 77–93.

Weber, L. (2013) *Policing Non-Citizens*. London: Routledge.

Weber, L. and Pickering, S. (2011) *Globalization and Borders: Death at the Global Frontier*. London: Palgrave.

Welch, M. (2011) The sonics of crimmigration in Australia: Wall of noise and quiet manoeuvring. *British Journal of Criminology*, 52: 324–344.

Wonders, N. (2007) Globalisation, border reconstruction projects and transnational crime. *Social Justice*, 34: 33–47.

8 Attributing criminal responsibility for workplace fatalities and deaths in custody

Corporate manslaughter in Britain and Ireland

David M. Doyle and Joe McGrath[1]

This chapter examines the divergent means of imposing criminal responsibility for corporate manslaughter in two comparable common law jurisdictions: Ireland and England and Wales. First, it explores the methodological limitations of gauging the true extent of work-related fatalities in both jurisdictions and investigates, insofar as is possible, the interplay between gender and workplace deaths across selected member states of the European Union. Secondly, the chapter traces the development of the law of corporate manslaughter from the imposition of corporate criminal liability via the common law 'identification doctrine' to the proposals for law reform in Ireland and the introduction of a direct corporate liability homicide offence in the UK. Thirdly, the chapter accepts the challenge set by Jeremy Horder to take 'the intellectual leap out of the Marxist moral-political rut in which corporate manslaughter scholarship has largely been stuck' and explores a provision of the Corporate Manslaughter and Corporate Homicide Act 2007, which has been neglected by criminologists and criminal law scholars – the application of the legislation to deaths in custody – an aspect of the Act, which was unsurprisingly very controversial at the time (Horder, 2012: 116). Building on the literature that examines the applicability of the 2007 legislation to National Health Service Trusts (Horder, 2012) and to the police (Griffin and Moran, 2010), this chapter opens up this area of inquiry in a context where it has hitherto been unexplored and investigates the potential liability of HMPS as an organisational body in light of the statute.

Work-related fatalities in comparative perspective

Homicide (whether murder, manslaughter or infanticide) is one class of violent crime where the contemporary police figures in Ireland and the UK are considered to provide a reasonably accurate count (Office for National Statistics, 2015: 27). As Ian O'Donnell observes, it would be wholly exceptional for an unlawful death not to be thoroughly investigated or not to be contained in the official figures (O'Donnell, 2002). The limitations of crime statistics more generally have been well documented, but the interpretation of workplace fatality statistics is also laden with methodological difficulties (Almond, 2013: 11–14). Although work-related fatalities do not appear to be subject to the same underreporting issues as non-fatal accidents in the workplace, it can be stated with some confidence that the true extent of work-related deaths is not reflected in the official statistics. For instance, deaths resulting from work-related road traffic collisions and long-term occupational illnesses such as cancer are excluded from the fatality statistics in Ireland and the UK (Drummond, 2007, 2008; HSE, 2015). Attributing chronic ill-nesses and deaths to occupational exposure is almost impossible given the genu-ine difficulties with case identification – 'disease processes are often complex, multi-causal and can have a long latency period' (Russell et al., 2015: 21) – but work-related road traffic deaths are also difficult to quantify due to limitations in data collection systems (Drummond, 2007: 6). This is so even though a growing body of literature indicates that road traffic fatalities contribute significantly to, and in certain common law jurisdictions, comprise the largest single category of work-related injury deaths (25). It thus seems reasonable to surmise that the range of work-related deaths that come to the attention of the Health and Safety Execu-tive (Britain) and Health and Safety Authority (Ireland) provide only 'a consistent record of a subset of work-related injuries and deaths' (Russell et al., 2015: 21).

Yet despite these limitations, the 'official' figures reveal that there are almost as many workplace deaths as homicides in Ireland annually (Kilcommins et al., 2004: 130). 'Sadly', as the Chief Executive of the Irish Health and Safety Author-ity pointed out, 'there were 48 work-related deaths in 2012' (HSA, 2013: 3), while there were sixty cases of murder and manslaughter in the same year. This, of course, is not to suggest that all workplace deaths can be attributed to employers breaking the law, but it does appear that Irish citizens are almost as likely to be 'wounded or killed at work, sometimes because their employer has broken the law, than they are to be attacked and harmed by a stranger' (Kilcommins et al., 2004: 130). Furthermore, while at least there is some possibility that such an assailant may be detected and prosecuted, '[there] has never been a prosecution of a corporate entity for manslaughter in Ireland' (LRC, 2005: 4). At the time of writ-ing, there is still no corporate manslaughter legislation on the Irish statute book, although the Law Reform Commission (LRC) has recommended its introduction (Carolan, 2011: 157–174), and the latest of a series of private members' bills was introduced in the Seanad in June 2013. By contrast, an entirely new homicide offence that can *only* be committed by organisations was enacted in the UK in 2007. This direct corporate liability homicide offence marked the abandonment of the identification principle as the method of attributing liability to companies and organisations that may now be held criminally responsible for 'unlawful homi-cide where previously there was no unlawful homicide and no homicide offence committed by anyone' (Ormerod and Taylor, 2008: 591). The UK is not the only jurisdiction to create a specific homicide offence for corporations that cause death – the Australian Capital Territory (ACT) introduced an offence of this type in 2003 – but the legislative act of passing an offence into law does not necessarily mean that the provision will be implemented in practice (Almond, 2013: 35–37).

There were, for instance, only six offences of corporate manslaughter recorded in England and Wales in the four-year period after the legislation came into force in April 2008 (Office for National Statistics, 2013). This chasm is particularly apparent when the police statistics are juxtaposed to workplace fatality statistics. To put it otherwise, there were 114 fatal injuries in the workplace between March 2011 and April 2012, but there were only two corporate manslaughter offences recorded in the same twelve-month period (Office for National Statistics, 2013). By contrast, there were almost five times as many homicides in the UK as deaths in the workplace (550 and 114, respectively), although it would appear to be stretching credulity to suggest that only two of these work-related fatalities were the outcome of gross negligence or blatant law breaking.

The examination of national data comparability on accidents at work also poses serious methodological challenges (Brenner and Hopkins, 2006: 10–12). International comparisons are fraught with difficulty due to differences in definitions of workplace accidents and reporting systems *inter alia*, but some basic insights can be attained from the ESAW collected by the Statistical Office of the EU, Eurostat (HSE, 2015: 7–8). Similar to the steady overall reduction in work-related deaths across the EU, the reports of the HSA and the HSE illustrate that there has been a downward trend in the rate of work-related fatality in Ireland and the UK in the period 1998–2013, although the decline has become somewhat less pronounced in the UK in more recent years (HSE, 2015: 2; Russell et al., 2015: 72). Yet despite the decrease in the number of reported workplace fatalities between 1998 and 2013, Ireland had the eighth highest workplace fatality rate in the EU15 countries in 2012, with more than twice the UK rate of workplace fatalities per 100,000 workers (Eurostat, 2012). The standardised fatality incidence rates in 2012 vary significantly among the EU15 civil law jurisdictions ranging between 0.72 in the Netherlands and 2.71 in Portugal. Other civil law jurisdictions, such as Sweden (0.80), Germany (0.90) and Denmark (1.18), also have low fatality rates, while the Irish rate (1.43) remains relatively stable, hovering just above the national EU15 average. By contrast, the standardised incidence rate for the UK (0.58 per 100,000) was considerably lower than the corresponding EU15 rate (1.3) and that of many other EU member states, including Italy (1.29), Spain (1.99) and France (2.64). Table 8.1 shows the latest standardised rates of fatal accidents at work published by Eurostat.

What is also clear from the Eurostat data is that there is a strong gender difference in the standardised fatality incidence rates. The 2012 statistics reveal that the risk of fatal accidents is quite unequal between males and females across the EU15 countries and that the female fatality rate is relatively low (0.12 per 100,000 workers in 2012) compared with the male fatality rate (2.02 per 100,000 workers). All told, there were 1,402 fatal accidents recorded in the EU15 countries in 2012, 48 of which were female fatalities. It is evident, therefore, from this succinct analysis that the problem of (reported) workplace fatalities in the EU15 countries is predominantly a male one, with the available statistical evidence revealing that women were less likely than men to die at work. Of course, this disparity between the sexes is partially explained by 'employment patterns within occupations and industries', but it does appear that this is not a uniquely European trend (Hoskins, 2005: 37; BLS, 1994–2013).

Table 8.1 Standardised incidence rates of fatal accidents at work in the EU15 countries, 2012

EU15 Countries	Total Rate (number)	Men Rate (number)	Women Rate (number)
United Kingdom	0.58 (85)	0.88 (83)	2 (0.05)
Netherlands	0.72 (26)	1.09 (26)	0.0 (0)
Sweden	0.8 (21)	1.12 (20)	0.18 (1)
Germany	0.9 (258)	1.45 (247)	0.1 (11)
Denmark	1.18 (20)	1.85 (20)	0.0 (0)
Greece	1.2 (18)	1.88 (18)	0.0 (0)
Italy	1.29 (237)	1.98 (233)	0.07 (4)
Ireland	1.43 (18)	2.19 (18)	0.0 (0)
Belgium	1.46 (30)	2.27 (30)	0.0 (0)
Finland	1.62 (23)	2.55 (22)	0.13 (1)
Spain	1.99 (168)	3.18 (165)	0.1 (3)
Austria	2.37 (51)	3.91 (51)	0.0 (0)
France	2.64 (350)	4.05 (328)	0.4 (22)
Portugal	2.71 (91)	4.36 (88)	0.28 (3)
Luxembourg	2.91 (6)	4.57 (6)	0.0 (0)
EU15	**1.3 (1402)**	**2.02 (1355)**	**0.13 (47)**

Attributing corporate criminal responsibility in Britain and Ireland

Although there is an increasing clamour to criminalise organisations that are in some way responsible for workplace deaths, the criminal law was 'developed with flesh-and-blood human beings in mind', so offences, and serious offences in particular, generally require both an illegal conduct element (*actus reus*) and a 'guilty mind' element (*mens rea*) (Gobert, 2008b: 61). As companies do not have minds of their own, the law has struggled to find coherent, consistent and fair methods to ascribe fault to companies (Gobert, 1994: 393; Wells, 2001: 86–99). Criminal liability may, however, be imposed via the identification doctrine, where a sufficiently senior manager, the 'directing mind and will' of the company, has perpetrated the crime or bears responsibility for the crime. In *Lennard's Carrying Co. Ltd v Asiatic Petroleum Co. Ltd* ([1915] AC 705: 713), a case concerning civil liability under statute for goods lost at sea, Lord Haldane LC noted the difficulties of locating a 'directing mind' in a company, stating 'its active and directing will must consequently be sought in the person of somebody who for some purposes may be called an agent, but who is really the directing mind and will of the corporation, the very ego and centre of the personality of the corporation'. In *HL Bolton (Engineering) Co. Ltd v TJ Graham & Sons Ltd* ([1957] 1 QB 159), concerning a statutory entitlement to renew a lease, Lord Denning developed the basis for the doctrine by analogising the company with a human. He noted (172) that servants and agents are merely the hands of the company, but the directors and managers are the brains of the company, 'who represent the directing mind and will of the company, and control what it does. The state of mind of these managers is the state of mind of the company and is treated by the law as such'.

These dicta were subsequently cited in *Tesco v Nattrass* ([1972] AC 153), a prosecution for false advertising. Lord Diplock (199) noted that the company itself may set out who acts as the directing mind and will of the company in its memorandum of association, through the actions of its board of directors or through its shareholders at the general meeting. Viscount Dilhorne (187) stated that such a person or persons would have 'actual control' of the company or some of its actions, though exactly who constitutes the directing mind and will of a company would naturally vary from company to company. Lord Reid (171) noted that these persons include the directors, the managing director, and senior officers of the company who 'carry out the functions of management and speak and act as the company' but that this would generally exclude 'subordinate' officers because 'they carry out orders from above and it can make no difference that they are given some measure of discretion'.

The identification doctrine has been successfully invoked to prosecute small companies or 'one-man' companies, where the actions of the company are easy to associate with the manager. For example, in *R v Kite and OLL Ltd* ([1996] 2 Cr. App. R.(S.) 295), a small company with an uncomplicated management system was convicted of the deaths of four school children who drowned in a canoeing accident because its managing director knew the safety systems in place were inadequate (McShee, 2008: 12). Similarly, in *R v Jackson Transport (Osset) Ltd* (Health and Safety Bulletin, November 1996), the one-director company was convicted of manslaughter because it had not provided equipment and training to an employee who died when sprayed with toxic chemicals while cleaning a tanker. It has, however, been more difficult to successfully prosecute larger companies, with more complex systems for organising responsibility (Sealy and Worthington, 2010: 145).

In *R v P&O Ferries* ([1991] 93 Cr. App. R. 72), the company was acquitted of corporate manslaughter when one of its ferries capsized while sailing with its doors open, killing 193 people, because none of the other natural defendants facing manslaughter charges could be identified as the controlling mind and will of the company. This was the case despite a previous inquiry conducted by Sheen J which concluded, 'all concerned in the management, from the members of the Board of Directors down to the junior superintendents, were guilty of fault in that all must be regarded as sharing responsibility for the failure of management. From top to bottom the body corporate was infected by the disease of sloppiness' (Department of Transport, 1987: 14). Similarly, in *Attorney-General's Reference (No 2 of 1999)* ([2000] 2 Cr. App. R. 207), a large company employing 2,700 people was prosecuted for manslaughter when a high-speed train and a freight train collided, killing 7 passengers. The company had allowed the trains to operate with the safety systems turned off but it was acquitted because no specific 'directing mind' could be found liable for manslaughter.

Convictions for manslaughter against large companies are hard to achieve because their organisational structures, their internal lines of decision making and accountability, the geographical scope of their operations and the nature, volume and complexity of their transactions can all give rise to ambiguities such that responsibility can become diffused and fragmented throughout these organisations (Minkes and Minkes, 2008; Wolgast, 1992). In large corporations, for example, senior managers cannot be involved in all aspects of the daily business of the company, so they set policies that are implemented by lower-level officers. This can mean that 'the subordinate has worked out all the details of the boss's predetermined solution, without the boss being specifically aware of all the eggs that have to be broken', a solution that 'relieves superiors of too much knowledge, particularly guilty knowledge' (Jackall, 1988: 20). This may insulate managers from the criminal actions of subordinates, so that 'a business inevitability is converted into a legal defence' (Gobert, 1994: 401).

As regards the Irish jurisprudence, Horan (2011: 30) notes that 'there is an absence of comprehensive judicial scrutiny in this jurisdiction on the identification doctrine', though there are a number of civil cases which identify the actions of corporations with their senior officers. In *R v Justices of County Cork* ([1906] 2 IR 415), concerning an application for a beer-dealing licence by Beamish & Crawford Ltd, it was suggested that the acts, omissions and reputation of the company could be inferred through that of its management. In *Taylor v Smith* ([1991] 1 IR 142: 166), a case concerning whether a company could commit conspiracy with its 'sole controlling agent and mind of the company', McCarthy J cited with approval Viscount Haldane LC in *Lennard's*, noting that the company acts through natural persons that are the directing mind and will of the company. In *Superwood Holdings plc v Sun Alliance and London Insurance plc* [1995] 3 IR 303), the Supreme Court determined that a company could potentially be civilly liable for insurance fraud where it was possible to identify that the directing mind and will of the company was responsible for it. While noting Ussher's (1986: 38) warning that 'attempts to relate parts of an organisation to corresponding parts of the human body was a medieval pastime', Denham J (330) cited and accepted the directing mind test in *Lennard's Carrying Co. Ltd*, noting that 'the appropriate test is to apply the essential principle expounded by Lord Haldane to an Irish company in a practical manner and determine who was in control of the relevant issue'. In *Howard v Irish Life & Permanent* ([2006] IEHC 419), a case concerning an order for costs sought by the Revenue Commissioners, the case law on the identification test is not cited, but O'Sullivan J appeared to accept the principle, stating, 'it would be unfair if, for example, knowledge in the possession of an employee of a branch of the respondents were to be imputed in the present context to the respondent itself in the absence of any evidence that this knowledge constituted the directing mind and will of the respondent'.

Drawing these threads together, the current status of the identification doctrine in criminal cases is unclear in Ireland. Horan (2011: 33) cautions, 'the decisions in *Howard*, *Superwood* and *Taylor* were not concerned with criminal liability and accordingly these precedents are not necessarily authorities in support of the identification doctrine in the context of corporate criminal liability nor do they preclude the option of the attribution doctrine'. Nevertheless, it is of note that the identification doctrine has been endorsed in civil cases in Ireland, and a number of English authorities seem to indicate that the doctrine is applied in criminal and civil law in the same way because it 'has been developed with, no divergence of approach, in both civil and criminal jurisdictions, the authorities being cited indifferently in the other' (*El Ajou v Dollar Land Holdings plc* [1994] 2 All ER 685; *Meridian Global Funds Management Asia Ltd v Securities Commission* [1995] 2 AC 500).

More recently, in *Meridian Global Funds Management Asia Ltd v Securities Commission* ([1995] 2 AC 500), the Privy Council seems to have taken a broader approach to attributing criminal liability to companies in a case concerning the failure to register the purchase of securities as required by statute in New Zealand. The Court of Appeal determined that the rules by which acts are attributed to companies, the rules of attribution, are determined by the specifics of the companies' constitutions, the rules implied by company law, the rules of agency and vicarious liability. However, these rules may not always provide comprehensive instructions, so the court 'must fashion a special rule of attribution for the particular substantive rule . . . [to determine] whose act (or knowledge or state of mind) was for this purpose intended to count as the act etc. of the company' (507). The court concluded that the purpose of the substantive rule in this instance was to ensure immediate disclosure, in fast-moving markets, of the identities of those buying large volumes of shares in public issuers. In order to prevent the law being frustrated, the court could infer intention to the company from the person authorised to perform the transaction, even if he was not the directing mind and will of the corporation. Otherwise the company would not have to report these transactions until senior management were aware of them, and that 'would place a premium on the board paying as little attention as possible to what its investment managers were doing' (511).

This broader approach, which has proven popular in other common law jurisdictions (Forlin and Smail, 2013: 502), was sharply circumscribed in *Re Attorney General's Reference (No. 2 of 1999)* ([2000] 2 Cr. App. R. 207). The Court of Appeal determined that the identification doctrine was the only appropriate test for ascribing criminal liability for gross negligent manslaughter to companies. The directing mind and will of the company had to have been grossly criminally negligent as a pre-condition to criminal liability. Rose LJ (211) explained that the identification theory 'was developed in order to avoid injustice: it would bring the law into disrepute if every act and state of mind of an individual employee was attributed to a company which was entirely blameless'. The broader approach taken in *Meridian*, when it was required, was only appropriate for statutory offences that would otherwise be frustrated, and identification remained the appropriate doctrine for ascribing liability for common law offences. This was the view of the court despite the fact that the identification doctrine was originally developed to address statutory offences (Gobert and Punch, 2003: 69).

Similarly, in *St. Regis Paper Co. Ltd v The Crown* ([2012] 1 Cr. App. R. 14), a prosecution for filing false environmental pollution reports, the Court of Appeal applied the stricter identification doctrine detailed in *Tesco*. It determined that it was not necessary to relax the approach in *Tesco* in order to avoid 'emasculating' the legislation, noting that the company had already been convicted on fourteen counts of strict liability offences (184). Moses LJ (185) determined that the 'conventional approach' was to apply *Tesco* and ask whether the technical and environmental manager was 'in actual control of the operations of the company in relation to the submission of records and not responsible to another person for the manner in which he discharged his duties in the sense of being under that other person's orders'. As this manager reported to numerous layers of management above him and acted in defiance of the company's clear environmental policy standards, the court determined that he did not fall 'within the category described by Viscount Dilhorne as someone who was in actual control of the operations of a company or part of them and not responsible to another person in the company for the manner in which they were discharged' (185).

It is difficult to state with complete certainty whether it is the identification principle in *Tesco* or the attribution principle in *Meridian* that ought to apply, not only because *Meridian* may only apply to statutory offences, but also because its application seems to turn on the statute being interpreted (Ashworth, 2009: 150). The impact of the wider *Meridian* approach in Ireland is also still unclear, though it has been referenced briefly in a number of Irish cases. In *Crofter Properties Ltd v Genport Ltd* ([2002] IEHC 26), McCracken J cites the rules of attribution detailed by Hoffman LJ in *Meridian*, and although the parties seemed to accept them, the Court did not actually consider the issue in further detail. In *Fyffes v DCC* ([2009] 2 IR 417), a civil action for insider dealing, Laffoy J cited Viscount Haldane LC in *Lennard's* and noted that it was applied by the Supreme Court in *Superwood*. She further cited Hoffman in *Meridian*, noting that in cases where the application of the directing mind and will test would defeat the purpose of the substantive rule, the court could fashion special rules attributing intent to companies. However, specific statutory provisions determined the attribution of liability in this case, so *Meridian* was not applied.

Gross negligence manslaughter

Companies cannot form subjective intent or be subject to the mandatory life sentence in prison, so companies cannot commit the offence of murder in English and Irish law (Wells, 2001: 109; LRC, 2003: 89–90). By contrast, companies may commit gross negligence manslaughter at common law. The House of Lords laid down the test for gross negligence manslaughter in *R v Adomako* ([1995] 1 AC 171). In that case, an anesthetist did not notice that the tube from a ventilator became dislodged during eye surgery causing the patient to have a cardiac arrest and die. Lord Mackay determined that the jury could make a determination of gross negligence manslaughter where the defendant had breached his duty of care and that breach had caused the loss of life, provided that the breach amounted to gross negligence. In making that determination, the jury would have to consider the extent to which his conduct departed from the proper standard of care, given all the circumstances in which he found himself at the time. In *R v Misra and Srivastava* ([2004] EWCA Crim 2375), where a patient died when he was not treated for an infection following routine knee surgery, the Court of Appeal subsequently determined that this test did not breach Article 7 of the European Convention of Human Rights (ECHR) for lack of certainty.

The Irish courts have also considered cases of gross negligence manslaughter resulting in deaths by actions or omissions. In *DPP v Dunleavy* ([1948] IR 95), the Court of Criminal Appeal laid down the test for gross negligence manslaughter. In that case, a taxi driver killed a cyclist when he was driving on the wrong side of the road with his headlights switched off at night. Davitt J in the Court of Criminal Appeal, while noting that manslaughter by negligence is difficult to precisely and concisely define for all circumstances, stated that the test is whether the accused fails to observe standards thought objectively necessary in the circumstances, where the negligent act results in death and the fatal negligence was of a very high degree involving the risk or likelihood of substantial personal injury to others. This test was subsequently endorsed and applied in *The People (DPP) v Cullagh* (unreported, Court of Criminal Appeal, 15 March 1999), a case in which a child was killed when a rusty cable holding a chairoplane at a funfair snapped. More recently, noting that this offence was not unconstitutional for vagueness, Charleton J in *Joel v DPP* ([2012] IEHC 295) reiterated, 'criminally negligent manslaughter arises where the death of another person is caused in circumstances which objectively amount to a very high degree of negligence and which, in the circumstances in question, to any reasonable person the fact that a serious risk was unjustifiably taken with the life of another would be apparent'.

Despite a clearly articulated test for gross negligence manslaughter, there is no record of a successful prosecution being taken against companies for this offence in Ireland. Identifying this as a lacuna in the law, the Law Reform Commission recommended the introduction of a new statutory offence of corporate manslaughter, based on the common law offence of manslaughter by gross negligence, formulated around a breach of duty as set out in *Dunleavy* (LRC, 2005: 15–19). The offence would apply to all 'undertakings', where this means 'a person being a body corporate or an unincorporated body of persons engaged in the production, supply or distribution of goods or, the provision of a service whether carried on for profit or not' (116). It sets out a restructured version of the identification doctrine to address the 'paradox of size', whereby the doctrine operates to 'disproportionately affect small organisations where the controlling mind is easy to identify' (29). The actions of 'high managerial agents', including directors, managers and other similar officers or persons who purport to act as such, are considered in determining whether there has been a breach of duty, but they do not have to be the directing mind and will of the corporation. The court may also have regard to a wide variety of factors, including the regulatory environment in which the entity is operating. Companies convicted of this offence may be subject to an unlimited fine, determined by the court. High managerial agents may be subject to accessorial liability for 'grossly negligent manslaughter causing death' if the company has already been so convicted. These agents may be subject to an unlimited fine, a period of disqualification as the court sees fit and imprisonment of up to 12 years. Though an attempt was made to pass a version of this bill in 2007, this effort lapsed. Reflecting on the failure to pass legislation in this area,

McGrath (2015: 117) observes, 'this was a period of talk, inquiry, investigation and consciousness-raising but often not of action or change. The need to address corporate wrongdoing was beginning to enter the consciousness of legislators and citizens alike but the efforts to act on these sentiments lacked commitment'.

By contrast, though its introduction was also significantly delayed, the Corporate Manslaughter and Corporate Homicide Act was enacted in the UK in 2007 (Gobert, 2008a). Despite its title, however, the offence can be committed not only by public and private companies, but also by unincorporated organisations, including government departments and public bodies, as specified in Schedule 1 to the Act. The legislation specifically provides that a duty of care is owed to anyone who is detained at a 'custodial institution' (CMCHA, s2(7)). Most of the legislation entered into force on the 6 April 2008, although the custody provisions were not effective until 1 September 2011 to allow the relevant organisations to prepare for their application (SI 2011/1867). The Act abolishes the existing common law offence of gross negligence manslaughter for companies and although individuals cannot be held liable under the Act, they remain subject to the common law on manslaughter and health and safety law. A relevant organisation is guilty of the new offence 'if the way in which its activities are managed or organised (a) causes a person's death, and (b) amounts to a gross breach of a relevant duty of care owed by the organisation to the deceased' (CMCHA, ss. 1(1)(a) and 1(1)(b)). By looking at the organisation as a whole, rather than a particular layer of management, 'the old limitations of the identification doctrine are gone. . . . It will now be possible to examine the shortcomings of a wide variety of individuals within the organisation to prove a failure of management by the organisation' (Ormerod and Taylor, 2008: 602). However, the offence can be committed 'only if the way in which its activities are managed or organised by its senior management is a substantial element in the breach' (CMCHA, ss. 1(3)), a construction that does not make the actions of the non-senior managers irrelevant, provided they do not render the senior managers' actions less than substantial (Ormerod and Taylor, 2008: 604). The breach is gross 'if the conduct alleged to amount to a breach of that duty falls far below what can reasonably be expected of the organisation in the circumstances' (CMCHA, s. 1(4)(b)). People are involved in 'senior management' if they 'play significant roles in (i) the making of decisions about how the whole or a substantial part of its activities are to be managed or organised, or (ii) the actual managing or organising of the whole or a substantial part of those activities' (s.1(4)(c)). As such, the legislation implements a 'qualified aggregation principle' because it characterises 'the [company's] management failure as the aggregate of those (groups of) individuals' failures; and (2) because whilst the failures might be found in and aggregated from a variety of places within the company, there is a proviso or qualification that failures must include to an appropriate (substantial) extent, failure or failures by senior management' (Ormerod and Taylor, 2008: 594–595). The mechanism for attributing liability is therefore broader than that of the identification doctrine. An individual natural person, as a directing mind and will of the company, does not need to be found criminally liable for the death in question in order for the company to be held criminally responsible. The organisations can be punished by unlimited fines, remedial orders and adverse publicity orders (CMCHA, ss. 1(6), 9, and 10).

The enforcement of the legislation has, however, been limited and uneven. Field and Jones (2013: 239–246) note that 'the Government's Regulatory Impact Assessment projected that the Act will not generate more than 10 to 13 successful prosecutions per annum, despite the fact there are on average 196 workers per year fatally injured in the United Kingdom'. In fact, however, only six cases had concluded by late 2014, and all offenders were small companies, despite the fact that the legislation was designed to make it easier to prosecute large companies with more complex organisational structures (Field and Jones, 2014: 158). Just one of these involved the successful prosecution of a company for the death of a non-worker in circumstances where an eleven-year-old girl was struck by a ski-boat (*R. v Prince's Sporting Club Ltd*, unreported 22 November 2013 (Crown Ct (Southwark)). Moreover, there was merely one trial (the other five corporate offenders had pleaded guilty), suggesting that the state had pursued only the most obvious and egregious cases. It seems likely that this is not for lack of bad-enough cases but 'the result of those with responsibility to investigate and prosecute lacking the necessary resources, co-ordination and training' (Slapper, 2013: 92). It has also been suggested that 'there has been a clear trade-off between guilty pleas for the CMCH charge and dropping those against individual directors (whether for manslaughter or health and safety offences)' because those charges have been withdrawn when such corporate guilty pleas have been entered (Wells, 2014: 861). Moreover, the offenders have been subject to fines less than the £500,000 minimum penalty recommended by the Sentencing Guidelines Commission (Sentencing Guidelines Council, 2010: para. 24). Accordingly, the evidence suggests that prosecutions for corporate manslaughter remain overwhelming directed at small privately held companies for the deaths of their employees.

The custody provision (section 2[1][d])

The methodological deficiencies and technical complexities of the 2007 Act have been well rehearsed, but the 'most controversial category of duty' in the legislation is, as Ormerod and Taylor (2008: 600) note, 'that relating to duties arising from detention'. Yet the fact that scholars have tended to focus on the duty owed by private companies to their employees, almost to the complete exclusion of the duty owed by custodial institutions to those detained, has meant that the application of the 2007 Act to the 'ugly side of public service activity' has not been subject to much academic scrutiny (Horder, 2012: 115). This is particularly evident in the prison context where a considerable number of reports over the last decade have repeatedly offered evidence of inadequate screening and formal risk assessment, not to mention insufficient and inexperienced staffing, overcrowded conditions and recurrent weaknesses in the implementation of the Prison Service suicide and self-harm prevention procedures (ACCT) (HMCIP, 2014: 29; PPO, 2014a: 5). Furthermore, there is evidence – despite the effect of deaths in custody on both the individuals and establishments involved (Liebling, 2002: 201–202) – that certain prisons still fail to give sufficient attention to implementing and reinforcing the recommendations of the Prisons and Probation Ombudsman, who investigates all deaths in prison custody, in fulfillment of the procedural duty under Article 2 of the ECHR (Owers, 2009: 1537). The 'dangerous perpetuation of negligence, idleness, indifference, inefficiency and the arbitrary cost-cutting' does not, to use Horder's words, 'only affect the safety of workers' (Horder, 2012: 116).

The clamour to ensure the applicability of the 2007 Act to the Prison Service and other 'carceral' spaces can, however, be only properly understood when one places the number of custodial deaths in comparative perspective. For instance, there were 150 deaths among British workers (almost all of which occurred in the pursuit of private corporate activity) between April 2012 and March 2013 (HSE, 2015). By contrast, there were 182 deaths in prison custody in the same period, 51 of which were classified as 'self-inflicted' (Ministry of Justice, 2014: 7). To put it another way, prisoners in this period were more likely to take their own lives than construction employees were to be killed at work (HSE, 2015). However, these statistics disguise the extent to which both workplace fatalities and self-inflicted deaths in prison custody are gendered. Although the rate of workplace fatality in Britain is one of the lowest in Europe, there were still 439 deaths among Britain's workers in the four-year period between April 2009 and March 2013, and most of the victims of work-related fatal accidents were male. Similarly, there were 313 self-inflicted deaths in prison in the same period, of which 9 of the deceased were female. Thus, after the sharp upward trend in prison suicides by females between 1998 and 2003, the number has declined in recent years. In 2013, for instance, women represented 4.6 per cent of the prison population in the UK and accounted for 2.6 per cent of self-inflicted deaths. This marked a notable decrease to the figures presented by the Corston Report (2007), which was triggered by the self-inflicted deaths of 6 women at HMP Styal in a twelve-month period between 2002 and 2003. The 2007 report highlighted that women represented only 6 per cent of the prison population in 2003 but that they accounted for 15 per cent of self-inflicted deaths (Corston, 2007: 19). In light of these figures, it seems reasonable to surmise that both workplace deaths and prison suicides have become predominantly a male preserve in the UK in recent years.

That said, it would be misleading to suggest that all self-inflicted deaths in prison custody can be attributed to grossly negligent management practices or to grossly negligent actions by prison staff, but it should also be borne in mind that a prisoner is almost entirely dependent on the prison to safeguard his or her health and safety during what may be a lengthy or an indeterminate sentence and that this should supersede the 'countervailing considerations and warrants of placing the relevant organisation under an ongoing duty of care' (Horder, 2012: 137). This argument was perfectly encapsulated by Lord Hunt (688 HL Official Report (5th Series), col GC 187), who asserted:

> The power lawfully to deprive an individual of his or her liberty must be one of the most serious responsibilities there can be. The duty of care owed to

an individual in detention, where he cannot act freely in his own interests, is onerous and profound.

In this regard, it is also important to point out that the House of Lords in the case of *ex parte Amin* [2003] (UKHL 51, para. 21), the Zahid Mubarek case, was unanimous in rejecting the government's argument, successful before the Court of Appeal, that 'an allegation of negligence leading to death in custody, though grave enough in all conscience, bears a different quality from a case where it is said that the state has laid on lethal hands' and held that systemic failures leading to deaths called for *even greater* scrutiny. Lord Bingham, for instance, said 'a systemic failure to protect the lives of persons detained in custody may well call for even more anxious consideration and raise even more intractable problems'.

So by virtue of schedule 1, the offence of 'Corporate Manslaughter' not only applies to private companies but also in some measure to all 'public bodies the performance of whose functions are most likely to involve causing deaths' (Horder, 2012: 117). These include, *inter alia*, the Ministry of Defence, the Department of Health and HMPS. Yet although the 2007 Act defines the scope of the duty, the nature of the duty is simply described as the duty owed under the law of negligence by the organisation to 'someone for whose safety the organisation is responsible' (CMCHA, 2007, s 2(1)(d)). Although it is well established in the law of tort that an organisation responsible for the detention of a person owes that person a duty to take reasonable care in respect of that person's health and safety, conjecture remains with regard to the exact extent to which that duty extends (Matthews, 2008: 66). Thus far, there has been no judicial consideration of the scope of the duty of care to prevent prisoner deaths at the hands of other prisoners, but the courts have held, in respect of self-inflicted deaths, that the duty to take reasonable care encompasses a duty to take reasonable steps to prevent a person from committing suicide, but only where the custodians *knew or ought to have known* that the individual prisoner was a suicide risk (66). The Court of Appeal in *Orange v Chief Constable of West Yorkshire Police* ([2002] QB 347: para. 43) did state, however, that given the increased risk of suicide among prisoners, there was an obligation, within the custodian's general duty of care for the prisoner's health and safety, to take *reasonable steps to identify* whether or not a prisoner presented a suicide risk. These decisions would suggest that the 2007 Act may only be applicable where the prisoner was being monitored under the Prison Service suicide and self-harm prevention procedures (ACCT) at the time of his self-inflicted death or where appropriate measures had not been taken to identify the known risk factors or 'triggers' (PPO, 2014b).

What is more clear, however, is that the offence is only committed if the death is caused by the way in which the custodial institution's activities are managed and organised by its senior management, and this must be a 'substantial element' in the gross breach of a relevant duty of care to the deceased. The first limb of this definition is, as Griffin and Moran (2010: 370) observe, a 'reflection of the common law "directing mind" test', but the 'second part of the definition removes any requirement on the part of a senior manager to possess a directing influence in the organisation or management of a relevant organisation's activities and policies'. Accordingly, it would appear that the liability of a prison 'may now ensue without the necessity of establishing that a senior manager obeyed policy or instructions dictated by the organisation's directing mind' (370). In other words, the prison service could potentially be prosecuted for manslaughter if gross failures of senior management cause the death of a detainee. Liability, however, appears to be excluded where the death is due to a public policy decision not to allocate appropriate resources to the Prison Service (CMCHA, s 3(1); Horder, 2012: 131–132).

The common law identification principle is also reformed further by virtue of the fact that an organisation's liability may now also be established by 'aggregating the cumulative conduct of a collective of senior managers' (Griffin and Moran, 2010: 370). Although the concept of aggregation was rejected by the trial court in the *Herald* case, the 2007 Act appears to accept aggregated fault in a limited form and makes it possible to convict a prison on the basis of collective failings that *must include*, but are not restricted to, failings on the part of senior managers. Take, for example, the murder of Zahid Mubarek, who was killed by his cellmate, Robert Stewart, at Feltham YOI in March 2000. Stewart had been 'manifesting extreme racist views in correspondence, and was diagnosed during the criminal proceedings as a psychopath' (Keith, 2006: 6). On arrival at Feltham, Stewart was placed in a cell with Mubarek, and brutally attacked him with a wooden table leg. Had Feltham YOI been prosecuted for the death of Zahid Mubarek under the 2007 Act (had it been in force at the time), it is reasonable to assume that the case would have succeeded. In this regard, the findings of the subsequent investigation into the murder conducted by the Commission for Racial Equality (2003: 162) are particularly noteworthy:

> Actions which should have protected Zahid were not taken because of the interaction of a number of factors. The pressure of prisoner numbers, the perception of staff shortages, limited resources and poor management had created a climate in which indifference, negligence, corner-cutting and non-compliance with specific and clear HM Prison Service requirements had become the norm.

Section 8 of the Act also stipulates that juries *must* consider any evidence that shows an alleged breach of health and safety legislation. This may have particularly important consequences in the prison context where the Health and Safety at Work Act of 1974 is largely inapplicable and cannot be invoked by prisoners who suffer breaches of it, even though Standing Order 6A (15) allows for prison inspections by the HSE, and HMPS has been censured four times since 1999 (Livingstone et al., 2008: 232). This is also significant in that the Act states that should a violation of health and safety legislation be established, juries are permitted to take into account whether 'attitudes, policies, systems or accepted practices within the organisation' were likely to have encouraged any failure to meet safety standards or produced a tolerance of it. Perhaps a crown censure would be sufficient evidence to show HMPS failed to comply with health and safety legislation, but as the dicta of Hooper J in the *Mubarek* case ([2003] UKHL 51: para. 26) indicates, evidence of a prison's culture and ethos *may* be decisive in certain cases involving deaths in custody:

> Zahid Mubarek was murdered in Feltham by a racist cell mate with 'an alarming and violent criminal record, both in and out of custody'. It is accepted that Zahid Mubarek was put in the same cell as his killer because of 'systemic failures'. Established procedures were not followed and there is an appalling history at Feltham of failure to comply with earlier recommendations. It seems likely (and it is certainly arguable) that there were serious human failings both at the wing level and at higher levels which have not been publicly identified.

Yet despite the merits of the custodial provision, it seems plausible to argue that the 'senior management' test renders section 2(1)(d) somewhat ineffective, because not only does it force 'the inquiry back onto the issue of identifiable individuals' (Ormerod and Taylor, 2008: 604), it also fails both to acknowledge the reality of how the suicide prevention procedures work in UK prisons and the complexity of the organisational structure within HMPS.

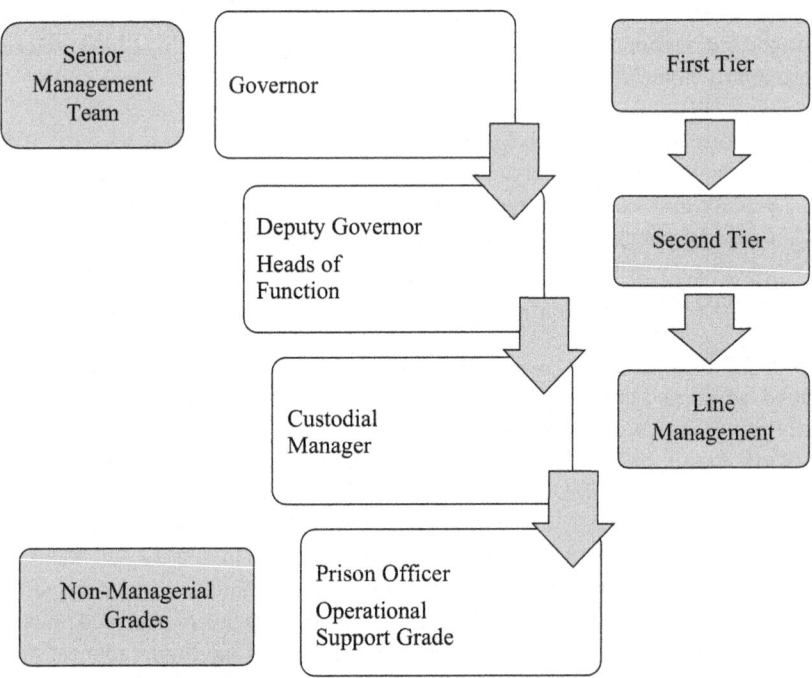

Figure 8.1 HMPS organisational structure since the introduction of the *Fair and Sustainable* working structures in April 2013

There have been three levels of management in HMPS since the introduction of the new *Fair and Sustainable* working structures on 1 April 2013. The first-tier definition of senior management (in effect, the 'directing mind' of the prison) consists solely of the office of prison governor, while the second tier comprises deputy governors and invariably heads of function. Although the SMT within a prison will be composed of members from both management tiers, proving a prison's liability based on the definition of 'senior management' in the 2007 Act may, in fact, 'mirror the difficulties' associated with establishing the guilt of private companies under the common law identification principle (Griffin and Moran, 2010: 371). For instance, the actual management control of the procedures to prevent deaths in prison custody are exercised in practice at a non-managerial level, and it is difficult to envisage how a prison officer could meet the criteria specified in the Act in terms of 'senior management'. Furthermore, even in the occasional instances where management is involved, it is at the level of first-line or third-tier management, and a custodial manager – a 'uniformed role' – would certainly not be classed as senior management within HMPS (NOMS, 2012: 8). Thus, in order to enable the Crown Prosecution Service (CPS) to establish a prison's liability for a death in a custodial setting, a custodial manager would have to be identified as a senior manager and involved in the suicide prevention process. This, of course, not only appears 'unduly restrictive' and 'threatens to open the door to endless argument in court as to whether certain persons do or do not constitute senior managers' (Clarkson, 2005: 683); it would also mean completely ignoring both the practical reality of the organisational hierarchy and the suicide prevention strategies within HMPS.

Furthermore, in its concentration on 'senior management', the Act fails to take account of the individual failings of a wider range of individuals within the organisation. Various inquests, thematic reviews and Chief Coroner Reports to Prevent Deaths (previously Rule 43 reports) reveal that a substantial number of avoidable deaths in custody can be attributed to failures by lower-ranking staff to properly implement the correct policies and procedures where a prisoner has been identified at risk. Of course, it could be argued that senior management must issue rules and guidance to staff, both orally and in writing, and that weaknesses in the implementation of the death avoidance procedures are at least partially attributable to a failure on the part of senior management to subject the processes to rigorous checks, but it should also be borne in mind that any case of corporate manslaughter must rest, as a prerequisite for success, on proof of a breach of a duty of care on the part of senior managers and that the senior management failure must be a *substantial* element in the breach of that duty. The term 'substantial element' is not defined by the Act of 2007 but rather a *question of fact* for the jury who must determine as a matter of causation whether the culpability of a senior manager was more than minimal, 'albeit not necessarily an absolute factor, in the breach of duty resulting in the person's death' (Griffin and Moran, 2010: 370). Therefore, other than in an unusual situation where a death in prison was directly attributable to a direction or instruction given by a governor, a deputy governor or a head of function ('something that is not usual during standard ACCT procedures'), it would be very difficult for the CPS to establish a prison's liability for the offence of corporate manslaughter (PPO, 2014a: 19). Even where a custodial manager is involved in the ACCT process, the difficulty in identifying a line manager as senior management may nullify the intent of section 2 (1)(d) and undermine the capacity of the Crown to successfully convict a prison for an avoidable death in custody.

There are, of course, other aspects to be critical of in the 2007 statute as originally enacted. Many of the criticisms made by legal scholars, such as the exclusive focus on organisational liability, the extension of the Act to such a diverse array of organisations, the exemptions to police officers and army officials, and the requirement of consent by the DPP to prosecute are persuasive and well founded. One eminent legal scholar (Gobert, 2008a: 415), for instance, has argued that:

> the extension of the bill in the final days before its passage to deaths in custody means that prisons can be prosecuted when deaths occur as a result of inadequate staff to provide comprehensive supervision of an undeniably violent prisoner population, where the inability to hire more staff is due to the budgetary constraints imposed by the government.

This example, he observes, is not intended to suggest that 'prisons should not be held accountable when their gross negligence causes death' or that all prisoners who are willfully exposed to organisational gross negligence are not deserving of protection, but rather that other more appropriate types of criminal legislation than the law of corporate manslaughter might be constructed to cover these type of situations (415–416). The new approach also provokes the broader question of whether it is the conviction of companies and public bodies that is the most significant facet or whether the punishment of organisations should be considered as important too (Ashworth and Horder, 2013: 154). A custodial institution can hardly be imprisoned, moderate fines can be swallowed up as operational costs, and severe fines may result in further reductions in the number of prison officers, which would inevitably have deleterious effects on the safety and welfare of inmates. Finally, there is also some evidence, both in the corporate and the custodial context, to suggest that perhaps the Act should have been extended beyond the limited (but high-profile) area of homicide (Gobert, 2008a: 419–422). Take, for instance, the remarks of Lord Ramsbottom, when speaking of Wormwood Scrubs during a debate on the bill. Although observing that there was 'no case of manslaughter', he recalled that 'there was extraordinarily bad behaviour by staff, brutality of prisoners and, over a number of years, management failure on a scale that I simply could not believe' (688 HL Official Report [Fifth Series], col GC 192).

Writing in 2008, James Gobert intimated that the symbolic significance of the 2007 Act may 'ultimately transcend its methodological deficiencies' and that the primary value of the Act may very well lie in the very fact of its existence (2008a: 413). If nothing else, it was anticipated that the Act would, at least, spur the prison service and a variety of other custodial institutions to satisfy themselves that the structures and systems for preventing deaths in custody were fit for purpose and coerce them to take a fresh look at their culture and ethos in this regard (425–432).

Furthermore, it was envisaged that the s.2(1)(d) duty would encourage the Prison Service to afford greater compliance with safer custody practices, as embodied in PSI 64/2011 and the ACCT document (v.5). As Lord Ramsbottom (688 HL Official Report [Fifth Series], col GC 193) put it:

> I hate the thought of coercion through a Bill, but this Bill, which is based on the duty of care and which should be shown to everyone in the charge of these authorities, is an appropriate weapon. I seriously believe that the Bill would energise the management system in a way that nothing else that I have come across in the past 10 years seems to have been able to.

Yet despite such optimistic pronouncements, there were more self-inflicted deaths in prison custody in 2014 than at any time in the last 10 years ('reversing a downturn in the previous decade') (HMCIP, 2014: 25), the Prison and Probation Ombudsman has called for a review of the Safer Custody strategy and ACCT to see if they are still fit for purpose and the Corporate Manslaughter Act has not yet been invoked for a single death in prison custody (PPO, 2014a: 5). What is more, it appears that even if proceedings were instituted against a prison for a death in custody, judicial interpretation of s.2(1)(d), and more particularly the senior management test, may prove evidentially problematic. Although the management of a prison will ultimately fall under the rubric of the SMT, the death avoidance and ACCT procedures are implemented, at best, at line management level and invariably at a non-managerial level. While it may be a rational supposition for a jury, in determining the liability of a prison, to conclude that the responsibility for the breach of a relevant duty should logically be attributed to members of the SMT, it should be borne in mind that an ability to deflect liability exists in any large organisation that is characterised by a system of complex management and operational structures (Griffin and Moran, 2010: 371). Of course, the ability to deflect responsibility has always been, and still appears to be at least in the prison context, a major limitation on liability, and like its predecessor the 'identification' principle did with medium- to- large-size corporate bodies, it fails to take into account that crucial strategic and, more importantly, operational decisions are frequently not only delegated but assigned to lower levels of management and operations than those granted policy authority over the prison's affairs (371). Both independent and anecdotal evidence suggests that this is certainly the case with Safer Custody. It is, nonetheless, unacceptable that a prison could be able to escape liability for a completely avoidable death in custody, especially when the fault element for the crime was possessed by a custodial manager or a prison officer who had authority to take operational decisions, simply because that person was not a member of the SMT.

Conclusion

This chapter analysed the difficulties associated with criminalising the predominantly male phenomena of culpable workplace fatalities in both Britain and Ireland. It was shown that proving the directing mind of the organisation responsible for the manslaughter, as a precondition to corporate criminal liability, was often too difficult an obstacle to surmount when prosecuting large companies with complex management systems. The attribution doctrine, which did not require the directing mind to be culpable for the purposes of criminal liability, offered greater flexibility for prosecutors seeking to impose liability but it also suffered from vagueness and has been disfavoured as a means of imposing criminal responsibility in recent times. Although the proposed corporate manslaughter legislation in Ireland appears to have stalled indefinitely, the CMCHA 2007 in the UK has embraced another method of attributing culpable misconduct to organisations. It adopted a 'qualified aggregation' test, whereby an organisation may be guilty of corporate manslaughter when individual failures can cumulatively constitute corporate failure, provided that senior management failures were a substantial element in the breach of duty owed to the deceased. Nevertheless, though the legislation extended criminal liability to all relevant public bodies that cause death, not just companies, the legislation has, thus far, been enforced primarily against small private companies for employee fatalities in the workplace. The CPS has yet to target HMPS for a death in custody, even though more deaths occur annually in prisons than in the workplace. Moreover, it is impossible to relegate this failing to the past. This chapter has demonstrated that it may prove extraordinarily difficult to subject HMPS to criminal liability in the future, even where there is a willingness to initiate proceedings, because the legislation imposes a requirement that the actions of senior management must have played a substantial role in the breach of duty resulting in death. This is compounded by the fact that the procedures to prevent deaths in prison custody are invariably exercised by uniformed officers who play no role in the management of the prison.

In addition to the difficulties of securing convictions in practice, there is also the difficulty as to what punishments the state should impose on this kind of public body. The trite observation that convicted organisations have 'no body to kick and no soul to damn' seems particularly ironic given that HMPS can hardly be imprisoned. Furthermore, it appears futile to fine a state-funded public body such as a prison, especially when this may reduce the resources it has available to safeguard the welfare and safety of prisoners and when the costs of such fines inevitably 'spill-over' onto the taxpayer. The 'spill-over' effect of punishment in more traditional corporate contexts has been well canvassed, with the literature noting that the fining of corporations may be more likely to affect innocent parties removed from the wrongdoing than to punish management who are directly responsible for the crimes. Indeed, it has been argued that the costs of such fines are imposed on employees who suffer layoffs, consumers who are charged higher prices for products and shareholders who do not receive dividends (Coffee, 1981; Fisse and Braithwaite, 1993). Yet, in terms of allocating responsibility, perhaps fining public bodies makes more sense than fining private companies. Politicians representing the concerns of taxpayers can put enormous pressure on prisons to reduce costs, without expressly encouraging illegal or unsafe actions, but without sufficiently resourcing these institutions to allow them to maintain safe conditions either. Imprisonment is the state's most powerful weapon of censure, designed to punish the most reprehensible of shared wrongs against the community, to reinforce the shared morality of that community (Durkheim, 1964; Marshall and Duff, 1998). The community is imposing the custodial sentence through the courts and thus it is at least arguable that the community should share the burden of responsibility for the conditions in which prisoners are detained too.

Yet wherever responsibility is attributed, it is difficult to avoid the conclusion that the criminal law – while necessary for holding corporations and public bodies criminally responsible when their gross negligence causes death – would have to be used much more extensively than it is at present to produce the level of deterrent effect required to prevent workplace fatalities or indeed deaths in custody (Almond, 2013: 178). Although the law of corporate manslaughter may serve a dynamic social purpose by leading corporations and public bodies on the values that should inform certain kinds of individual, collective and organisational behaviour, criminalisation is insufficient to bring about fundamental change on its own. Perhaps it will only be when work-related fatalities and deaths in custody are recognised as pressing public health issues that feasible prevention strategies will emerge to reduce the number of avoidable deaths both in custody and in the workplace (Bonner, 2000: 374; Herber and Landrigan, 2000: 541–545; Simon, 2010). Politicians, legislators and members of the public, who rarely respond sympathetically to calls for prisoners' rights, may respond more enthusiastically if such problems are reconfigured in this way.

Note

1   The authors thank Professor Paul Almond, Professor Mary Bosworth, Professor Shane Kilcommins and the reviewers for their comments on earlier drafts of the chapter. The usual disclaimers apply.

References

Almond, P. (2013) *Corporate Manslaughter and Regulatory Reform*. Basingstoke: Palgrave Macmillan.

Ashworth, A. (2009) *Principles of Criminal Law* (6th ed.). Oxford: Oxford University Press.

Ashworth, A. and Horder, J. (2013) *Principles of Criminal Law* (7th ed.). Oxford: Oxford University Press.

Bonner, R. L. (2000) Correctional suicide prevention in the year 2000 and beyond. *Suicide and Life-Threatening Behavior*, 30: 370–376.

Brenner, H. J. and Hopkins, J. (2006) Health and quality in work final report. Volume IV, Annex IV: Accidents at work. Available from: ec.europa.eu/social/BlobServlet?docId= 2133&langId=en

Bureau of Labor Statistics (BLS). (1994–2013) Census of fatal occupational injuries. Available from: www.bls.gov/iif/osh_nwrl.htm#cfoi

Carolan, B. (2011) Criminalizing corporate killing: The Irish approach. *Stetson Law Review*, 41: 157–174.

Clarkson, C. (2005) Corporate manslaughter: Yet more government proposals. *Criminal Law Review*, 9: 677–689.

Coffee, J. (1981) No soul to damn: No body to kick: An unscandalized inquiry into the problem of corporate punishment. *Michigan Law Review*, 79: 386–459.

Commission for Racial Equality. (2003) *The Murder of Zahid Mubarek*. London: Commission for Racial Equality.

Corston, J. (2007) *The Corston Report: A Report of a Review of Women with Particular Vulnerabilities in the Criminal Justice System*. London: Home Office.

Department of Transport. (1987) *MV Herald of Free Enterprise*. Report of Court No. 8074. Formal Investigation. London: HM Stationery Office.

Drummond, A. (2007) An investigation into the official data sources and collection methods. Available from: www.hsa.ie/eng/Publications_and_Forms/. . ./Drummond_Study.pdf

Drummond, A. (2008) A review of the occupational disease reporting system in the Republic of Ireland. Available from: www.lenus.ie/hse/bitstream/10147/76879/1/Areviewofoccupational.pdf

Durkheim, E. (1964) *The Rules of Sociological Method*. New York: Free Press.

Eurostat. (2012) Accidents at work (ESAW, 2008 onwards). Available from: http://ec.europa.eu/eurostat/web/health/health-safety-work/data/database

Field, S. and Jones, L. (2013) Five years on: The impact of the Corporate Manslaughter and Corporate Homicide Act 2007: Plus ça change? *International Company and Commercial Law Review*, 24: 239–246.

Field, S. and Jones, L. (2014) Are directors getting away with manslaughter? Emerging trends in prosecutions for corporate manslaughter. *Business Law Review*, 35: 158–163.

Fisse, B. and Braithwaite, J. (1993) *Corporations, Crime and Accountability*. Cambridge: Cambridge University Press.

Forlin, G. and Smail, L. (2013) *Corporate Liability: Work Related Deaths and Criminal Prosecutions*. West Sussex: Bloomsbury Professional.

Gobert, J. (1994) Corporate criminality: Four models of fault. *Legal Studies*, 14: 393–410.

Gobert, J. (2008a) The Corporate Manslaughter and Corporate Homicide Act 2007 – thirteen years in the making but was it worth the wait? *The Modern Law Review*, 71: 413–433.

Gobert, J. (2008b) The evolving legal test of corporate criminal liability. In Minkes, J. and Minkes, L (eds.) *Corporate and White-Collar Crime*. London: Sage, pp. 61–80.

Gobert, J. and Punch, M. (2003) *Rethinking Corporate Crime*. London: Butterworths.

Griffin, S. and Moran, J. (2010) Accountability for deaths attributable to the gross negligent act or omission of a police force. *Journal of Criminal Law*, 74: 358–381.

Health and Safety Authority (HSA). (2013) Annual report 2012. Available from: www.hsa.ie/eng/Publications_and_Forms/Publications/Corporate/annual_report_12.pdf

Health and Safety Executive (HSE). (2015) Statistics on fatal injuries in the workplace in Great Britain 2015. Available from: www.hse.gov.uk/statistics/pdf/fatalinjuries.pdf

Herber, R. and Landrigan, P. J. (2000) Work-related death: A continuing epidemic. *American Journal of Public Health*, 90: 541–545.

HM Chief Inspector of Prisons for England and Wales (HMCIP). (2014) Annual report 2013–14 (London: Stationery Office). Available from: www.justiceinspectorates.gov.uk/hmiprisons/wp-content/uploads/sites/4/2014/10/HMIP-AR_2013–14.pdf

Horan, S. (2011) *Corporate Crime*. Haywards Heath: Bloomsbury Professional.

Horder, J. (2012) *Homicide and the Politics of Law Reform*. Oxford: Oxford University Press.

Hoskins, A. B. (2005) Occupational injuries, illnesses, and fatalities among women. *Monthly Labour Review*, 128: 31–37.

Jackall, R. (1988) *Moral Mazes: The World of Corporate Managers*. New York: Oxford University Press.

Keith, B. (2006) *Report of the Zahid Mubarek Inquiry*. London: Stationery Office.

Kilcommins, S., O'Donnell, I., O'Sullivan, E. and Vaughan, B. (2004) *Crime, Punishment and the Search for Order in Ireland*. Dublin: Institute of Public Administration.

Law Reform Commission (LRC). (2003) *Consultation Paper on Corporate Killing*. Dublin: Stationery Office.

Law Reform Commission (LRC). (2005) *Report on Corporate Killing*. Dublin: Stationery Office.

Liebling, A. (2002) *Suicides in Prison*. London: Routledge.

Livingstone, S., Owen, T. Macdonald, A., Ní Ghrálaigh, B. and Law, H. (2008) *Prison Law*. Oxford: Oxford University Press.

Marshall, S. E. and Duff, R. A. (1998) Criminalisation and sharing wrongs. *Canadian Journal of Law and Jurisprudence*, 11: 7–22.

Matthews, R. (2008) *Blackstone's Guide to the Corporate Manslaughter and Corporate Homicide Act 2007*. Oxford: Oxford University Press.

McGrath, J. (2015) *Corporate and White Collar Crime in Ireland: A New Architecture of Regulatory Enforcement*. Manchester: Manchester University Press.

McShee, D. (2008) The History of the Corporate Manslaughter and Corporate Homicide Act 2007. In Davies, A. (ed.) *Corporate Manslaughter and Corporate Homicide Act: Special Report*. Cambridge: Workplace Law Group, pp. 9–16.

Ministry of Justice. (2014) Safety in custody statistics England and Wales update to March 2014. Available from: www.gov.uk/government/uploads/system/uploads/attachment_data/file/339067/safety-in-custody-to-mar-2014.pdf

Minkes, J. and Minkes, L. (eds.) (2008) *Corporate and White-Collar Crime*. London: Sage.

National Offender Management Service (NOMS). (2012) *Fair and Sustainable: Revision to Proposals for Working Structures in HM Prison Service Following the Consultation with Trade Unions*. London: Ministry of Justice.

O'Donnell, I. (2002) Unlawful killing past and present. *The Irish Jurist*, 37: 56–90.

Office for National Statistics. (2013) Crime statistics: Appendix tables – focus on: Violent crime and sexual offences, 2011/12. Table 1.02: Police recorded crime by offence, 1997 to 2011/12 and percentage change between 2010/11 and 2011/12. Available from: www.ons.gov.uk/ons/publications/re-reference-tables.html?edition=tcm%3A77–290621

Office for National Statistics. (2015) Crime in England and Wales: Year ending December 2014. Available from: www.ons.gov.uk/ons/dcp171778_401896.pdf

Ormerod, D. and Taylor, R. (2008) The Corporate Manslaughter and Corporate Homicide Act 2007. *Criminal Law Review*, 8: 589–611.

Owers, A. (2009) Prison inspection and the protection of prisoner's right. *Pace Law Review*, 30: 1535–1547.

Prison and Probation Ombudsman for England and Wales (PPO). (2014a) Learning from PPO investigations: Self-inflicted deaths of prisoners on ACCT. Available from: www.ppo.gov.uk/wp-content/uploads/2014/07/ACCT_thematic_final_web.pdf

Prison and Probation Ombudsman for England and Wales (PPO). (2014b). Learning from PPO investigations: Risk factors in self-inflicted deaths in prisons. Available from: www.ppo.gov.uk/wp-content/uploads/2014/07/Risk_thematic_final_web.pdf

Russell, H., Bertrand, M. and Watson, D. (2015) Trends and patterns in occupational health and safety in Ireland. Available from: www.hsa.ie/eng/Publications_and_Forms/Publications/Corporate/Trends_and_Patterns_in_Occupational_Health_and_Safety_in_Ireland.pdf

Sealy, L. and Worthington, S. (2010) *Sealy's Cases and Materials in Company Law* (9th ed.). Oxford: Oxford University Press.

Sentencing Guidelines Council. (2010) Corporate manslaughter & health and safety offences causing death. Definitive guideline. Available from: www.sentencingcouncil. org.uk/wp-content/uploads/web__guideline_on_corporate_manslaughter_accessible. pdf

Simon, J. (2010) Do these prisons make me look fat? Moderating the USA's consumption of punishment. *Theoretical Criminology*, 14: 257–272.

Slapper, G. (2013) Justice is mocked if an important law is unenforced. *Journal of Criminal Law*, 77: 91–94.

Ussher, P. (1986) *Company Law in Ireland*. London: Sweet and Maxwell.

Wells, C. (2001) *Corporations and Criminal Responsibility* (2nd ed.). Oxford: Oxford University Press.

Wells, C. (2014) Corporate criminal liability: A ten year review. *Criminal Law Review*, 12: 849–878.

Wolgast, E. (1992) *Ethics of an Artificial Person: Lost Responsibility in Professions and Organisations*. Stanford, CA: Stanford University Press.

Legislation and Statutory Instruments

The Corporate Manslaughter and Corporate Homicide Act 2007

The Corporate Manslaughter and Corporate Homicide Act 2007 (Commencement No. 3) Order 2011 (SI 2011/1867)

Parliamentary Debates

688 HL Official Report (5th Series), col GC 187

Concluding thoughts on homicide, gender and responsibility

Sandra Walklate and Kate Fitz-Gibbon

Our intention in bringing this collection together has been not only to demonstrate the extent to which a gendered lens facilitates a blurring of the boundaries between what is taken to be the 'private' act of domestic killing and the 'public' act of killing in wartime or institutional settings but also, in so doing, to add some nuanced understanding to the available conceptual maps used to make sense of killing in these different contexts. We took the seminal work of Kelly (1988), developed by Cockburn (2009), as our starting point for this collection. From that beginning, in this conclusion we sought to review the contributions in this book and hopefully to push at the boundaries of the way in which debates around gender, homicide and responsibility have been framed. Within this the question of how the law responds to acts of lethal violence has been central, both in terms of challenging the construction of responsibility as individual or collective as well as questioning the extent to which the criminal law is able to adequately account for gendered influences in the perpetration of violence. As the contributions throughout this collection reveal, these are not questions confined to the realm of the 'domestic' homicide but rather contestations surrounding the allocation of responsibility and debates surrounding the gendered nature of lethal violence permeating the wide range of contexts within which the crime of homicide is perpetrated.

Put simply, this collection has brought together a set of original contributions which focus attention on the ways in which the question of gender is more or less visible, in the different contexts in which illegal killing occurs. The visibility and salience of gender varies in how such events are actually experienced by the participants in them, the responses to such events (how they are defined, understood and acted on) and the academic debates constructed to make sense of them. All of these different contexts are also permeated by gendered understandings of responsibility. These understandings are in themselves multi-layered and multifaceted, as the chapters in this collection illustrate. Taken together this affords us with a complex conceptual matrix in which to make sense of killing comprising the following dimensions: public/private, visible/invisible, state/ intimate – a matrix permeated in different ways by gender itself and gendered understandings of responsibility. In this conclusion we endeavour to explore the extent to which an appreciation of this complexity can be translated into law.

In Chapter 1, Anette Ballinger considered the ongoing relevance of a landmark case of 'domestic' murder. This case saw Ruth Ellis hanged for the murder of her partner, David Blakely. Ruth Ellis was the last woman to be hanged in the UK. The nature of this case, and the circumstances surrounding it, as Ballinger discusses, were pivotal in introducing changes to the law on homicide, particularly the nature of the defences available to the accused. It was a case particularly influential in not only informing the legislation of 1957 which in the UK introduced the defence of diminished responsibility, but latterly has been a significant contributor to debates concerning how the law understands the defence of provocation. In those debates the challenge posed by what Ballinger refers to as the 'vengeful woman' has resulted in efforts to rethink the concept of provocation. That rethinking has endeavoured to widen understandings of what might count as provocation as not only determined by what a 'reasonable man' might do under particular circumstances but also to include provocative conduct constituting a 'slow burning fuse' assumed to be more typical of what a 'reasonable woman' might do. Yet, as Ballinger documents, despite efforts to appeal Ruth Ellis' conviction in the light of these recent developments, that appeal failed. The Court of Appeal was arguably both ethically and legally correct to reject this appeal on two grounds. The first reflects the principle of viewing each case through the legal requirements dominant at the time. The second reflects the undeniable admission made by Ellis in her own words; when asked what she intended to do with the gun in her possession, she replied that she intended to kill him – an admission she maintained until her execution.

Despite the failure of this appeal, the events surrounding this case and its consequences still provoke considerable interest. For Ballinger this is in part a result of the gendered assumptions underpinning the allocation of responsibility for what transpired. Thus, the court in overemphasising Ellis' admission of responsibility and underemphasising Blakely's irresponsibility took the concept itself as being neutral and given. Yet in the details of this case it is possible to discern that such neutrality is misplaced. The relationship between Ellis and Blakely was far from neutral. They belonged to different social classes, clearly had different levels of commitment to the relationship, with Blakely evidently having considerable power and influence over Ellis – the latter partially achieved through the alleged use of psychological abuse and physical violence. However, these complexities become lost in the legal desire to assign individual responsibility for what took place: a process clearly facilitated by Ellis' own admission. In this way the complex narratives of people's lives become transformed into a simple legal one. This case, and Ballinger's analysis of it, alerts us to the possibility that there is more at play here than simply understanding provocation as either immediate retaliation (the reasonable man response) or a slow burning fuse (the reasonable woman response). Here, who is made responsible, for what, and under what conditions are called into account – all of which, when taken together, miss the mark in making it possible for the law to stand for us all (Naffine, 2003). Moreover, as shall be seen, the legal presumptions that strain to make an individual responsible for what transpires not only removes the complexity of people's lives from the legal arena, it also renders those lives more manageable and controllable through the law. Thus the private world of intimacy is sanitised and made ready for public intervention by the state. Chapters 2 and 3 offer further close ups on this private world and some of the dynamics within it.

In Chapter 2, Julie Stubbs, in discussing murder, manslaughter and domestic violence, reminds us of the complexities that lie behind the interrelationship between these different issues. Of course, as she points out, what constitutes murder or manslaughter in a legal sense is contested and changing, offering up different interpretations and opportunities for defences and partial defences for such behaviours (as the case discussed by Ballinger gives some weight to). However, the connections between murder, manslaughter and the concept of 'domestic' are differently articulated. In different jurisdictions and, moreover, even in the same jurisdictions, these can be referred to as domestic homicide, intimate partner homicide, or domestic violence homicide. All of these labels presume that these acts are not only gender neutral but, as Stubbs discusses, also connote different contexts with potentially different actors involved; that is, with different victims and offenders, mothers, fathers, children, as well as intimate partners. However, there is one feature of intimate partner violence in particular that remains relatively constant over time and across cultures: within this framing of what counts as 'domestic', men and women are killed and are moved to kill under different circumstances. Thus whilst the statistical patterning of homicide as compared with femicide might vary, the underlying context that results in this act of violence does not vary so much. Put simply, men kill women out of jealousy. Women kill men for self-protection. Moreover, this kind of violent outcome occurs at different points in relationships, with the point of separation being one in which women are particularly vulnerable to this kind of extreme violence from their partners (see also Dekeseredy and Rennison, 2013; Mahoney, 1991).

Moreover, Stubbs's analysis usefully complicates this equation. She goes on to argue that when this equation is overlaid with differential experiences of structural inequalities, there is clear evidence to suggest that intimate partner violence is also racialised. In other words, for minority women, the likelihood of being a victim of murder is also a feature of the political economic context in which they find themselves. Hence, the relationship between gender and homicide is neither simple nor straightforward but needs to be understood in relation to other structural inequalities in people's lives: the question of intersectionality. The extent to which the law can appreciate and make judgments in the light of this kind of granularity is a moot point.

Stubbs offers some very interesting insights on the efficacy of the law, and/ or changes to the law, in responding to homicide in the context of 'domestic' violence. Interestingly, her analysis concurs with the observations made by Smart (1989) on the extent to which laws passed with an intention to support women's interests can be very quickly used to the very opposite effect. Stubbs's example of the Australian introduction of the 'one punch' laws illustrates this. When this kind of legislation is used in the context of a domestic homicide, sight can be lost of the fact that men who murder women also specialise in violence against women, in other words their use of a defence that implies a 'one-off' action frequently belies a history of the use of violence (see also Ball, 2012; Cullen, 2014). Of course, embedded in the recourse to law under these circumstances, by definition, calls upon some understanding of culpability (responsibility), and here again the strain towards rendering an individual responsible, his structural location notwithstanding, is still evident.

Whilst the chapter by Stubbs affords a more subtle understanding of the relationship between gender and homicide rendered more complex by structural inequalities, the chapter by Myrna Dawson takes an even closer look at how cases of intimate partner homicide are constructed and understood in the court process itself. Here the central focus is on the concept of intimacy. It is Dawson's contention that stereotypical assumptions about intimacy itself have pervaded understandings of and responses to intimate partner violence, whilst the salience of those assumptions remains to be examined systematically. Here she is referring to assumptions that dangerousness, gender and the recourse to violence, as they are practically articulated in the court process, are actually stereotypes about men's violence. So the extent to which the idea that offenders who kill intimate partners are much less dangerous than those who kill strangers has become deeply embedded in intimate partner violence, so much so that their potential effect has been ignored. Specifically these assumptions can be found in the search for reduced culpability. This search can be found in the presentation of mitigating emotions (the expressive violence of acts committed in hot blood usually associated with men's violence against intimate partners reminiscent of the issues raised by Ballinger) or presumptions of victim participation (being provoked, for example, by a partner's unacceptable behaviour), or indeed in the presumption that private acts of violence are not a threat to the social order articulated in the perceived lack of future dangerousness on the part of the offender. When taken together, these constitute the domain assumptions in which the criminal justice process constructs the 'normal' crime of intimate partner violence. Indeed, they carry with them historical traces about relationships, violence and desire also commented on by D'Cruze (2011).

So Dawson's analysis leads to a consideration of how and under what conditions these stereotypical assumptions of intimacy, in which crimes committed between partners in private, are deemed less threatening to the social order than when the same behaviour occurs in other contexts. In her fine-grained empirical work, it is possible to see the complex ways in which judges themselves draw upon these stereotypes in assigning culpability, future dangerousness, and participation in making sense of what transpires when there is a man, a woman, violence and a death. The role of alcohol in legal deliberations is also to be noted. This work, of course, constitutes only a preliminary exploration of the way in which the concept of intimacy is operationalised. However, here again it is also possible to catch sight of what is put in the foreground and what is left in the background, in particular the foregrounding of what goes in the private domain as being less threatening to the social order is particularly interesting and something that we shall return to at the end of this conclusion.

Kate Fitz-Gibbon's chapter offers a close examination of gender and homicide from a different angle. This chapter serves to remind us that the frequency with which men kill each other outside of the context of war is also a feature of making sense of the relationship between gender and homicide. The first three chapters take as given that men's recourse to violence, or indeed a woman's violent response to men's abusive behaviour, is generated by the question of what constitutes manhood. Thus, the normal expectations associated with men's 'hot blooded' responses to provocation are intimately connected with masculinity. However, how men express their masculinity may vary within and across contexts of violence. Indeed, in the first three chapters of this book we have been offered an insight into different dimensions in the expression of that masculinity, all tied together by the propensity for lethal violence. Fitz-Gibbon offers an analysis of how that propensity manifests itself in a particular gendered setting, not that of intimacy but of young men committing lethal violence against other young men. This chapter explores original data on the processing of young men charged with committing this kind of crime and affords some insight into how the court process constructs and understands the dangerous and irresponsible masculinity these young men are presumed to possess.

This empirical work draws on a qualitative examination over ten years of cases of child-perpetrated homicide in the state of Victoria. Set against the backcloth of the seminal work of Connell and others around masculinity, Fitz-Gibbon's analysis reveals the extent to which the court proceedings drew on concepts of irresponsible masculinity in assigning culpability and responsibility to these offenders. Interestingly, in the fine detail of these cases it is possible to discern contested understandings of what constitutes responsible behaviour (the defence of carrying a knife for protection proving to be unconvincing to the court, for example) alongside the presence of alcohol consumption as a contributory factor. Taken together, these kinds of factors are illustrative of the culture of violence valued by some young men and documented elsewhere in the literature as a key feature of a 'good night out' (see *inter alia* Tomsen, 1997; Winlow and Hall, 2006). Even in circumstances where the collective presence of the violence was a key feature of the act perpetrated, the child/young man before the court was assigned individual responsibility for his willingness to participate. Though this was not always done without sympathy or understanding. Fitz-Gibbon's analysis also alerts us to the presence of a judicial discourse of what she terms 'vulnerable masculinity'. Here the courts alluded to the problems faced by young men in general, and socially marginalised young men in particular, in negotiating perhaps family breakdown or being a refugee from a violent and volatile situation. Arguably these narratives constitute efforts to contextualise responsibility. So in these narratives – whilst it is possible to discern the presence of more populist discourses of young men 'at risk' that might focus on the surface manifestation of the articulation of those risks, from knife crime, to alcohol abuse, to a culture of violence – these same young men are also 'at risk' from the situated life experiences in which they find themselves and their capacity to respond to those circumstances within the scripts of masculinity available to them.

Mooney has observed (2007): how can violence be a public anathema and a private commonplace all at the same time? Part of the answer to this question lies within the perpetuation of the gendered assumptions about the non-threatening world of the private. In that world, what it is to be a man is legitimated in laws suffused by gendered understandings of responsibility expressed in their ultimate form in acts of homicide, femicide and legal responses to these acts. At the same time, much of men's violence as perpetrated against each other, as Fitz-Gibbon's analysis alludes to, is the product of collective male violence and the values assigned to it. This is nowhere more evident than in the context of war.

In wars, people are killed. That these acts of killing, even contemporarily, involve for the most part men killing other men is indisputable. Moreover, acts such as these are also deeply implicated in visions of how heroic acts in war might be understood, and in some respects military masculinity constitutes the epitome of the kind of masculine values and behaviour to which many men aspire, grains of which can also be identified in Fitz-Gibbon's analysis of collective male violence. However, all of this presumes that such acts of killing are perpetrated 'legitimately': on behalf of and in the interests of the state.

In Chapter 5, Walklate and McGarry explore how such acts are framed and understood when they occur illegitimately. Their chapter encourages us to think about what murderous behaviour in war might look like, the extent to which it is related to presumptions of gender, and how the question of responsibility is addressed. Their two chosen case studies reveal not only some interesting parallels with the debates that occur around 'domestic' murder but also some interesting consistencies between how such behaviour is responded to and understood in what are considered to be two very different domains. For example, the exploration of 'hot emotion', 'flight to the front' (in reference to My Lai) or the presence of posttraumatic stress disorder (in reference to My Lai and Marine A) not only carries implicit gendered assumptions about masculinity and its vulnerabilities, it also reflects implicit denials of the context in which these actions occurred. By definition, of course, war is considered to be a threat to the social order (not so with domestic murder, as was observed above). Yet the strains to render some acts of killing more threatening to that order than others remain. Specifically this chapter illustrates that the search to render individuals responsible for murderous behaviour in war (as illustrated in the available explanations for case studies considered in this chapter), even when evidence exists for collective responsibility, ensures that the legitimacy or otherwise of the war itself remains beyond question. In leaving this legitimacy, and hence, responsibility, as the 'elephant in the room', as Walklate and McGarry's analysis suggests as a consequence, we see the individuals who perpetrated these acts (deemed illegitimate by the state), yet the role of the state in legitimating the context in which those acts occur remains unseen and unspoken. Thus, murderous behaviour in war is not a question of how ordinary men could do extraordinary things. The answer to that is simple. The more pertinent issue might be why this is thought to be the question at all. In asking it, which issues are foregrounded and which are left relatively untouched? It is the case that the issues raised by Cockburn (2009) are certainly sidelined when individual responsibility is assumed but are put centre stage in the analysis by Walklate and McGarry.

The desire to search for individual responsibility for murderous behaviour, even in the context of the collective act of war and conflict, is given closer scrutiny in Chapter 6 by Anette Bringedal Houge. In a detailed analysis of the case files of the fifteen defendants convicted for murder by the International Criminal Tribunal for the former Yugoslavia (that number of convictions indicating the level of impunity available for such acts), Houge illustrates the power of legal discourses that search for individual responsibility either by constructing the men before the court as deviant or ordinary, but interestingly not as men. As with the case studies examined by Walklate and McGarry, Houge's work focuses on re-presentations of lethal behaviour that have occurred in highly masculinized contexts. The conflict in the former Yugoslavia was overwhelmingly driven by men and perpetrated by men in all the forms of violence that resulted, including sexual violence, with the victims of killing for the most part also being men. Out of this highly sex-selective context it is remarkable that the ICTY has to date convicted only fifteen perpetrators: all men.

In presenting these men to the court, Houge's analysis reveals that prosecutors had recourse to two discourses. These men were either deviant (that is, had some kind of disorder or were opportunistic in their commission of sadistic acts of violence) or they were just ordinary men responding to situational pressures or in varying states of denial that their behaviours were in any way problematic. There are (at least) two interesting observations to be made about this analysis, the small number of successful convictions notwithstanding. First the strain in this process that has resulted in individual men, and not particularly powerful men in terms of this conflict, in being brought to the attention of the ICTY. Second there is a remarkable symmetry between the discourses used to make sense of homicide in this legal setting (designed as it was to address the international response to and public awareness of the excesses of violence used in this particular conflict) with those used for more mundane and ordinary homicides occurring in a domestic setting. Thus, as Walklate and McGarry observed in relation to Marine A, whose case was heard in a military court, even in the context of an international court, the drive to assign responsibility for those acts deemed illegitimate become constrained, circumscribed, and informed by understandings of similar acts, also deemed illegitimate but which occur in very different settings. Houge suggests that this symmetry is a reflection of wider social and cultural views existing outside the courtroom. However, it is possible to suggest that this symmetry also exists because to respond otherwise would call into account the need for the state to keep such acts from threatening the social order. Arguably this strain becomes even more apparent when deaths occur in institutions for which the state has direct responsibility. Or does it?

In Chapter 7, Alison Gerard and Tracey A. Kerr critically examined the 2014 death of a twenty-three-year-old Iranian asylum seeker, Reza Barati, killed in an Australian-funded detention centre housing male asylum seekers on Manus Island, Papua New Guinea. This analysis is situated against the backcloth of the highly politicised and global problem of migration to which Australia has adopted geographically particular responses. However, whilst the case study used in this chapter is situated within the Australian context, the issues it raises in terms of responsibility when deaths occur at contested borders that migrants are endeavouring to cross are not peculiar to Australia. The case study in this chapter poses equally pertinent questions for management of migration in Europe and beyond.

What this case study does in particular is point to the ways in which the processes of responsibility that might be assumed to lie with the state when a death occurs in a state-run institution to which someone has been assigned – not because of his criminal status but because of his marginal status as someone seeking asylum in that state – are silenced (Mathieson, 2004). In this case this happened in a number of ways, from pointing to problems with the asylum seekers themselves (for protesting against the conditions in which they were being held), to the problems inherent in creating an all-male facility in which this particular individual was housed, to the problems associated with the organisation assigned to protect this facility. Taken together, and perhaps not surprisingly, these strategies facilitated the assignation of an individualised responsibility for what happened focusing very much on the events that led up to this death and what procedures and practices could be put in place to ensure that it did not happen again. However, all of this was done within a frame of what Gerard and Kerr label 'outsourcing responsibility' – in other words, laying the responsibility for what happened at the door of Papua New Guinea in which this facility is located despite the presence of voices suggesting otherwise. Nonetheless, to date the Australian state response and sovereignty in relation to migration policies remain unsullied by these debates. A feature of what Weber and Pickering (2011) have referred to as the diffusion of responsibility: a process, as implied above not peculiar to the Australian position on these issues. Moreover, the role of the state in policing the borders and the implications of that role when people are killed as a result of those policing practices, with a few exceptions, remain relatively unspoken. Yet in this chapter, and the previous two, there are clear pointers about this role and the extent to which it is implicit in ensuring a governable neoliberal subject (O'Malley, 2010).

A recurring theme in all of the above has been the strain towards assigning individual responsibility in cases of lethal violence. In the final chapter, David M. Doyle and Joe McGrath point to the difficulties of trying to stand outside of this. This chapter offers a comparative analysis of legal responses in Ireland and England and Wales designed to address the issue of corporate murder/manslaughter. Starting from an appreciation of the number of workplace deaths as compared with prison suicides, Doyle and McGrath proffer the suggestion that in recent years, death in both of these contexts has become a male preserve in the UK. Yet whilst there has been much noise about rendering corporations responsible for deaths in the workplace, particularly when those deaths can be shown to be a result of the failure to adhere to health and safety regulations, the diffusion of responsibility commented on by Weber and Pickering (2011), referred to above is even more difficult to work through within business corporations. Indeed, where there have been successful convictions, these have been mostly within small businesses.

What is even more noteworthy has been the reluctance to consider the appropriateness of this kind of legal response with the prison service even though deaths in custody match with recorded deaths in the workplace. Doyle and McGrath document some of the difficulties of calling such institutions to account. This is particularly the case because the legislation requires that actions of senior management itself need to be demonstrably implicated in any particular incident; and because senior management are unlikely to have hands-on day-to-day engagement with prisoners, such a requirement can be difficult to evidence. As yet, no prison has been called to account under this legislation, and the prospects of success appear limited given the current framework. However, rather as with some of the implications of Gerard and Kerr's analysis, this chapter suggests that such deaths might be better framed and responded to as a health issue. Yet, we start where we began, facing the problems posed by a legal framework that seeks to make an individual responsible for a lethal act, in a context in which responsibility for such violence may be multilayered and multifaceted.

This collection has added some considerable nuanced understanding of the different ways in which gender and gendered understandings of responsibility permeate acts of killing. These nuances are demonstrated in a number of different ways. First, what counts as being masculine and being feminine in terms of both perpetrator and victim behaviours not only inform and frame how people respond to the circumstances in which they find themselves – they also frame how the legal process responds to them. From Ruth Ellis to Marine A, we find powerful examples of the ongoing presence of these kinds of assumptions. This observation may not in itself be new, but placing the salience of these issues in the context of war alongside the context of 'domestic' murder tellingly reveals how powerful these constructions are. Second, the presence of gender in this way continues to pervade struggles to interpret and or reform the law. These struggles have come to the fore in the context of intimate partner violence in particular but are present in other contexts too. Third, why this presence still persists might lie in underlying assumptions about intimacy. This question has yet to be subjected to closer critical scrutiny. Arguably, whether in the realm of the private, non-threatening, domestic killing or the world of the public, more threatening, wartime killing, there is much value in considering how intimacy between the various actors has been understood and how that understanding informs responses to these acts. This adds a new and deeper nuance for our understanding of the relationship between gender and the recourse to lethal violence. Fourth and further to this, the chapters here point to the ongoing strain towards rendering an individual responsible for lethal violence regardless of context. That strain is illustrated in the discourses from the ICTY to explanations for deaths in detention centres. The desire to render this gendered individual responsible for acts in which others carry equal if not more responsibility, evidenced most notably in the silencing of the role of the state, reveals much about who and what is to be protected when the social order is threatened by illegitimate lethal violence. This gendered understanding of responsibility, its reproduction in the law, its role in preserving the social order and its contribution towards maintaining the state in a particular shape and form are ripe for further theoretical and empirical investigation.

References

Ball, R. (2012) *Human Rights Implications of 'Unlawful Assault Causing Death' Laws: Briefing Paper.* Melbourne: Human Rights Law Centre.

Cockburn, C. (2009) The continuum of violence. In Linke, U. and Smith, D. T. (eds.) *Cultures of Fear: A Critical Reader.* London: Pluto Press, pp. 158–173.

Cullen, J. (2014) WA's "one-punch" law: Solution to a complex social problem or easy way out for perpetrators of domestic violence. *Griffith Journal of Law and Human Dignity,* 2: 52–77.

D'Cruze, S. (2011) Sexual violence in history: A contemporary heritage? In Brown, J. and Walklate, S. (eds.) *Handbook of Sexual Violence.* London: Routledge. pp. 23–51.

Dekeseredy, W. and Rennison, C. M. (2013) Comparing female victims of separation/divorce assault across geographical regions. *International Journal for Crime and Justice,* 2(1): 65–81.

Kelly, L. (1988) *Surviving Sexual Violence.* Oxford: Polity.

Mahoney, M. R. (1991) Legal images of battered women: Redefining the issue of separation. *Michigan Law Review,* 90(1): 1–94.

Mathieson, T. (2004) *Silently Silenced: Essays on the Creation of Acquiescence in Modern Society.* Hook, Hampshire: Waterside Press.

Mooney, J. (2007) Shadow values, shadow figures: Real violence. *Critical Criminology,* 15: 159–170.

Naffine, N. (2003) Who are law's persons? From Cheshire Cats to responsible subjects. *Modern Law Review,* 66(3): 346–347.

O'Malley, P. (2010) Resilient subjects: Uncertainty, warfare and liberalism. *Economy and Society,* 39(4): 488–509.

Smart, C. (1989) *Feminism and the Power of Law.* London: Routledge.

Tomsen, S. (1997) A top night: Social protest, masculinity and the culture of drinking violence. *British Journal of Criminology,* 37(1): 90–102.

Weber, L. and Pickering, S. (2011) *Globalization and Borders: Death at the Global Frontier.* London: Palgrave.

Winlow, S. and Hall, S. (2006) *Violent Night: Urban Leisure and Contemporary Culture.* London: Berg.

Index

Note: Italicized page numbers indicate a figure on the corresponding page. Page numbers in bold indicate a table on the corresponding page.